Economic Policy, COVID-19 and Corporations

This book addresses the economic impact of the COVID-19 outbreak on Central and East European countries and examines the effect the pandemic has had on organizations in the region. It focuses on the widely understood business environment, covering companies' responses to the crisis, the role of institutions in stabilizing markets, and the reshaping of global business trends.

The book is a complex and multidimensional work that draws its roots from distinct yet simultaneously interlinked research areas. All of the chapters, whether they refer to macro-, meso-, or micro-perspectives, always highlight how crises – global and regional – change the global trends we have observed in business in the last 20 years. The book includes the most topical issues that delineate public discourse on firms' resilience. In this way, it 'connects the dots' and uncovers the missing links necessary for any reader wishing to understand the specificity of contemporary companies' responses to unexpected events such as pandemics or geopolitical crises. Further, it tackles questions such as what role institutions play in building the adaptive capacity of companies, how companies build their resilience capacity for 21st-century crises, and what the significance is of the uncertainty, the information asymmetry, and the bounded rationality concept on the company's decision-making process.

The book will find a broad audience among academics and students across diverse fields of study, as well as practitioners and policymakers. It is a key reference for all those who want to better understand the complex nature of uncertainty, crisis management, and its implications, not only for CEE countries but, first and foremost, the business environment.

Katarzyna Mroczek-Dąbrowska, PhD, is Associate Professor at the Poznań University of Economics and Business, Department of International Competitiveness.

Aleksandra Kania, PhD, is Assistant Professor at the Poznań University of Economics and Business, Department of International Competitiveness.

Anna Matysek-Jędrych, PhD, is Associate Professor at the Poznań University of Economics and Business, Department of International Competitiveness.

Routledge Studies in the Economics of Business and Industry

The Rural Enterprise Economy
Edited by Birgit Leick, Susanne Gretzinger and Teemu Makkonen

The Evolution of Contemporary Arts Markets
Aesthetics, Money and Turbulence
Andrés Solimano

The Economics of Corporate Trade Credit in Europe
Julia Koralun-Bereźnicka and Dawid Szramowski

The Economics of the Global Oil and Gas Industry
Emerging Markets and Developing Economies
Edited by Joshua Yindenaba Abor, Amin Karimu and Runar Brännlund

The Professional Standards of Executive Remuneration Consultants
Calvin Jackson

International Trade and the Music Industry
Live Music Services from the Caribbean
Lisa Gordon

Sustainability Management in the Oil and Gas Industry
Emerging and Developing Country Perspectives
Edited by Joshua Yindenaba Abor and Amin Karimu

Economic Policy, COVID-19 and Corporations
Perspectives from Central and Eastern Europe
Edited by Katarzyna Mroczek-Dąbrowska, Aleksandra Kania and Anna Matysek-Jędrych

For more information about this series, please visit www.routledge.com/Routledge-Studies-in-the-Economics-of-Business-and-Industry/book-series/RSEBI

Economic Policy, COVID-19 and Corporations

Perspectives from Central and Eastern Europe

Edited by
Katarzyna Mroczek-Dąbrowska,
Aleksandra Kania and
Anna Matysek-Jędrych

Routledge
Taylor & Francis Group
LONDON AND NEW YORK

First published 2023
by Routledge
4 Park Square, Milton Park, Abingdon, Oxon OX14 4RN

and by Routledge
605 Third Avenue, New York, NY 10158

Routledge is an imprint of the Taylor & Francis Group, an informa business

British Library Cataloguing-in-Publication Data
A catalogue record for this book is available from the British Library

ISBN: 978-1-032-38498-6 (hbk)
ISBN: 978-1-032-38524-2 (pbk)
ISBN: 978-1-003-34542-8 (ebk)

DOI: 10.4324/9781003345428

Typeset in Bembo
by Apex CoVantage, LLC

Contents

Figures

Tables

Editors' biographies

Katarzyna Mroczek-Dąbrowska, PhD, is Associate Professor at the Poznań University of Economics and Business, Department of International Competitiveness. Her main research areas include international competitiveness of firms and industries, transaction costs, and the internationalization process of industries. She is the author and co-author of published works covering, among others, the Global Financial Crisis and its impact on strategies of Polish enterprises and the impact of Brexit on the EU-27 cohesion. Professor Mroczek-Dąbrowska is a National Representative of Poland in the European International Business Academy and works on several international research and teaching projects, cooperating with universities and consulting companies in the United Kingdom, Belgium, and Slovenia.

Aleksandra Kania, PhD, is Assistant Professor at the Poznań University of Economics and Business, Department of International Competitiveness. She has participated in national and international research and educational projects and coordinated the project within Erasmus + Strategic Partnership: Open Access Digital Video Case Library for Teaching International Business. She focuses her research on internationalization, coopetition, and innovation. She is a former Rotary Scholar in Mannheim, Germany, and an active AIB and EIBA member. For her doctoral thesis on innovative clusters in Baden-Württemberg and Greater Poland, she won the first prize in the national competition funded by Wolters Kluwer. Before her current research role, she worked for MNEs in Poland and in Germany.

Anna Matysek-Jędrych, PhD, is Associate Professor at the Poznań University of Economics and Business, Department of International Competitiveness. Her main research areas include macroeconomics and political aspects of international economics. She is the Director of the Executive MBA Program held in cooperation with Georgia State University in Atlanta, United States. Dr Matysek-Jędrych's expertise covers financial markets, institutional frameworks, and its impact on the economy's performance. Recently, she joined a research team on a project studying Brexit consequences on EU27 cohesion, and she conducts her own research in institutional determinants of macroprudential policy efficiency. She is the author of more than 50 scientific articles, chapters, and monographs, including two research projects for the National Bank of Poland (winner of grant competition among economists from Poland). She is also a member of the editorial and review board of the *Journal of Eastern European and Central Asian Research* (Webster University), the *International Journal of Emerging Markets*, and *Cross-Cultural & Strategic Management*.

Contributors' biographies

Anže Burger is Associate Professor of International Economics and Head of the Centre of International Relations at the Faculty of Social Sciences, University of Ljubljana, Slovenia. His research topics include international trade, international business, international factor movements, and industrial policy. He has published six monographs and more than 25 articles in a variety of international journals, such as *Journal of World Business*, *Journal of International Management*, *Empirical Economics*, *Journal of Happiness Studies*, *Economic Systems*, and *Service Industries Journal*. He was a visiting researcher at LICOS, Faculty of Business and Economics at KU Leuven (Belgium) in 2005, and at the University of Fribourg (Switzerland) and at the Dublin City University (Ireland) in 2019.

Dawid Cherubin is a PhD candidate at Poznań University of Economics and Business and specializes in critical geopolitics and foreign direct investment during and after the Covid-19 period.

Kamil Fijorek, PhD, is a researcher at the Department of Statistics at the Cracow University of Economics, lead statistician in the 'Instrument Szybkiego Reagowania' project, and lead biostatistician in one of the LIDER projects. Interested in computational statistics (R programming) and econometric models for binary, categorical, time-to-event, and other non-normal variables.

Marta Götz is a professor at the Vistula University and graduate of the Poznań University of Economics and Business, Aalborg University (AAU) in Denmark; she has carried out projects funded by the NCN, NAWA, and the Visegrad Fund. Her research interests include foreign direct investment (FDI), clusters, Industry 4.0, and international competitiveness.

Łukasz Jabłoński, PhD (dr hab.) in Economics, associate professor, researcher, and academic teacher in the Department of Macroeconomics at the Cracow University of Economics. Since 2021, he has been a member of the Polish Economic Association. His research interests cover economic growth in relation with income inequality and human capital acquisition.

Andreja Jaklič is Full Professor and Researcher at the Centre of International Relations and Vice Dean for Research at the Faculty of Social Sciences, University of

Ljubljana, Slovenia. Her research includes studies on international trade, foreign direct investment, global value chains, and internationalization strategies. She has published over 50 scientific articles in scientific journals, several monographs, and book chapters. She is a co-founder and executive board member of the Academy of International Business Central and Easter European Chapter (AIB-CEEC) and is active in several editorial boards and as a board member of the European Academy of International Business (EIBA) between 2010 and 2016.

Iris Koleša is a teaching and research assistant at the Faculty of Social Sciences, University of Ljubljana, Slovenia (FSS UL). She holds a PhD in International Business from the School of Economics and Business at the University of Ljubljana, a second cycle master's degree in diplomacy, and a bachelor's degree in marketing communications and public relations from FSS UL. In her research, she focuses on business internationalization, international employee mobility, diaspora entrepreneurship, and inter-organizational networking. She is a recipient of several awards and recognitions for her academic work. She is also an experienced communication expert with relevant practical skills in science communication and business support.

Wojciech Marciniak is a graduate of Poznań University of Economics and Business and specializes in the current macrotrends, including reshoring and nearshoring.

Marta Wajda-Lichy, PhD in economics, is a researcher and academic teacher in the Department of Macroeconomics at the Cracow University of Economics as well as the coordinator of the EU program Jean Monnet Module. Since 2012, she has been a member of the Polish Economic Association. Her research interests cover international trade, economic integration, and economic development of middle-income countries.

Acknowledgments

This book would not be possible without the publisher and the series editor, who supported our idea from day one. We are grateful for all support on our quest to prepare the volume. We would like to thank all contributing authors who trusted us as we embarked on this, on what turned out to be a long and both professionally and privately adventurous journey. We would like to thank the entire Routledge team for the arduous technical assistance in the preparation of this volume for publication.

Chapter 3, 8, and 9 of this contribution draw on the final results of the 'Determinants of company's adaptability to crisis situation – the case of Covid19' project. The project was co-financed by the Polish National Agency for Academic Exchange within the Urgency Grants program.

1 Why do we never learn?

A history lesson on crisis management

Katarzyna Mroczek-Dąbrowska, Aleksandra Kania, and Anna Matysek-Jędrych

Although a potential pandemic has been on the Global Risk Map of 2019, few took it as a severe threat. Yet, the SARS outbreak in 2003, with around 8,000 people infected and 774 deceased, cost the global economy an estimated 50 billion USD; the MERS outbreak in 2015 in South Korea caused 200 infections and took a toll of 38, but amounted to an estimated 8.5 billion USD loss (Oh et al., 2018). The pandemic outbreaks were relatively small in scale (restricted to specific areas such as, e.g., Ebola in 2014–2016) and hence lulled countries into complacency (Huber et al., 2018), labelling a full rollout of the pandemic as not a probable event.

And thus, the 2019 outbreak of the COVID-19 pandemic took global society, policymakers, health systems, and businesses by surprise. One by one, countries implemented severe measures – border closure, mobility restrictions, lockdowns, and curfews – in the hope of reigning in the COVID-19 virus. Only then did the global dependencies built through years of intensive globalization process start to appear. Companies offshoring their activities to other locations; companies being part of global value chains; companies dependent on global procurement – all entities suffered due to disruptions in operations, 'infecting' co-dependent industries and the international market.

And so, the question emerges: why do we never learn? The history of economics clearly shows that we should expect unexpected shocks – of different nature, magnitude, and frequency – as they keep reappearing to disturb our development path. But if potential disturbances vary in magnitude and frequency, can we build resilience capacity to effectively manage a crisis? We believe we can, as although crises differ, the ways of designing, implementing, and executing a response plan – be it in the case of businesses or economies – have common baseline principles.

We bring you a volume on COVID-19 economic policies and business responses, in which we aim to assess the nature of the crisis, macroeconomic frameworks aiding businesses in overcoming the pandemic aftermath, and corporate strategies for mitigating losses and fostering the creation of resilience capacity in hopes of prompting discussion on how to exploit accumulated experiences for the future. We purposefully focus on Central and Eastern Europe (CEE). The CEE countries make for an interesting study as they have both suffered from the pandemic rollout and benefited (e.g., reshoring trend) due to geopolitical tensions among the world leaders.

DOI: 10.4324/9781003345428-1

When we wrote these words in October 2022, Europe and especially CEE, has once again found itself at a crossroads with new threats emerging from around the corner: energy-market crisis, inflation crisis, and growing geopolitical tensions. With this volume, we hope to contribute to the debate on transferable good practices in crisis and change management that are general and not event-specific.

The volume consists of 12 chapters, including this introductory chapter as well as the concluding one. The chapters address a variety of issues consistent with the volume's objectives. The discussion in the book takes a top-down approach, starting with the macroeconomic perspective and later on focusing on the microeconomic perspective and the company's response to COVID-19. We discuss the recent pandemic concerning previous crises that CEE countries have suffered from, especially referring to the Global Financial Crisis of 2008. We relate strategies to the geopolitical context that played a significant role in rolling out global trends during lockdown periods.

Chapter 2, written by Wojciech Marciniak and Katarzyna Mroczek-Dąbrowska, focuses on the nature of the crises, their cyclical character, and the reasons underlying their occurrence. Each crisis is different and has a different genesis, yet in the end – when looked at closely – similarities and patterns in transmission channels, response, recovery plans, etc., are revealed. Chapter 2 is a natural continuation of thoughts highlighted in Chapter 1. It is the first vital step to understanding how economies function and discussing crisis management.

Chapter 3, by Anna Matysek-Jędrych, focuses on institutions as 'creators' of the game's rules, whose main task is to stabilize the economy by minimizing uncertainty. In the wake of the COVID-19 crisis, two actors played critical roles in designing the institutions: central banks and national governments. In particular, central banks acted under a monetary policy mandate, while governments made adjustments to institutions in the areas of fiscal and structural policy. The chapter aims to qualitatively discuss the impact of institutions on the companies' resilience in the face of the crisis caused by the COVID-19 pandemic.

Chapter 4, written by Marta Götz, discusses the complexity and dynamics of Eurozone (EZ) reforms in response to successive crises (the Global Financial Crisis and the outbreak of the COVID-19 pandemic). Eurozone membership is often perceived as a factor in determining resilience capacity, and thus it re-emerges with redoubled strength during crisis time. Conducted analysis allows for identifying possible opportunities and threats associated with Eurozone enlargement, especially in the context of CEE countries. However, the temptation for quick and easy answers concerning EZ membership – binary decisions and definite opinions based on definite cost–benefits analysis – should be avoided and replaced with balanced and broader discussion, with arguments being substantiated rather than ascertained.

Chapter 5, by Marta Wajda-Lichy, Łukasz Jabłoński, and Kamil Fijorek, focuses on the question of how the COVID-19 pandemic affected the macroeconomic environment for doing business in Central and Eastern European economies. The authors look closely at GDP fluctuations and fiscal policy adjustments as essential areas of the new macroeconomic environment for companies in pandemic and post-pandemic times.

Having discussed monetary and fiscal responses to COVID-19, the author of Chapter 6 – Marta Wajda-Lichy – takes a close look at the consequences of the COVID-19 pandemic for foreign trade in Central and Eastern European countries. Since the CEE economies differ in the level of trade openness and trade structure, the strength of their responses to the pandemic shock varied. This chapter aims to present how the COVID-19 pandemic affected the CEE economies' trade openness and dependence.

Chapter 7, written by Dawid Cherubin, constitutes a link between macro- and microeconomic perspectives. It discusses geopolitical events related to international relations in light of the conflict between the US and China before and after the COVID-19 pandemic. It touches upon the phenomenon of reshoring that has become a new trend in international business, shifting previous global trends. The chapter focuses on CEE countries' role in the reshoring process in light of intensifying geopolitical tensions.

Chapter 8, written by Aleksandra Kania, concerns companies and their exposure to the COVID-19 pandemic. Lockdowns and health-focused restrictions have forced companies to adapt to certain changes. However, not all industries were equally exposed to the COVID-19 impact. The chapter attempts to answer why some industries are more sensitive to external shocks and others are not. The chapter discusses the impact of globalization and global supply chains and their effect on contemporary business models.

Chapter 9, prepared jointly by Katarzyna Mroczek-Dąbrowska, Aleksandra Kania, and Anna Matysek-Jędrych, focuses on building the company's adaptive capabilities in the case of Poland. While various authors differ in the conceptualization of resilience, they all refer to a company's ability to contend with a disruption. Disruption can be seen as external and internal occurrences that alter the status quo. The chapter is designed to fill the gaps on what makes some companies more resilient to disruptions than others. The authors aim to answer the following research questions: what are the critical sources of the company's resilience following the COVID-19 pandemic in developed economies, and what are the implications of a company's resilience for improving both the rate and the speed of adaptability?

Chapter 10, written by Anže Burger, Iris Koleša, and Andreja Jaklič, depicts the case of risk management during systemic crises in Slovenia. This exploratory study provides a typology of resilience strategies that firms employ to cope with or avoid crises' negative consequences and capitalize on the opportunities they present. Using empirical evidence on firms' responses to the pandemic from two surveys conducted among international businesses after the first wave of the 2020 COVID-19 outbreak and combining cluster and regression analyses, the authors identify four groups of businesses based on the different strategies they use to confront the economic downturn. The study has theoretical and practical implications for planning, designing, monitoring, and implementing crisis management strategies in business that lead to stable or improved performance – i.e., capitalization on organizational resilience.

Chapter 11, prepared by Iris Koleša and Andreja Jaklič, focuses on COVID-19 government emergency support for foreign affiliates in Slovenia. First, it provides an overview of measures available to companies immediately after the pandemic had been 'announced.' Second, it shows how affiliates of multinational enterprises (MNEs) perceive and evaluate different types of government support in their host country and how they use and integrate emergency measures into their recovery plans. The findings offer rare insights into the propensity and ability of foreign affiliates to benefit from national support measures and encourage consideration of how foreign affiliate support can contribute to the recovery of small economies.

Chapter 12, a summary of the considerations in this volume, collects and presents the most critical conclusions synthetically. The most important lessons for the Central and Eastern European region from recent vital events in the economic history of the whole world, i.e., the crisis caused by the COVID-19 pandemic, geopolitical turmoil, including Russia's aggression against Ukraine, and the technological revolution, are presented.

All chapters are at the same time interconnected and individual. Each depicts an individual study area but simultaneously contributes a brick to the main volume's topic: effective crisis management in response to the COVID-19 pandemic in Central and Eastern Europe. The chapters relate to one another, invoking global macro trends and discussing them in the case of individual businesses and their experiences.

References

Huber, C., Finelli, L. & Stevens, W. (2018). The economic and social burden of the 2014 Ebola outbreak in West Africa. *The Journal of Infectious Diseases, 218*(5), 698–704.

Oh, M.Y., Park, W.B., Park, S.W., Choe, P.G., Bang, J.H., Song, K.H., Kim, E.S., Kim, H.B. & Kim, N.J. (2018). Middle east respiratory syndrome: What we learned from the 2015 outbreak in the Republic of Korea. *Korean Journal of International Medicine, 33*(2), 233–246.

2 Nature of a crisis

How has it changed and affected the firms?

Katarzyna Mroczek-Dąbrowska and Wojciech Marciniak

Introduction

We live and function in a VUCA world. VUCA stands for the volatility, uncertainty, complexity, and ambiguity of the contemporary world. Volatility means that a certain process is unexpected or unstable and we might not be able to predict its duration. Uncertainty means that we lack information and the event's basic cause and effect remain unknown. Complexity means that the situation has interconnected parts and factors. Finally, ambiguity means that the situation has no precedents, and causal relationships are unknown. The VUCA world is therefore vulnerable and susceptible to crisis.

Crisis is a complex and multifaceted phenomenon, a state of organisational ineffectiveness when usage of most critical elements does not allow for effective performance (Fischbacher-Smith, 2014). Crisis is both a state and a process. It is a state since it describes the outcome in which the organisation finds itself – an inability to face a disturbance. But at the same time, it is a three-phase process: crisis of management, where the disturbance evolves to a threatening degree; crisis of operations, where organisation seeks to contain the ever-growing disturbance; and crisis of legitimation, where the organisation seeks to recover from its negative effects. In other words, crisis is "a fundamental challenge to the effectiveness of an organisation in terms of its abilities to prevent, mitigate, or respond" to a disturbance (Fischbacher-Smith, 2014, p. 427).

Crisis is characterised by spatial and temporal settings. Since the term is often used around the events that "push" an organisation to the edge of its capabilities, time and space are crucial when discussing it. Organisations may have built an effective set of resilience capabilities; however, certain circumstances (e.g. recent disturbances in global value chains) or sensitive timing (e.g. lockdowns) may trigger the crisis to escalate. In such a way, an organisation's resilience capabilities are overcome by the rapid shift in the environment. An organisation's development results from interactions with its ecosystem and internal adaptations and adjustments to the strategies. However, the further the organisation is moved from its targeted development path, the more prone it is to spiral into a crisis. Therefore, the organisation's awareness and ability to recognise and mitigate potential threats is a key element of crisis management (Fischbacher-Smith, 2012).

DOI: 10.4324/9781003345428-2

Looking back at recent disturbances in the global economy and especially in Europe, certain questions arise: what is the nature of the contemporary crises, and how do they differ from one another? How can organisations build their resilience capabilities, and are these capabilities sustainable in time? What does it mean for a company to be resilient, and is this resilience generic or crisis-specific? The remainder of the chapter is led by these questions. Firstly, the discussion focuses on the nature, characteristics, and specificity of contemporary crises. Secondly, two major disruptions of the twenty-first century – the Global Financial Crisis (GFC) and COVID-19 crisis – are discussed. The final section covers the similarities and differences of the invoked crises.

The nature of the crisis

Over many centuries, human civilisation has experienced multiple economic crises. Some date as far back as BCE 33, when the execution of forgotten property law in ancient Rome started a credit crunch and a crash in real estate prices. Another crisis of bygone days, the Tulip-mania of 1637, was one of the first recorded speculative bubbles. It occurred when the prices of tulip bulbs rose to unprecedented heights and then fell sharply. In recent history, we have observed more frequent occurrences of global crises. Globalisation led to the higher growth of multiple economies at the cost of the growing risk, meaning that a crisis in one country was likely to spread through international links, like a virus, into others. Due to the emergence of multinational corporations and the intensification of international trade, a crisis in one country affects many others. The more connected two countries are, the more effects of a crisis in one will spread to another.

The two most recent global crises are the GFC of 2007–09 and the COVID-19 pandemic. They are starkly different in reasons and mechanisms. However, both led to the misfortune of countless people and became the top subject of numerous debates in governments and national banks around the globe. Yet, what never fails to astonish is the fact that we – widely understood society, economists, policy makers – still treat "crisis" as a surprising occurrence even though history has taught us otherwise. Economies are cyclical in nature. Business cycles can be short – what is credited to e.g. seasonal changes; or long – what stems from e.g. transformative changes. Burns and Mitchell (1946) – one of the first to define a business cycle – claim that it is a cyclical yet irregular fluctuation of economic activity resulting in significant changes in economic output. One economic cycle is completed through a series of four stages: expansion, peak, contraction, and finally trough. Contraction followed by trough is what we colloquially associate with crisis. And yet, as Jasiński (2009) rightly points out, we misinterpret the crisis as a recession. To Jasiński, crisis means the inability to further grow or even sustain the achieved development stage. The term economic crisis is also commonly interchanged with terms like economic slowdown, economic crash, or economic depression. Figure 2.1 is an attempt to briefly summarise the key differences between those concepts.

As indicated in Figure 2.1, any term that depicts change in the real economy sees drop in GDP as the initial signal for a potential crisis. However, it is commonly

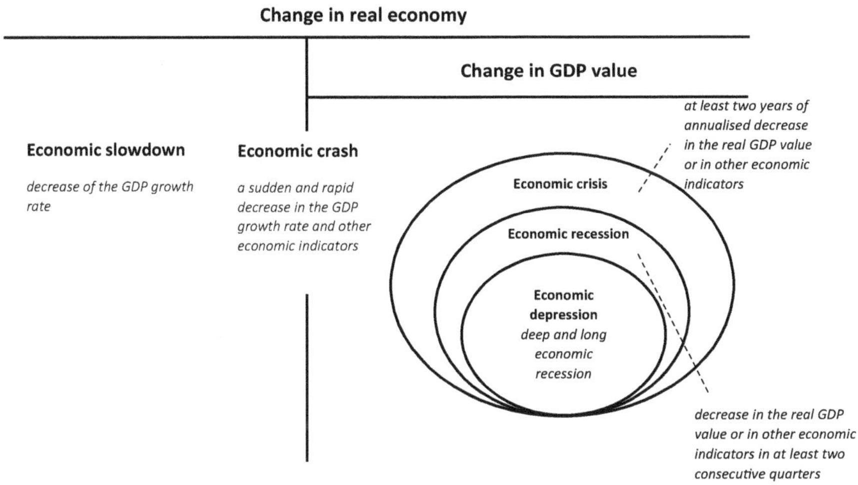

Figure 2.1 Crisis-related terms and their relationships

Source: own elaboration based on Dzikowska & Trąpczyński (2017, p. 45)

acknowledged that the timespan of change in GDP value is what distinguishes the terms. To talk about a crisis, we need to observe at least two years of annualised decrease in the real GDP value. Economic recession is similar but is observable in a shorter period, of at least two consecutive quarters. Economic crash, on the other hand, is much more sudden and the drop is much more severe.

And the bubble bursts – Global Financial Crisis

Years of unprecedented growth, greed taking over Wall Street, and lack of proper control in the US finance sector led to the most significant financial crisis since the Great Depression of the 1930s. It affected most of the developed countries around the world. The GFC is one of the best-described crises in economic literature and was the breaking point at which many policymakers realised the need to take lessons and impose greater scrutiny on the financial and banking sector of the economy (Adamowicz, 2013; Adamowicz & Adamowicz, 2018).

Though the GFC began in the late 2000s, the crisis had roots dating back to the previous century and multiple government interventions in the US housing market. During the 1990s, the president of the United States, Bill Clinton, led the administration to changes that, among others, exempted credit default swaps (CDS) from regulation and put more pressure on banks to lend money to low-income citizens. A few years later, in 2000, the US stock market crashed due to the overvaluation of tech companies. This resulted in the Federal Reserve (FED) deciding to cut the interest rates to record lows. In effect, credits became more affordable, and bank deposits less profitable, making investors look for alternative places to protect their capital from inflation higher than interest rates. Demand for housing rose, and as a consequence, prices went up, too. Investors could buy and quickly sell the new properties for a profit. Many retail investors jumped on the bandwagon, along with big institutional investors. However, numerous families that bought a new property with the intention of making a quick profit could not afford it in the first place. It was possible for them only because subprime mortgages were secured by state-funded institutions: Federal National Mortgage Association (FannieMae) and Federal Home Loan Mortgage Corporation (FreddieMac).

The financial sector has its fair (if not most significant) share of the blame as well. At the core of this blame lies greed or the naivety that housing prices would continue to grow. This resulted in banks offering mortgages to people with too low of an income to repay the debt. Banks were aware of this but, knowing that the prices of properties were on the rise, they thought they would profit regardless. Moreover, bankers began selling mortgage-backed securities (MBS) and CDS. An MBS is a bond made up of home loans allowing the investor essentially to loan money to the bank and indirectly get someone's mortgage payments as a repayment scheme. A CDS, sold worldwide, operates on the basis that when bank "A," in exchange for payment from bank "B," is obliged to secure the loan and, in the event that the borrower of bank "B" fails to pay back their loan, pay it instead of the borrower. The pivotal ingredient in this situation was the revision of the law prohibiting banks from combining two types of banking: investing banking and deposit and credit banking. From 1999 till 2007, in perfect conditions for buying a property, investors could refinance or sell a house after a year or two, with its value rising by 15–20%. At the same time, the bank was selling MBS, where an investor could get a 15% return on investment (ROI). The same bank servicing the mortgage was collecting interest payments plus provisions and could simultaneously sell MBS based on the mortgages it services, thus earning from two streams on the same assets. That gave incentive for bankers to approve more mortgages to sell more MBS.

The system worked when the housing prices rose. The changes began with the FED, which decided to raise interest rates and, as a result, increased the cost of mortgage instalments. This heavily burdened the budgets of US families, and many became unable to pay back their loans. Banks began to take over properties and put them up for sale. Increased supply led to a fall in prices. The housing bubble broke, and the effects spilt across the globe. International banks in many developed countries began to publish losses due to their involvement in risky securities.

In the first attempts to fix the situation, the biggest banks managed to access additional capital. Shares in banks like Merrill Lynch, Goldman Sachs, or Lehman Brothers were bought by hedge funds from Asia and the Middle East. However, not everyone managed to weather the storm. The bankruptcy of Lehman Brothers on September 15, 2008, is still one of the most memorable moments of the crisis. Many expected the bank to be bailed out by the state. In the aftermath, at least 100 banks and institutions selling mortgages in the US were bought out or bankrupted during 2007. The crisis started out in the financial sector, but it quickly spread to the construction industry and others. This led to a general fall in share prices on the stock market. Future retirees were a severely affected social group, as falls on Wall Street erased 2.3 billion USD from the US pension funds. The same happened in many countries, as investors often copy behaviours present on Wall Street.

The last decade of the twentieth century was a time of successive growth of developing economies. In many countries, structural and economic reforms led to production and international trade growth. This in turn led to greater stability of their financial systems. The crisis of 2007 significantly impacted continuous growth in developing countries as the effects of what happened in the US spilt across continents. Central and Eastern European countries (CEECs) were affected mainly by the crisis of trust. Foreign investors, aware of growing foreign debt and the low stability of banking systems in developing countries, moved their assets to what were perceived as safe harbours for capital, e.g. US bonds or commodities like gold. As a result, many currencies depreciated. Ironically, the newly formed international links – especially in banking and trade – led to significant losses among many emerging market countries. Before 2007, many Western banks offered loans to the governments and companies in CEECs, which accelerated the growth in this region. Moreover, CEECs were heavily reliant on trade with Western Europe, which was deeply affected by the crises. This reliance meant a slowdown in growth and production outputs and a rise in unemployment.

Expect the unexpected – the COVID-19 pandemic

The year 2020 brought a crisis incomparable to those before – the global pandemic of COVID-19. The new virus managed to infect people in every country and forced governments to halt production, lock people at home, and close their borders, even in the EU. The event's unpredictability and its rarity make it a perfect example of what economists call a "black swan" event (Gorynia et al., 2022).

The first cases of people infected with the new coronavirus were recorded in late 2019 in Wuhan, China. It is still not certain what the original cause of the virus was. The Chinese government was slow to react and only implemented city lockdown on 23 January 2020. By then, the virus was already spreading. The first cluster of COVID cases in Europe was recorded on 21 February, and in the US, initial major outbreaks began in mid-March. On 23 December, COVID reached Antarctica, thus infecting people on every continent (Booker, 2020). The global presence of COVID-19 caused not only health crises but also a deep economic and social crisis.

The impact of the pandemic on the global economy was threefold. Firstly, it put significant pressure on each country's health services, often exposing years of negligence and insufficient government funding. Hospitals were overrun with patients and at the same time remained significantly understaffed. Governments had to spend significant parts of their budgets to buy additional beds, masks, and respirators. OECD countries experienced an average 5% growth in health service-related expenditures in 2020 alone (OECD, 2022a). The second impact was the cost of actions taken to suppress the spreading of the virus – implementing home lockdowns, enforcing border closures, and maintaining curfews. Many governments weighed the costs and benefits of imposing lockdowns, knowing it would disrupt the whole economy (cf. Chapter 3). However, the effects differed between countries. For instance, after the lockdown, UK imports and exports fell in the second quarter of 2020 and rose in the third quarter after restrictions were eased (Onyeaka, 2021). In developing economies like Kenya, the global lockdown led to an increase in weekly exports by 12% and a decline in imports by 28% (Socrates, 2020). The last type of influence can be described as the global economic slowdown. COVID disrupted the interconnected global economy, leaving supply chains broken for months. China, where the virus originated, is the biggest exporter and represents 16% of global exports. Moreover, nearly 20% of intermediate products come from China. COVID-19 hit the global supply chain at its core by disrupting the most critical player in global trade and, arguably, the country that gained the most from decades of globalisation (PwC, 2022). The pandemic shook stock markets, the price of crude oil, and other commodities and led to mass unemployment and an elevated rate of extreme poverty. Disruptions in the global supply chain led to empty store shelves and common shortages of food and medical supplies. Due to the shortages, many countries imposed export bans, ironically leading to more shortages. Those bans, new to the established supply chains, hampered their elasticity. Numerous companies went bankrupt, and governments had no option but to ignore growing debts and loosen their public borrowing restrictions. The total global debt rose to 30% of GDP in 2020, the highest annual increase since the 1970s (Kose et al., 2021). The lockdowns and reduced lending opportunities decreased the value of currencies, thus making it harder to repay the debt in USD. Some of the least developed countries struggled as many foreign direct investments (FDIs) decided to pull out of their operations (which at the time of the crisis was perceived as risky), in turn worsening credit ratings of those economies. Over the year 2020, more emerging markets and developing economies (EMDEs) – around 30 – had their sovereign credit downgraded than in the nine years since 2010 (Kose et al., 2021). Moreover, countries faced additional fiscal struggles due to increased social protection programmes and reduced tax revenue inflow.

The global pandemic triggered the most prominent economic response from governments since the Second World War, including the most significant fiscal stimulus in decades. The response can be divided into two stages. The first stage focused on protecting household incomes, which were struggling due to lockdowns, supporting the health system, and protecting employment. It was mainly conducted by direct transfers, increased unemployment benefits, and wage subsidies. The latter recovery stage began after the restrictions eased. Only then could the investments in public infrastructure and incentives to support private consumption have a more significant impact. During the first stage, countries used both direct and indirect fiscal support. In countries without strong social support and progressive taxation, we have seen more funds placed into direct support. Countries like Canada, the USA, and Australia are a few examples where direct support represented most of the support. In other parts of the world, where social support was more common, like Europe or Japan, policymakers focused more on indirect support (Hudson et al., 2021).

The first coronavirus cases recorded in CEECs date to February and March 2020. During the first months, the region did not experience high infection rates as was observable in other part of Europe, especially Italy. However, the implementation of lockdowns and border closures led to significant losses for the developing countries of the Eastern EU, especially in the second quarter of 2020 when, on average, GDP fell by 8.64% (OECD, 2022b). Central and Eastern Europe went through the first half of 2020 in relatively good shape. However, the second half brought the second wave of COVID-19 infections and again struck local economies, this time harder. Since CEECs' economies are not as homogenous as many assume, the responses taken by governments and central banks differed. Hungary provided an enormous anti-crisis response of 13.6% of GDP, where 60% represented liquidity support and 40% direct fiscal support. It implemented the highest tax reliefs among CEECs. The national bank of Czechia was the most conservative in the region and decided to cut interest rates while introducing the second biggest anti-crisis support in the region – equal to 12.3% of GDP (ING, 2020). Polish response ranked third in size at 11.3% of GDP. It mainly focused on protecting jobs and sustaining household incomes. So far, it is difficult to say whose approach was the most successful; nevertheless, all CEECs seem to have similar quarterly GDP growth since the fourth quarter of 2020, ranging between 0.9 and 1.6% on average until Q1 of 2022 (OECD, 2022b). Many commentators highlighted the fact that, thanks to the EU teamwork approach, the countries fared better than they would have separately. The question of how important for CEECs was the fact that they had power over their monetary policies outside the Eurozone is a question for a longer discussion.

GFC and COVID-19 crises – similar or different?

The global pandemic was the first major crisis since the GFC. After the initial shock, many began looking for similarities and lessons that could be brought out from the previous crisis to manage the new one (Graff et al., 2021). Both crises were worldwide, and both disrupted the global economy. However, there are significant differences. The main one lies in their causes. The GFC's roots lay in the financial sector's flaws and the housing market's speculative bubble. Financial causes of the GFC affected almost all sectors of the economy; on the other side, the pandemic worsened the situation of the society in general, but some, like big-pharma companies responsible for the development of vaccines or digital service companies like Zoom, thrived. During the GFC, the financial sector was hit first; the construction industry followed in some countries due to numerous mortgage defaults; combined with the decrease in lending, it led to a downturn that spread to the rest of the economy. During the COVID-19 crisis, neither the financial nor the construction industry was affected to a greater extent. Supply bottlenecks and shortages raised some challenges but to a lesser degree than during the GFC. It is important to mark that the economic crisis of 2020 was triggered by a highly transmittable virus, which threatened the lives of people across the globe, not by economic disturbance or financial wrongdoing. The economic problems of the GFC originated from the US financial and banking sector and mainly affected the countries connected to the US. Neither China nor India recorded a single quarter of negative growth during the GFC. However, the COVID-19 pandemic was present in every country and thus led to economic crises almost everywhere.

Table 2.1 COVID-19 crisis versus the Global Financial Crisis

Feature	*COVID-19 crisis*	*Global Financial Crisis*
Primary source of the crisis	Coronavirus (medical dimension, Chinese market)	Subprime mortgage segments (financial dimension, American market)
Primary nature of the crisis	Human, determined by the growing number of infections	Financial, mostly limited to banking crisis
Direct transmission channels	Globally synchronised lockdowns (sudden stop in economic activity) Supply chain disruption Financial markets (sharp repricing with the increase of uncertainty, flight to safe assets, rush to liquidity) Credit market (lenders hold back on extending credit) Unemployment (increase in the risk of defaults)	Financial markets (dramatic fall of commodity prices, increased exchange rate volatility) Credit market and banking sector channel (global liquidity squeeze, problems of "mother" banking institutions) International trade (weaker global demand) FDI channel Stock exchange market
Scale of the crisis	Global	Global (with dominance of highly developed countries)
Primary anti-crisis policy measures	Fiscal policy-related	Monetary policy-related
Anti-crisis policy nature	Act fast and do whatever it takes	Whatever it takes
Uncertainty level	Extremely high	Very high
Process	Crisis is immediately and completely spreading across the real economy, evaporating supply and demand simultaneously	Crisis gradually spread from the financial markets to the real economy (gradual contagion process)

Source: own elaboration

According to the World Bank data, in 2020, out of 215 countries, approximately 86% recorded negative or lower than 1% GDP growth annually. In comparison, in 2009 it was less than 60% (The World Bank, 2022). Both crises increased unemployment, yet not in the same way. The unemployment caused by the GFC was slowly growing from 5.8% in January 2008 until it reached its peak of 8.7% in September 2009; it took nine years for the unemployment rate – of the OECD countries – to return to the level seen in 2008. The volatility of the unemployment rate was much higher during COVID-19. In January 2020, it stood at 5.4% and reached 8.8% three months later. The unemployment rate returned to 5.4% in December 2021 (OECD, 2022c). The origins of the crises can explain the difference. The GFC led to layoffs in construction and manufacturing industries that lasted for a few years (Scanni, 2021). The banking system was struggling, so there was little incentive and optimism to invest, which led to steady growth in unemployment. During the COVID-19 pandemic, the hardest hit industries were leisure and hospitality.

The pandemic practically restrained all movement as people began to be put under quarantines and lockdowns. Therefore, all hotels, cinemas, fun parks, and similar entertainment units had to stop all operations without explicit knowledge of when it would be possible for them to resume work. Lockdowns and uncertainty led to massive layoffs in a short period of time. After a few months, with the increased rate of vaccinations, governments started to slowly lift previously imposed restraints. The easing allowed businesses to resume operations and employ the necessary staff again. By July 2022, most countries returned to an unemployment rate at the same level as before the pandemic began. When comparing unemployment statistics during GFC and the pandemic, we can describe the GFC chart as the slope and the pandemic as the cliff. Reactions implemented by policymakers during the two crises had to be tailored to match the causes, and therefore they differed. In order to mitigate the adverse effects of the GFC, policymakers focused the global response on fiscal and monetary stimulus. The monetary response was mainly based on the quantitative easing programmes and tools intended to inject money into the economy; the fiscal response was generally deployed in the form of tax measures. When COVID-19 started, initial opinion was that the economy was just put on pause; when the restrictions lifted, economic activity should jump back to the same levels as before due to the accumulation of funds and pent-up demand. However, as the realisation of the scale and risk to the economy grew, government response and support were much swifter and more extensive than in the case of the GFC. It was clear that policymakers had learned their lessons from the previous crisis and knew that quicker decision-making would help avoid bankruptcies and loss of human capital. This time there were fewer debates over the necessity of government intervention.

An interesting comparison can be drawn from the statistics representing the average household debt among the OECD countries. From 2020 to 2021, the percentage grew from 125% to 204%. However, between 2007 and 2009 it barely rose, just by 2%. That can be explained by the fact that the GFC was partially caused by the inability of households to pay interest on their mortgages, so when the crisis broke, they could not take any more credits. However, during the pandemic, the crisis causes were not rooted in the flaws of the banking system, so people often borrowed money to support budgets affected by lack of work during lockdowns. Historically low interest rates were just another incentive to do so. Moreover, we found that banks took lessons from the GFC. Since 2008, many G20 reforms have come into place, and at the beginning of 2020, banks had much more capital and liquidity and were less leveraged than in 2007. It allowed them to mitigate rather than amplify macroeconomic disruptions.

Conclusions

The easiest way to describe the differences between the two crises is to say that GFC had a weaker impact over a longer period, while the pandemic caused a massive short-lasting shock to the global economy. Luckily, we can see that policymakers learned vital lessons from the previous crisis and took swift and decisive actions to intervene. The same can be said about the banking sector, which was better prepared to mitigate issues rather than raise them the way it did in 2007. What can be learned from both crises is the humility we need to embrace in our limitations of economic predictions. It is paramount to remember lessons of past crises and how we coped with them, as well as to be prepared for the unexpected that can come in the future.

References

Adamowicz, T. (2013). Przyczyny i skutki I fazy kryzysu finansowego lat 2007–2009 w wybranych krajach na świecie (Causes and Results of the First Phase of the Financial Crisis in 2007–2009 in Selected Countries). *Zeszyty Naukowe SGGW w Warszawie. Polityki Europejskie, Finanse i Marketing, 9*(58), 9–21.

Adamowicz, M. & Adamowicz, T. (2018). Przebieg i skutki światowego kryzysu finansowego lat 2007–2011 oraz działania antykryzysowe w Polsce (Process and effects of the world financial crisis of the years 2007–2011 and anti-crisis actions in Poland). *Prace Naukowe Uniwersytetu Ekonomicznego we Wrocławiu, 529*, 12–25.

Booker, B. (2020). The coronavirus has reached Antarctica. Now it's on every continent. *NPR*. Retrieved from: http://www.npr.org/sections/coronavirus-live-updates/2020/12/23/949552848/the-coronavirus-has-reached-every-continent-after-positive-cases-in-antarctica

Burns, A.F. & Mitchell, W.C. (1946). *Measuring Business Cycles*. New York: National Bureau of Economic Research.

Dzikowska, M. & Trąpczyński, P. (2017). Economic crises – Theoretical and empirical aspects. In M. Dzikowska, M. Gorynia, & B. Jankowska (Eds.), *International Competitiveness of Polish Companies during and after the Global Economic Crisis* (pp. 41–69). Warsaw: Difin SA.

Fischbacher-Smith, D. (2012). Getting pandas to breed: Paradigm blindness and the policy space for risk prevention. *Mitigation and Management. Risk Management, 14*(3), 177–201.

Fischbacher-Smith, D. (2014). Organisational ineffectiveness: Environmental shifts and the transition to crisis. *Journal of Organizational Effectiveness: People and Performance, 1*(4), 423–446.

Gorynia, M., Mroczek-Dąbrowska, K. & Matysek-Jędrych, A. (2022). Nowe relacje między Wielką Brytanią a Unią Europejską – perspektywa polskich przedsiębiorstw (New relations between Great Britain and the European Union – The perspective of Polish companies). In M. Gorynia, J. Kuczewska, & A.Z. Nowak (Eds.), *Polskie przedsiębiorstwo na jednolitym rynku europejskim. Wyzwania współczesności (Polish Company on the Single European Market. The Challenges of Contemporary Times)* (pp. 165–177). Warsaw: Polskie Wydawnictwo Ekonomiczne.

Graff, M., Abrahamsen, Y., Siegenthaler, M. & Domjahn, T. (2021). *Comparing the Coronavirus Crisis and the Financial Crisis: Eight Differences and Similarities*. Retrieved from: https://kof.ethz.ch/en/news-and-events/kof-bulletin/kof-bulletin/2021/10/Comparing-the-coronavirus-crisis-and-the-financial-crisis-eight-differences-and-similarities.html

Hudson, C., Watson, B., Baker, A. & Arsov, I. (2021). *The Global Fiscal Response to COVID-19*. Martin: Reserve Bank of Australia.

ING. (2020). The CEE fiscal and monetary response to Covid-19. *ING*. Retrieved from: https://think.ing.com/articles/the-cee-fiscal-and-monetary-response-to-covid-19

Jasiński, L.J. (2009). Gospodarka i teoria ekonomiczna po kryzysie (The Economy and economic theory after crisis). *Studia Ekonomiczne, 3–4*, 271–277.

Kose, M., Nagle, P., Ohnsorge, F. & Sugawara, N. (2021). *Debt Tsunami of the Pandemic*. Retrieved from: http://www.brookings.edu/blog/future-development/2021/12/17/debt-tsunami-of-the-pandemic/

Nacewska-Twardowska, A. (2021). Central and Eastern Europe Countries in the new international trade environment at the beginning of the 21st century: Global value chains and COVID-19. *European Research Studies Journal, 24*(3), 547–560.
OECD. (2022a). *OECD Health Statistics 2022*. Retrieved from: http://www.oecd.org/els/health-systems/health-data.htm
OECD. (2022b). *Quarterly Growth Rates of Real GDP*. Retrieved from: https://stats.oecd.org/index.aspx?queryid=350#
OECD. (2022c). *Unemployment Rate*. Retrieved from: https://data.oecd.org/unemp/unemployment-rate.htm
Onyeaka, H., Anumudu, C.K., Al-Sharify, Z.T., Egele-Godswill, E. & Mbaegbu, P. (2021). COVID-19 pandemic: A review of the global lockdown and its far-reaching effects. *Science Progress, 104*(2).
PwC. (2022). Impact of COVID-19 on the supply chain industry. *PWC*. Retrieved from: http://www.pwc.com/ng/en/assets/pdf/impact-of-covid19-the-supply-chain-industry.pdf
Scanni, G. (2021). *The Great Recession vs The Covid-19 Pandemic: Unemployment and Implications for Public Policy*. New York: Levy Economics Institute of Bard College.
Socrates, M. (2020). The effect of lockdown policies on international trade flows from developing countries: Event study evidence from Kenya. *World Trade Organization*. Retrieved from: http://www.wto.org/english/news_e/news20_e/rese_15dec20_e.pdf
The World Bank. (2022). *World Development Indicators*. Retrieved from: https://databank.worldbank.org/reports.aspx?source=2&series=NY.GDP.MKTP.KD.ZG&country=#

3 Institutions as stability warrantors

Can institutions help safeguard companies from crises?

Anna Matysek-Jędrych

Introduction

Every crisis, particularly one that lasts a long time or causes profound changes, makes us see the world around us and the conditions in it differently. At the same time, the crisis is that specific period during which individuals, but also – or perhaps especially – companies count on support from the government and other entities involved in stabilizing the market. The crisis caused by the COVID-19 pandemic was no different in this aspect from earlier ones: the global financial crisis, the Brexit-induced crisis, or the debt crisis of Southern European economies (the so-called PIGS: Portugal, Italy, Greece, and Spain). In each of these cases, companies directly or indirectly affected by the crisis were expected to support the creation of conditions that would allow them to continue operating in the market.

A crisis affects business entities operating in the market in various ways. There are many reasons for this: internal, resulting from the characteristics of individual entities and their inbuilt resilience to the crisis; and external, resulting from environmental conditions. Recently, it has been increasingly recognized that 'institutions matter' (Aoki, 2001) for understanding both the diverse economic performance of different economies (macroeconomic approach) and the diverse financial and market performance of organizations and firms operating in the various markets (microeconomic approach).

This chapter aims to analyze and assess what was the role of the governments and central banks as two crucial stabilizing entities in creating the companies' resilience toward the COVID-19 crisis.

The chapter is structured as follows: the first section presents theoretical considerations regarding the basic concepts used in the analysis, i.e., institutions and institutional change, while the second section presents the conceptual framework for the study. The following part is devoted to the qualitative analysis of the impact of institutions on the companies' resilience in the face of the crisis caused by the COVID-19 pandemic, taking into account the institutions that existed before the crisis (the rules of the game created by central banks of Central and Eastern European countries, CEECs, versus some advanced economies) and the institutional change (i.e., the new rules of the game introduced by central banks in the face of the crisis).

DOI: 10.4324/9781003345428-3

Institutions: genesis, meaning, and institutional change

The three labels 'institutions,' 'institutional,' and 'institutionalism' have spread over the past 40 years across political, economic, and other social science disciplines. In all of these disciplines, the institutional perspective emerges from the basic consideration that human activity (as individuals and as a part of a firm), including activity of an economic nature, is embedded and structured within a larger institutional system, which is usually stable (Veblen, 1904 [1975]; Weber, 1978; North, 1990). Regardless of the scientific discipline, the attention of researchers has focused on diagnosing how the system of institutions reduces uncertainty in human behavior, how it affects the regularity and stability of decisions or actions taken, and how much the issue of embeddedness matters.

Both institutionalism and neo-institutionalism have a broad intellectual heritage that helps to shape them in the social sciences, starting from the German historical school (represented by Max Weber and Werner Sombart), which have had a profound impact on the foundations of institutionalism (Hodgson, 2004), through the so-called old institutionalism, mainly in the American economic and political sciences (represented by Richard T. Ely, Westel W. Willoughby, Thorstein Veblen) and old institutionalism in sociology. The intellectual foundation of institutionalism is diverse, which does not help unravel terminological and semantic disputes.

Even though the use of the term institutions has become widespread in the social sciences, there is still no consensus on the very definition of the term (cf. Hodgson, 2006). Table 3.1 contains a simplified overview of the definitions of institutions, paying particular attention to the meaning and shedding light on the implications of using one specific definition as part of the analysis.

Several cognitive and pragmatic conflicts emerge from a mere review of selected definitions of the term institutions (cf. Table 3.1): are we taking into account only formal rules, or should we also consider informal ones? Are institutions 'material objects' or instead a cultural pattern? Are institutions locally embedded, or are they broad and patterns without any boundaries? Are institutions pre-existing for human actions, or are they a product of human activities, etc.

The number of conflicts or disagreements is not limited to those mentioned above. Recent contributors have considered the conflicts previously mentioned so that the definitions they have created seem to be a reasonable compromise. One of the authors who proposed such a definition is Scott (1995, 2008, p. 48), according to whom 'institutions are comprised of regulative, normative and cultural-cognitive elements that, together with associated activities and resources, provide stability and meaning to social life.'

Another concept that is crucial in understanding the role of institutions in stabilizing the market is institutional change. Institutional change – like the concept of institutions – is the subject of many controversies. In general, there are three distinct approaches to this phenomenon:

- First, some researchers do not perceive changes as a crucial and meaningful phenomenon from the institutional system perspective. These researchers include

Table 3.1 Institutions – definition and meaning

Author(s)	*Definition*	*Meaning/implications*
Commons (1931, p. 649)	'collective action in control, liberation and expression of individual action. Collective action ranges all the way from unorganized custom to the many organized going concerns, such as the family, the corporation, the trade association, the trade union, the reserve system, the state'	Institutions are perceived through the lens of collective actions being consequences of some 'working rules' formed by law, statute, administrative decisions, etc.; Commons emphasized the role of 'transactions' in economic interactions
Veblen (1919 [1990], pp. 239-240)	'men's present habits of thought tend to persist indefinitely, except as circumstances enforce a change. These institutions which so have been handed down, these habits of thought, point of view, mental attitudes and aptitudes, or what not, are therefore a conservative factor'	Institutions are part of social settings (their framework is wider than mere economic or political) and have a causal role in shaping human behavior, instincts, and habits
Selznik (1957, p. 16)	'To institutionalize means to infuse with values'	An institution is an organization that has moved from being just an instrument to the level of a meaningful community
Meyer & Rowan (1977)	Institutions are wide cultural and symbolic patterns, rationalized and impersonal prescriptions, rational myths that infuse and diffuse in the organizational world'	Cultural and symbolic patterns and rational myths are becoming more and more similar, and homogeneous, making us deal with organizational and behavioral isomorphism
Shepsle (1986, p. 74)	"*Ex-ante* agreement about a structure of cooperation that economizes the transaction costs reduces opportunism and other forms of agency 'slippage' and thereby enhance the prospects gains through cooperation"	As a representant of the rational-choice type of neo-institutionalism, Shapsle perceives an existing institutional framework as being rational and efficient, hence having a positive impact via organizational and behavioral solutions
North (1990, p. 3; 2005, p. 48)	"Institutions are rules of the game in a society or, more formally the humanly devised constraints that shape human interactions"	There are formal and informal institutions; while the formal one can be learned and imitated by economies from the best institutions from better-performing countries, informal ones are embedded into the society, which created them inert and difficult to change
Knight (1992, p. 2)	'Institution is a set of rules that structure social interactions in particular ways'	

Source: author's compilation

institutional changes in the analysis, only to diminish their importance. According to them, the institutional system is coherent, and the subsystems that make it up are closely interconnected through complementarity. This created a picture of deep-rootedness and almost unshakeable stability, even in the face of external shocks. Ultimately, these researchers point to small, progressive, marginal, and non-consequential alterations (Whitley, 1999; Zeitlin & Herrigel, 2000). Other contributions pay attention to the inherent feature of the institutional system, which is 'flexibility to stability.' This feature is due to mechanisms built into the system that facilitate adapting to changes without breaking the overall system logic (Offe, 1995; Pempel, 1998; Quack & Morgan, 2000).

- Second, other scholars point to the exogenous, dramatic shocks that cause a radical and profound reconfiguration that reaches the foundations of institutions (Westney, 1987; Djelic, 1998). Particularly noteworthy is that these researchers almost ignore the gradual, slow, and even evolutionary changes in institutions in their discussions. At the same time, they emphasize that the significance and consequences of changes caused by exogenous shocks are more significant for the institution system than slow and incrementally occurring changes. Moreover, the latter only recognize in an analysis that covers an extended time frame.
- Third, there is a growing number of contributors who argue that gradual changes can be of great significance for the institution (Streeck & Thelen, 2005; Mahoney & Thelen, 2010). There are at least four different types of institutional change: displacement (introduction of a new rule in place of the removed one); layering (introduction of a new rule on top or alongside the existing ones); drift (change in the impact of institutions due to the shift in the environment); and conversion (revised implementation of existing rules due to their strategic shift).

Conceptual framework

In particular, the conceptual framework for the study conducted is formulated, including fundamentals of neo-institutional theory, analyzed through the lens of firms' behavior and their economic decision-making process. This theory suggests that business behavior is not always the outcome of rational decisions aiming to maximize financial performance (Meyer & Rowan, 1977; Zucker, 1977; DiMaggio & Powell, 1983; Powell & DiMaggio, 1991; Scott, 1995). This is because it has been recognized that the decisions and behavior of individual managers and entire organizations are also shaped by external factors existing in the environment, such as regulations, norms, values, beliefs, and traditions – i.e., institutions in the sense of the rules of the game prevailing in the market (cf. Figure 3.1). Various stakeholders create these institutions (e.g., the government creating regulations, professional industry agencies introducing standards, consumers who impose their beliefs or values, employees deep-rooted in a particular culture, the media and citizens, etc.). All of them can, on the one hand, exert their pressure to stimulate change and shape specific behavior. On the other hand, they can be a source of conditions that guarantee stability, primarily by reducing uncertainty.

Organizations respond to the pressures and expectations of various stakeholders and adapt to the prevailing rules in the market because they need to gain legitimacy to be considered socially acceptable (Meyer & Rowan, 1977). At the same time, they must consider the transaction costs that result from those rules (Coase, 1937; Williamson, 1975). Scott (1995) proposed a certain analytical framework to better understand how environmental factors shape organizational behavior. According to Scott (1995), there are three types of institutions (referred to by him as pillars) that provide legitimacy to an organization's behavior by influencing its structure and decision-making process. These three pillars of institution form respectively (Scott, 1995):

- regulative institutions,
- normative institutions, and
- cognitive institutions.

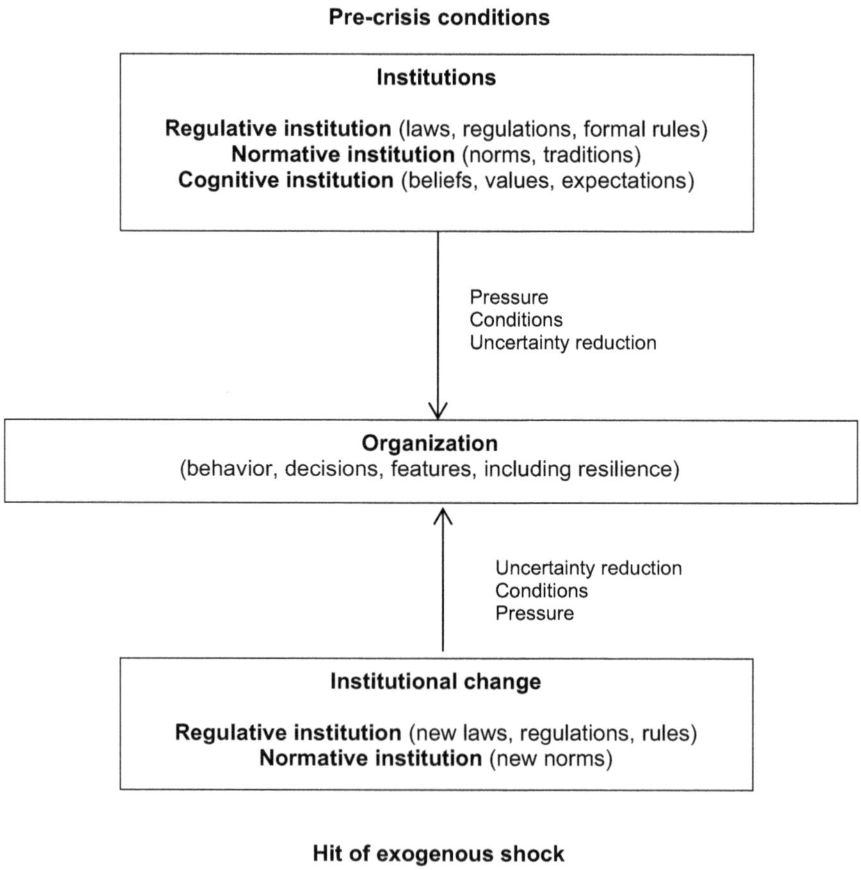

Figure 3.1 Institutions' impact on firm's stability: a conceptual framework

Source: own elaboration

Regulatory institution refers to acting within the framework of market rules, laws, and regulations. Government agencies – by creating laws – put pressure on organizations, which in turn must comply with legal and regulatory requirements to gain regulative legitimacy. The second pillar (i.e., normative institution) focuses on rules imposed by industry agencies, associations, and academic institutions. These stakeholders exert a kind of pressure on companies (known as normative pressure) to act under the norms and traditions. Wanting to gain normative legitimacy, organizations are forced to meet the expectations of these stakeholders by aligning their behavior with existing norms. The cognitive institution is created by so-called take-for-granted expectations, which can be linked to values and beliefs shared by stakeholders. In its nature, a cognitive institution appears to be culturally embedded. By analogy with the regulative and normative institutions mentioned earlier, organizations respond to these 'take-for-granted' expectations to gain cognitive legitimacy.

Organizations respond to stakeholder pressure, expressed in the form of the three pillars of institutions, and consequently gain legitimacy by conforming to regulations, norms, values, beliefs, and expectations (Meyer & Rowan, 1977; Zucker, 1977; Powell & DiMaggio, 1991; Scott, 1995).

The second element of the conceptual framework for the research is institutional change. Given the research subject (i.e., the impact of institutions on stabilizing the situation of companies in the context of the crisis caused by the COVID-19 pandemic), the institutional change included in the model is of a sudden and profound character and caused by an exogenous shock. By nature, this change is mainly related to regulations, rules, and legal norms (regulative and partly normative institutions) and, to a limited extent, to beliefs, values, and traditions (cognitive institution).

Central banks as creators of new institutions in the face of the COVID-19 pandemic

The action taken by different countries' central banks in the face of the COVID-19 pandemic crisis was unprecedented in terms of speed of action, the scope of action, and the scale of action. Undoubtedly, the experience of the Global Financial Crisis (GFC) and the decidedly belated response of central banks to that crisis was significant factor in the rapid and decisive response by central banks in the face of the COVID-19 pandemic. The multifaceted policy reaction of central banks worldwide benefited from extensive institutional change implemented in response to the GFC. This change in financial infrastructure and institutions contributed to a great extent to keep tensions in the global financial markets manageable.

In response to the crisis caused by the pandemic, the world's central banks have taken several measures that can be classified into five distinct groups (cf. Table 3.2):

- an interest rate cut to ease tensions in the financial markets, but also as a factor boosting aggregate demand and supporting economies to fight the economic slowdown,
- the programs of asset purchases (quantitative easing policy) in response to the growing dysfunctions of financial markets and, as a result of the increase in commercial bank lending, as a driver of aggregate demand,

- regulatory easing, e.g., reduction in the requirements for liquidity and capital buffers, reduction in the level of countercyclical capital buffer, and other instruments of macroprudential policy to ensure that banks do not reduce the value of loans distributed to meet regulatory standards,
- liquidity and credit provisions – often in cooperation with governments – to support the provision of credit to business entities to ensure that viable firms can survive the crisis and be able to increase production and support employment,
- foreign exchange policy, which played a crucial role in alleviating strains in the foreign currency market.

Table 3.2 shows that central banks used a range of tools covering all five categories. The basic monetary policy tool – interest rate level – was only an initial and relatively small part of the response. Nevertheless, this tool has been reinforced by so-called forward guidance, i.e., a conditional commitment about the evolution of the policy rate in the future. Central banks started to rely on this additional policy tool in the aftermath of Global Financial Crisis, aiming to influence the private sector's expectations of future policy direction (Woodford, 2013; Morris & Shin, 2018). The speed and extent of the institutional change created by central banks as their response toward the pandemic crisis largely depended on the central banks' past experience, in particular that of the GFC. On the one hand, it was extremely fast and even aggressive with tools that have been used during the GFC and have proved effective, e.g., purchases of government bonds and liquidity provision to financial sectors. On the other hand, the reaction was slower and much cautious regarding new tools or new areas of application (e.g., purchases of corporate bonds).

Table 3.2 Central bank measures in the face of the COVID-19 pandemic

		Advanced economies								*Central and Eastern European countries*			
Tool category	*Measures*	*US*	*EA**	*JP*	*GB*	*CA*	*CH*	*NO*	*SE*	*CZ*	*HU*	*PL*	*RO*
Interest rate	Policy rate cut	+			+	+		+	+	+	+	+	+
Lending operations	Liquidity provision	+	+	+	+	+		+	+	+	+	+	+
	Targeted lending	+	+	+	+		+		+			+	
Asset purchases	Government bonds	+	+	+	+	+			+		+	+	+
	Corporate bonds	+	+	+	+	+			+		+		
	Other private	+	+	+	+	+			+		+		
Reserve policy	Remuneration						+						
	Requirement ratio	+										+	
	Compliance										+		
Foreign exchange	USD swap line		+	+	+	+	+	+	+				
	Swaps										+		
	Spot intervention						+			+			

Notes: * European Central Bank policy represents also policies for some CEECs, i.e., Estonia, Latvia, Lithuania, Slovakia, and Slovenia

Source: based on Cantú et al. (2021)

Initially, central banks used the primary tool, the interest rate, in response to deteriorating financial market conditions. The sudden and often drastic cut in interest rates by central banks was intended to support aggregate demand to stimulate consumption and help economies to rebound. Central banks across the world used a so-called recession toolkit that has been developed during the GFC: cut fast and aggressive to the effective lower bound (ELB) and supplement this institutional change of the environment with the forward guidance (Bernanke, 2020). In advanced economies, interest rates, which were kept low during the crisis, did not provide much opportunity to reduce rates (cf. Australia, UK, US, New Zealand). In other developed countries (Switzerland, Japan, Sweden, and the eurozone), interest rates had already reached zero or negative levels before the pandemic crisis, blocking central banks from using this essential tool. Emerging market economies from Central and Eastern European countries decided to cut policy rates more aggressively since they had space to lower rates (cf. Figure 3.2).

It should be stressed that the transmission mechanism of the COVID-19 crisis to the real economy differed significantly from the shocks that caused earlier crises: first, severe containment measures imposed on the real economy (lockdowns, social distancing, etc.) led to an economic slowdown and then propagated to the financial markets and financial institutions. Due to the abovementioned nature of the crisis (which is not typical for financial crises), one of the most effective tools used by central banks in response to COVID-19 covers liquidity assistance and credit provision. In CEECs, around 70% of lending operations policies entailed newly established programs (Cantú et al., 2021). The core aim of the central banks was to mitigate any constraints on the availability of credit (and thus to stimulate the aggregate demand). The main difference between the new policies and the existing ones was the scale of private sector inclusion (significantly higher in the new policies) and the term (substantially longer in the new policies).

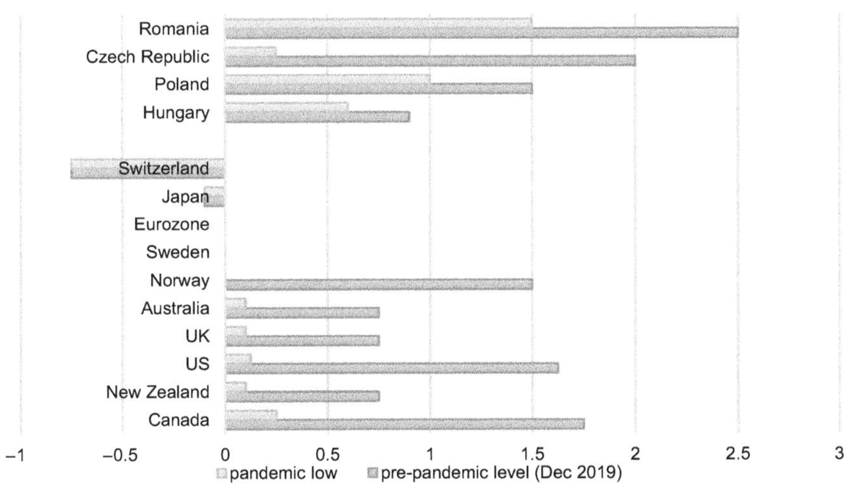

Figure 3.2 Central bank policy rates: pre-COVID to pandemic low

Source: own elaboration based on central banks' data

The vast majority of central banks have used the banking sector as a transmission channel for increasing lending to the corporate sector (regardless of the sector supported, size of the companies, etc.). Some of them allowed companies other than commercial banks to participate in the repo operations (e.g., the Czech National Bank permitted insurance companies and pension funds). In the next step, some central banks decided to act more directly, promoting credit availability to a range of private sector companies, including nonfinancial companies. These programs – including targeted lending – were intended to support viable companies to withstand the pandemic and restart growth once it ebbed. For example, the Federal Reserve, the Bank of Japan, the Bank of England, and the National Bank of Poland established lending policies designed to support specifically small and medium enterprises with funds available at favorable terms.

Another category of central banks' response to the COVID-19 crisis was asset purchase programs. When comparing advanced countries and emerging European countries' approaches, the following issues can be identified:

- in advanced counties, less than 50% of the programs introduced were new, while in emerging countries, the share of new programs was over 90% (i.e., advanced countries' central banks have broader experience in using asset purchase as a tool of monetary policy),
- in advanced economies, the asset purchase programs played a key role – comparable to the liquidity support programs – in responding COVID-19 crisis, while in emerging European economies, it has a relatively limited application (Arslan et al., 2020),
- in advanced economies, the existing programs were expanded in size and the types of assets purchased. In contrast, in emerging economies, the programs have been mostly limited to government securities (cf. Figure 3.3).

In the environment of low-interest rates, some central banks decided to significantly reinforce liquidity support by implementing changes in the reserve policy. Some of them (the Federal Reserve and the National Bank of Poland) were able to quickly free up a large amount of liquidity support to the financial institutions by lowering the reserve requirement ratio. The Central Bank of Hungary – the only one from the analyzed cases – announced measures related to compliance, i.e., changes on instruments that count as reserves. In general, reserve policy has not left central banks much room for maneuver due to historically low ratios and not rather non-active other tools of that policy.

A comparative analysis of the central bank's communication policy versus accurate monetary policy decisions provides interesting conclusions. Significant disproportionality is discernible for many central banks (cf. Figures 3.4–3.9). Central banks of the Czech Republic, Poland, and Romania have largely dominated their communication policy with announcements concerning the primary tool of monetary policy, the interest rate. In all three cases, interest rate policy announcements accounted for nearly 70% of the total. While the intensity of use of various monetary policy instruments was quite similar, the high share of tools in the 'other' category by the Czech central bank is characteristic. The 'other' category contains actions and announcements on technical changes to facilities, loan guarantee programs, and changes to the central bank's law.

The communication policy used by central banks is specifically designed to stabilize the expectations of market participants. Still, at the same time, the content of the message reflects the state of the public's knowledge of monetary policy. The latter factor may explain the divergence between developed countries (Eurozone and the US) and emerging European economies.

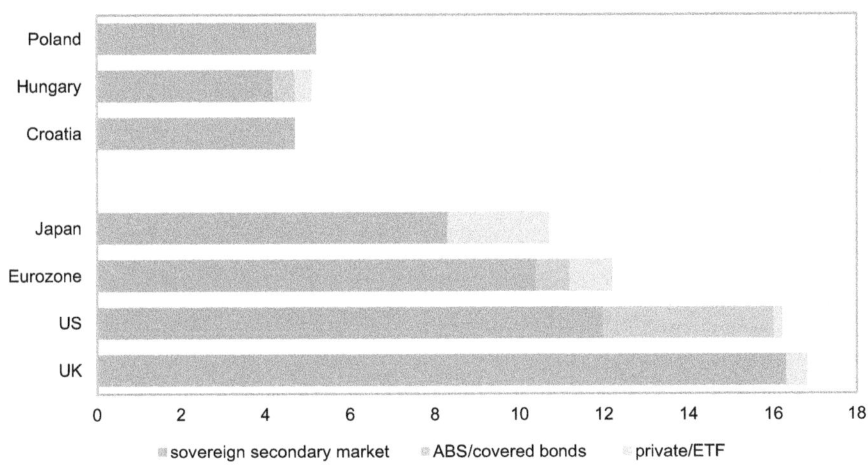

Figure 3.3 Central bank asset purchases programs: advanced countries versus CEECs

Source: own elaboration based on IMF and central banks' data

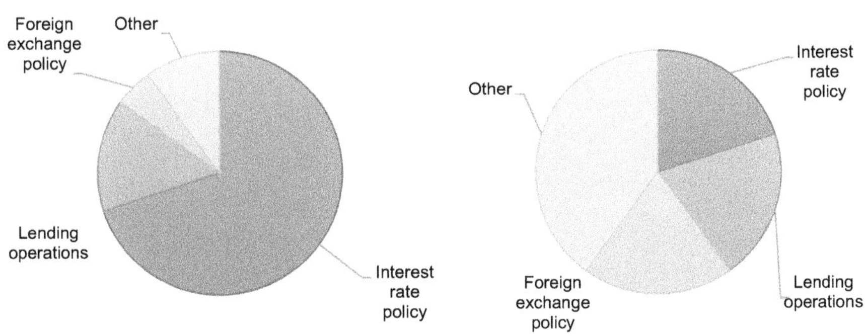

Figure 3.4 Communicating vs using central bank policies – Czech Republic

Source: own elaboration on Cantú et al. (2021)

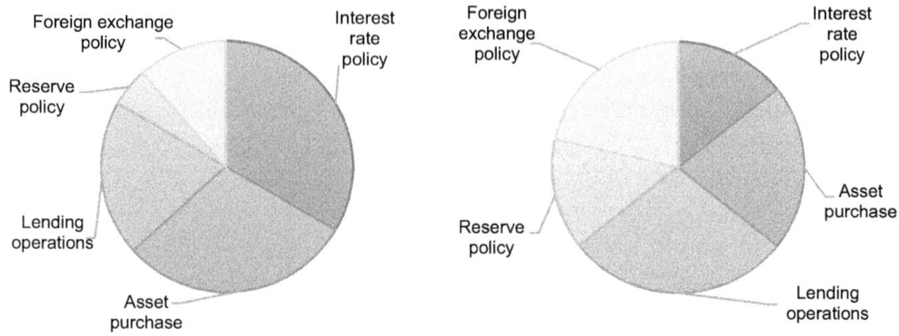

Figure 3.5 Communicating vs using central bank policies – Hungary case

Source: own elaboration based on Cantú et al. (2021)

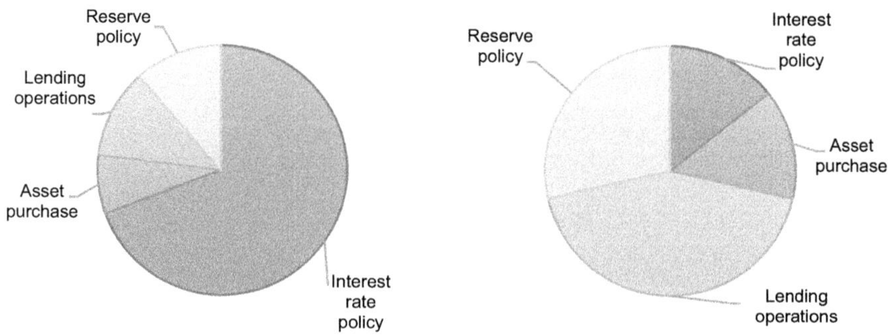

Figure 3.6 Communicating vs using central bank policies – Poland case

Source: own elaboration based on Cantú et al. (2021)

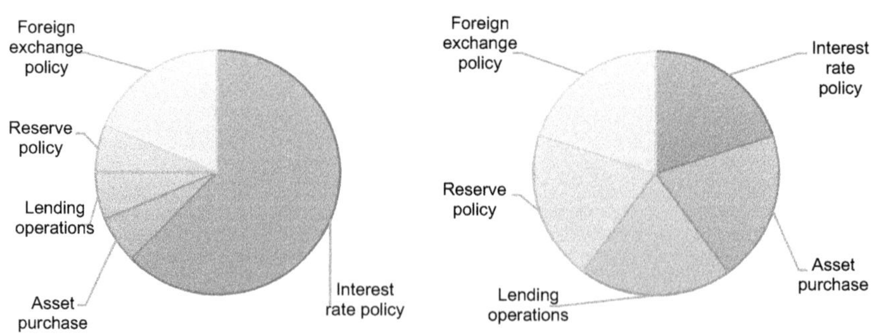

Figure 3.7 Communicating vs using central bank policies – Romania

Source: own elaboration based on Cantú et al. (2021)

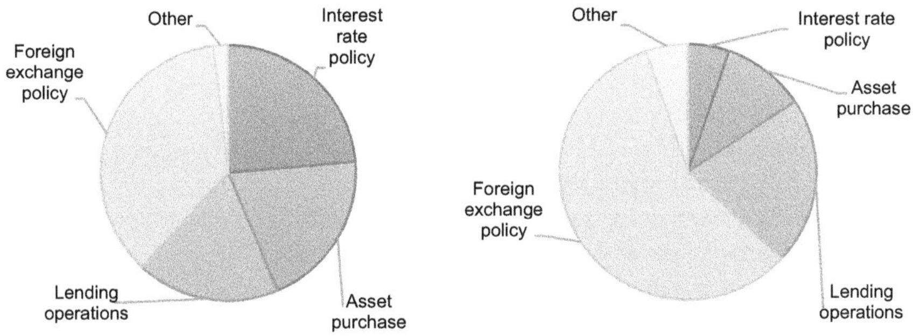

Figure 3.8 Communicating vs using central bank policies – Eurozone

Source: own elaboration based on Cantú et al. (2021)

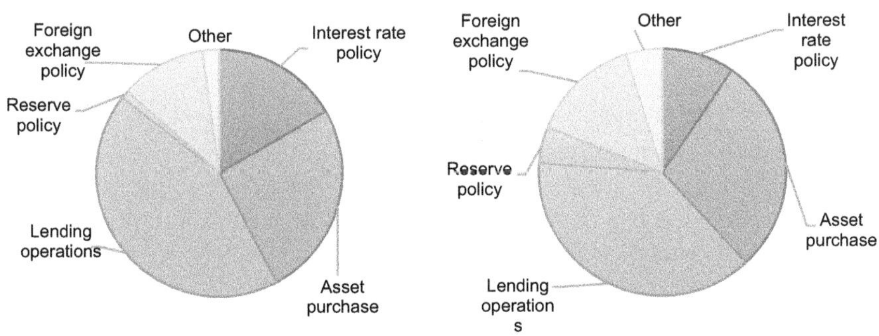

Figure 3.9 Communicating vs using central bank policies – US

Source: own elaboration based on Cantú et al. (2021)

Conclusions

The COVID-19 pandemic was a shock that simultaneously affected real economies through demand and supply transmission mechanisms. The scale of the pandemic shock was reflected in the unprecedented actions central banks took, in terms of both the speed and variety of monetary policy tools.

The natural behavior of central banks across the world is to follow the standards set by the largest financial market 'players,' i.e., the Federal Reserve of the US and the European Central Bank. However, the response of CEECs central banks reflected some specific factors faced by those still emerging economies. Their reactions must be adapted to the specific economic conditions, including significant capital outflows and sharp currency depreciation, which did not appear in developed countries. These specific economic conditions – which undoubtedly amplified the impact of the crisis – were also not experienced by some CEEC countries already part of the eurozone (Estonia, Latvia, Lithuania, Slovakia, and Slovenia).

Introduced quickly and on a large scale by central banks, the institutional change was designed to stabilize financial markets while creating conditions for strong economic recovery. Overall, the actions taken by the CEECs central banks were effective in stabilizing the financial markets. Still, the landscape for monetary policy and central banks has fundamentally changed and raised many new challenges. First, interest rates have been decreased to a very low level (zero in some countries), which could leave central banks without the tool needed to pursue their mandate. Second, the policy of asset purchases has left central banks with substantial balance sheets. Third, the COVID-19 crisis was the first test for the post-Global Financial Crisis regulatory and macroprudential framework. Fourth, the critical challenge facing central banks will come from pressure from politicians and financial market participants regarding the growing informal mandate. The experience of first the Global Financial Crisis and then the crisis triggered by the COVID-19 pandemic leads us to expect that central banks will be forced to consider the moral hazard implications of their policies and develop ways to address them.

Acknowledgments

This contribution draws on the final results of the 'Determinants of company's adaptability to crisis situation – the case of Covid19' project. The project was co-financed by the Polish National Agency for Academic Exchange within the Urgency Grants program.

References

Aoki, M. (2001). *Toward a Comparative Institutional Analysis*. Cambridge: The MIT Press.

Arslan, Y., Drehmann, M. & Hofmann, B. (2020). Central bank bond purchases in emerging markets economies. *BIS Bulletin, 20*.

Bernanke, B. (2020). The new tools of monetary policy. *Presidential Address to the American Economic Association*, 4 January. Retrieved from: https://www.aeaweb.org/articles?id=10.1257/aer.110.4.943 (accessed date: 10.09.2022).

Cantú, C., Cavallino, P., De Fiore, F. & Yetman J. (2021). A global database on central banks' monetary responses to Covid-19. *BIS Working Papers, 934*.

Coase, R. (1937). The nature of firm. *Economica, 4*, 386–405.

Commons, J.R. (1931). Institutional economics. *American Economic Review, 21*(4), 648–657.

DiMaggio, P.J. & Powell, W.W. (1983). The iron cage revisited: Institutional isomorphism and collective rationality in organizational fields. *American Sociological Review, 48*(2), 147–160.

Djelic, M.-L. (1998). *Exporting the American Model*. Oxford: Oxford University Press.

Hodgson, G. (2004). *The Evolution of Institutional Economics*. London: Routledge.

Hodgson, G. (2006). What are institutions? *Journal of Economics Issues, 40*(1), 1–25.

Knight, J. (1992). *Institutions and Social Conflict*. Cambridge: Cambridge University Press.

Mahoney, J. & Thelen, K. (Eds.) (2010). *Explaining Institutional Change. Ambiguity, Agency, and Power*. Cambridge: Cambridge University Press.

Meyer, J. & Rowan, B. (1977). Institutionalized organizations: Formal structure as myth and ceremony. *American Journal of Sociology, 83*, 340–363.
Morris, S. & Shin, H.S. (2018). Central bank forward guidance and the signal value of market prices. *AEA Papers and Proceedings, 108*, 572–577.
North, D. (1990). *Institutions, Institutional Change and Economic Performance*. Cambridge: Cambridge University Press.
North, D. (2005). *Understanding the Process of Economic Change*. Princeton: Princeton University Press.
Offe, C. (1995). Designing institutions for East European transition. In J. Hausner, B. Jessop, & K. Nielsen (Eds.), *Strategic Choice and Path-dependency in Post Socialism*. Aldershot: Edward Elgar.
Pempel, T. (1998). *Regime Shift: Comparative Dynamics of Japanese Political Economy*. Ithaca: Cornell University Press.
Powell, W.W. & DiMaggio, P.J. (Eds.) (1991). *The New Institutionalism in Organization Analysis*. Chicago: The University of Chicago Press.
Quack, S. & Morgan, G. (2000). National capitalism, global competition and economic performance: An introduction. In S. Quack, G. Morgan, & R. Whitley (Eds.), *National Capitalism, Global Competition and Economic Performance*. Amsterdam and Philadelphia: Benjamins.
Scott, R.W. (1995). *Institutions and Organizations*. London: Sage.
Scott, R.W. (2008). *Institutions and Organizations* (3rd ed). London: Sage.
Selznik, P. (1957). *Leadership in Administration*. New York: Harper & Row.
Shepsle, K. (1986). Institutional equilibrium and equilibrium institutions. In H. Weisberg (Ed.), *The Science of Politics*. New York: Agathon Press.
Streeck, W. & Thelen, K. (2005). Introduction: Institutional change in advanced political economies. In W. Streeck & K. Thelen (Eds.), *Beyond Continuity: Institutional Change in Advanced Political Economies*. Oxford: Oxford University Press.
Veblen, T. (1904 [1975]). *The Theory of Business Enterprise*. New York: New American Library (Reprinted (1975), New York: Augustus Kelley).
Veblen, T. (1919 [1990]). *The Place of Science in Modern Civilisation and Other Essays*. New York: Huebsch (Reprinted (1990) with a new introduction by Samuels, W.J., New Brunswick: Transaction Books).
Weber, M. (1978). Economy and society. In G. Roth & C. Wittich (Eds.), *Economy and Society*. Berkeley: University of California Press.
Westney, D.O. (1987). *Imitation and Innovation. The Transfer of Western Organizational Patterns to Meiji Japan*. Boston: Harvard University Press.
Whitley, R. (1999). *Divergent Capitalisms*. Oxford: Oxford University Press.
Williamson, O. (1975). *Markets and Hierarchies*. New York: Free Press.
Woodford, M. (2013). Forward guidance by inflation-targeting central banks. *Paper Presented at the Conference Two Decades of Inflation Targeting: Main Lessons and Remaining Challenges*, Sveriges Riksbank, 3 June.
Zeitlin, J. & Herrigel, G. (Eds.). (2000). *Americanization and Its Limits*. Oxford: Oxford University Press.
Zucker, L.G. (1977). The role of institutionalization in cultural persistence. *American Sociological Review, 42*(5), 726–743.

4 Reflections on the challenges of future Eurozone expansion on the example of Poland

Avoiding the crisis with a common currency?

Marta Götz

Introduction

This chapter aims to assess the accession of a new country to the euro area (the enlargement of the euro area in the example of Poland) in the context of the reforms of the common currency area, and thus to diagnose the related challenges – potential opportunities and threats. Firstly, there is a need to determine what institutional changes have recently taken place in the architecture and governance of the euro area (EA), and then to describe the existing adjustments and the mode of Poland's convergence/divergence with the Eurozone (EZ). Finally, an attempt to outline the further path towards integration with the euro area is made, including the challenges that such integration brings. The analysis refers to various conceptual frameworks and is set in the broader context of the latest euro area reforms initiated after the 2008+ crisis and the measures taken in response to the outbreak of the COVID-19 pandemic.

The members of the Eurozone are already 19 countries of the Union, and there are still eight outside: Bulgaria, the Czech Republic, Denmark, Poland, Romania, Sweden, Hungary, and Croatia. The benefits and costs of participation in the monetary union have been repeatedly and widely discussed in economic literature (Małecki, 2009). Despite these reservations, efforts to join the EZ are being made by the successive European Union (EU) member states. Croatia and Bulgaria are seeking to become the twentieth and twenty-first countries to adopt the single currency. They are also joined by Romania (Forbes, 14.05.2018). The entry of new countries into the Eurozone, despite the debt crisis after the global financial collapse in 2008 and repeated predictions of the collapse of the EZ, shows that the common currency is still attractive. Demertzis (2022) argues that the euro had come of age. The last 20 years have seen two "once-in-a-lifetime" crises. There have been enough opportunities to assess the EZ members' willingness to continue within EZ. Regardless of the reasons, countries have chosen to defend the euro by implementing progressively more mutualised instruments. The EU's decisive response during the pandemic resulted from appreciating the importance of collective action in such circumstances.

This chapter is organised as follows. First section discusses the reforms and changes in the EZ architecture and governance since the 2008+ crisis and includes also the latest COVID-19 pandemic-induced developments in this respect. The next

DOI: 10.4324/9781003345428-4

part reviews the main economic similarities and differences between Poland as one of the pre-ins EZ members and EZ itself, as well as the current state of the convergence process. Finally, based on these considerations, challenges for future EZ accession and membership will be presented.

Eurozone reforms so far . . .

The membership in EZ as a common currency area is regulated by the treaties and framed in so-called Maastricht criteria, which stipulates the benchmark values of selected indicators. The economic crisis, which revealed various irregularities of the incomplete architecture of EMU, was a cold shower that led to strengthening supervisory mechanisms and enforced better coordination of economic policies. Before the 2008+ economic crisis erupted, joining the Eurozone was mainly conditioned by meeting the nominal convergence criteria (Vasiloiu, 2019). However, due to the multiple, often unexpected problems experienced by the Eurozone members during the crisis, EZ bodies launched a variety of measures aiming to improve EZ resilience. In consequence, the conditions for new candidates became more complex. Gradually, new requirements imply reaching a high level of real convergence, maintaining macroeconomic balance, or joining the Banking Union (BU). Among the reforms already carried out in the euro area, it is worth mentioning first of all the creation of the European Stability Mechanism (ESM) and the construction of the BU. ESM was created in order to offer assistance to the member states experiencing public finance problems. The lending capacity of the mechanism is financed through Member State contributions in relation to their GDP and regulated by the ESM Treaty. It is supposed to provide a permanent framework for financial assistance to euro area countries and hence to safeguard financial stability in the euro area. Banking Union is the EU's bank supervision and resolution regime, operating under EU-wide rules. It aims to ensure that the banking sector in the euro area and across the EU is safe and sound and that insolvent banks are restructured or wound down without using taxpayers' money and with minimal impact on public finances and the real economy (Götz, 2012). All Eurozone countries and willing EU countries outside the zone belong to the BU. All countries that adopt the euro in the future will automatically become members of the Banking Union. In addition to the institutional reforms mentioned earlier, it should be noted that since March 2015, the European Central Bank (ECB) has joined central banks conducting so-called unconventional monetary policy in the form of quantitative easing (QE) to stimulate bank lending and boost the economy. The 2008 crisis, brought to the surface the shortcomings of the EMU construction, aggravated the economic crisis in some member states (MS) (Czerniak & Smoleńska, 2019). Lack of safety mechanisms or common supervision over the banking sector caused certain disintegration of European financial markets (a decrease in cross-border transactions, divergence in risk assessment of MS). Hence, euro area reforms since the crisis aimed at the reintegration of banking systems of the euro area under single supervision, the introduction of risk-sharing (via financial markets as well as stabilisation mechanisms) and greater synchronisation of business cycles. New economic governance mechanisms and institutions were introduced (Pisani-Ferry, 2014; Sandbu, 2017), and, as argued by Czerniak & Smoleńska (2019), these reforms have importantly changed the ratio of costs and benefits of new candidates adopting the euro, including Poland.

EZ has indeed undergone extensive reconstruction for several years. It began shortly after the outbreak of the financial crisis, which prompted the MS to reform fiscal institutions and start building a Banking Union. Still, in many key areas, no decisions were made, primarily due to fundamental differences in interests of MS. This evolution should be closely watched by the EU pre-ins that are bound by membership, but still not decided on the accession date. The reforms proposed would result in important institutional and legal changes that Poland should consider when deciding to join the euro area (Götz, 2020). However, as noted, interpretation and reception of planned reforms in the EU have been anything but clear, ranging from heralding them as a game-changer, to scepticism; opinions that propositions are either misconceived, fall short of the current needs, or have an inappropriate sequence.

However, not only did the 2008+ crisis initiate the actions towards redesigning euro area architecture and management, but another critical moment was the COVID-19 pandemic breakout. In this respect, Next Generation European Union (NGEU) should be seen as an extraordinary fund to support Europe's post-pandemic recovery, with a focus on green and digital dimensions. To finance it, as agreed in the summer of 2020, the European Commission will borrow a total of around €800 billion on the capital markets until the end of 2026, or an average of €150 billion per year (Forsal, 2021). In the longer term, the issuance of debt under the NGEU should have the effect of making the euro area more resilient to economic shocks and making the euro more attractive as a global transaction currency. This effect is to be expected by linking the NGEU fund to reforms that will strengthen the growth potential and internal cohesion of the euro area. Incidentally, member states had to structure their national recovery plans in such a way as to allocate at least 37% of the funds to green transformation and a minimum of 20% to digitalisation. The issuance of Corona bonds will create a new class of so-called safe assets. "Safe assets" mean liquid financial assets that maintain or increase their nominal value even during a deep recession. A "new class", in turn, means that the bonds under the NGEU are not linked to a specific country, but have a community character. While average spending in the overall EU budget is around 1% of EU GDP per year, the next generation increases it by another 0.7% of GDP (Dorn et al., 2021). The debt-financed fund will be raised by the EU but backed by guarantees from the MS. The fund aims to provide mutual support in times of crisis and to speed up the recovery from the Corona crisis.

Jones et al. (2021) argue that in some circumstances European integration proceeded through a pattern of failing forward: in an initial phase, lowest common denominator intergovernmental bargains led to the creation of incomplete institutions, which in turn sowed the seeds of future crises, which then propelled deeper integration through reformed but still incomplete institutions – thus setting the stage for the process to move integration forward. Howarth & Quaglia (2021) apply such a "failing forward" approach (learning from setbacks and making the necessary adjustments to move on) to analyse reforms to Eurozone economic governance to tackle the COVID-19–related crisis of EMU. This crisis highlights both spillovers from major asymmetries in EMU and weaknesses in the incomplete economic governance of the Eurozone. As they claim, the NGEU financial package fails to address and, rather, contributes to existing asymmetries, thus sowing the seeds of future crises.

Heinemann (2021) argues that the establishment of a sovereign debt restructuring mechanism (SDRM) would be one of the important issues in the robust EMU constitution. Yet, the topic seems to be taboo in the official debate, which is primarily due to political economy expectations: low-debt countries support an EMU constitution with an insolvency procedure, whereas a coalition of high-debt countries and EU institutions oppose it. Hence, in such a situation, possible political–economic equilibrium for coping with sovereign insolvencies would be an institutional set-up without an SDRM but with some hidden transfers. The recent response to the COVID-19 solvency shock confirms this prediction.

COVID-19's first reactions at the EU level encompass the ECB's launch of a large programme of asset purchases and the European Commission temporarily shutting down budget rules and lifting state aid rules (triggering an "escape clause" in fiscal rules), as the MS themselves were initially inward-looking; they unilaterally closed borders and focused on crisis management at home. The second round of measures included actions aiming at restarting the European economy, guided by the principle to repair, restore, and reconstruct the economies.

The first round showed that ECB again serves as the last resort, "the only game in town" bearing too much of the burden, implying asymmetry and more to be done by fiscal policy.[1] Through indiscriminate support, the EU unwillingly promoted the "survival of the fittest" – a situation where only those with the "richest parents" (i.e., governments that can afford generous stimulus) survive. Mutualisation (sharing the debt), like monetisation (EBC purchasing in primary markets sovereign bonds), proved again to be a rather toxic topic in the EU. The "COVID-19 pandemic is the latest example of the failure of the EU to deliver one of the most the most basic raisons d'être of a union of states, namely, the effective provision of union-level public goods" (Georgiou, 2020). Nevertheless, the EU recovery fund (NGEU) is supposed to ensure that the EU MS do not drift further apart after the pandemic and will provide €390 billion to MS through grants and €360 billion through repayable loans. It means that for the first time, the EU is raising funds from financial investors in such a large volume that apparently – as judged by the massive demand for the first Covid-related EU bonds – they are looking for "safe havens", and with the EU as a debtor, they are even accepting negative interest rates (Heimberger, 2021). As such success demonstrates the formidable potential of EU bonds backed by MS, it could be used for future EU programmes addressing challenges such as climate change and digitalisation. EU issuance of up to €750 billion in bonds to finance the EU recovery plan might in the future be a model for tackling common problems such as climate change. Another initiative, SURE (Support to mitigate Unemployment Risks in an Emergency), was meant to enable national governments to borrow at preferential rates in order to finance higher unemployment and related social transfers. The funds raised by issuing EU bonds are passed on to the MS to help governments keep workers in their jobs during the pandemic. All in all, an extraordinary EU fiscal response to this pandemic is demonstrated by the European Recovery and Resilience Fund (part of Next Generation, which as some claim might be seen as the litmus test for CFC central fiscal capacity for EMU; Beetsma et al., 2021); the Sure Program to finance the explosion of unemployment benefits; the Pandemic Crisis Support Line of the ESM to fund the drastic increases in health expenditures; and the strengthening of the guarantees programme by the European Investment Bank – extraordinary in speed, amount, cohesion, and unity (Fernández Méndez de Andés, 2022). However, they have been one-time programmes and emergency actions thus far, and hence it remains open as to whether they will become a structural part of EU architecture.

Various proposals have been tabled against the background of the risk of disintegration of the euro area in the long run, also causing resentments and recriminations (core-burden; periphery-conditionality). Despite an avalanche of measures and initiatives, the general perception in capitals was that the EU's response has been too little, too late. However, what exactly was expected and how much EU involvement was envisaged varies considerably. Questions arise as to whether more or less coordination is needed; fear of neglect of or even discrimination against non-Eurozone members by the rest of the Eurozone emerged, and, likewise, expectations of economic and financial burden-sharing and concerns about the transfer of additional competencies to the EU. EU-wide Covid-19 management revealed the need to put more energy into finding ways of sharing both the benefits and the burdens of EU membership.

De Grauwe & Ji (2022) analysed the emergence of the pandemic in 2020 and revealed that it has not led to a new debt crisis in the Eurozone, even though the shock produced by Covid-19 was at least as large as the 2008 crisis. The fact can be attributed to the new governance of the Eurozone, which skilfully prevented this shock from evolving into a full sovereign debt crisis, though it does not imply that the Eurozone now has matured and become less fragile in nature. This is because ECB faces 19 sovereigns, none of which has authority over the ECB, and hence none of these governments can force the ECB to provide liquidity in times of crisis. This uncertainty concerning the ECB's role as a lender of last resort in the government bond markets will continue to make the Eurozone a fragile construction. Codogno and van den Noord (2020) show that the introduction of a Eurobond together with fiscal capacity at the centre would produce macro-stabilisation benefits for both the EZ "core" and "periphery" – had a Eurobond/fiscal capacity existed at the onset of the 2008+ crisis, the recession would have been much more muted, and with much less need for unconventional monetary policy.

In summary, the 2008+ financial crisis and the outbreak of the Covid-19 pandemic were two watershed moments for the process of redesigning EZ architecture and its governance. The various mechanisms put in place at that time received mixed reviews and provoked ambivalent reactions ranging from criticism of being too little too late, to praise of the ground-breaking nature of these solutions, even described as a milestone and "Hamilton moment" for Europe (Odendahl & Springford, 2020). Much has been accomplished, but much still needs to be done.

Attitudes and achievements so far

The basic dilemma that pre-in countries' decision-makers might face is how to balance the legitimacy of joining the Eurozone (due to the guarantee of fully benefiting from the changes taking place in it) with the probable difficulties it poses (due to the possible incomplete economic readiness to introduce the euro and in the face of significant uncertainty as to the direction of development of the euro area itself).

Analysing the level of integration in international networks or roles along global value chains (GVC) might be predictive of the potential benefits of euro adoption. The more the business is tied with EZ partners, the more it can benefit from the simplicity, transparency, and certainty resulting from euro adoption. The importance of foreign firms as measured by the value-added in foreign subsidiaries (FS), which can be emblematic of the integration level within GVC, shows that in all Central and European (CEE) countries this share has been increasing, though with some fluctuations (Götz & Jankowska, 2021). The higher the share, the larger the integration and the larger the potential benefits from adopting the common currency. Interestingly, the highest level of embeddedness in global production networks is shown by Hungary and Romania, which are not EZ members.

Trade with the 19 countries in the EZ remains vital for ECE non-EZ members – in particular for Poland, which is the sixth most important partner for the extra EA19 trade, followed by the Czech Republic, Hungary, and, interestingly, Romania (Götz & Jankowska, 2021). The higher the levels, the more the economy contributes to the total intra-EU trade and, hence, the larger the expected gains from using a single currency. Interestingly, the EZ membership does not seem to correlate with the level of ties. ECE countries that adopted common currency are not necessarily those particularly relevant for the total intra-EU trade. A very rough analysis shows that the magnitude of linkages and weight of the ECE country economy does not seem to be a good predictor of a country's decision to join the common currency area or to stay away. Poland and Hungary, despite being closely tied to mainly the German economy, have deliberately decided not to join the Eurozone in the foreseeable future. In general, it seems the Polish government's unwillingness to join the EZ is mainly justified by associated risk and costs outweighing the benefits. This is primarily due to the economic divergence and differences in GDP p.c. levels among EZ members and Poland and the fact the euro area continues to proceed through fundamental reorganisation.

The December 2021 Convergence Monitor with the Economic and Monetary Union prepared by the Macroeconomic Policy Department of the Ministry of Finance underlines that since Poland acceded to the EU, the relative income level of the population has been increasing, approaching the average level of other euro area MS, but Poland's GDP per capita is still slightly below the average of the CEE countries (Ministry of Finance, 2021). As noted in the monitor, the trend of a widening gap in the GDP structure between Poland and the euro area continued in 2020, especially concerning a higher share of industry and trade in the Polish GDP and a lower share of real estate and public services. A weakening of the similarity scale between Poland and the euro area is also observed in the case of investment structures. These divergences of economic structures do not affect the high level of similarity of business cycles, which is considered typical for the catching-up process. On the other hand, the disproportions observed between Poland and the euro area in terms of financial structures should be explained by, inter alia, the lower level of development of the financial sector, but as emphasised in the monitor, given the benefits arising from the stability of the traditional model of the banking system, the convergence to the state observed in the developed EMU countries should not always be considered as desirable. On the other hand, there is no doubt that the Polish economy needs to improve its competitive structure by developing non-price competitive advantages and increasing innovation. Importantly, the economic development of Poland takes place in the absence of excessive imbalances.

In economic terms, CEE "pre-ins" or "outs" could perform quite well inside as well as outside the EZ. Yet, the EU is clearly not only about economic benefits, as it represents shared commitments to European values. Eurozone membership was not a determining factor for economic success in CEE.

> There were both good and bad macroeconomic performances in both flexible and fixed-exchange-rate regimes of central European countries. The implication is that the Czech Republic, Hungary and Poland, as well as the other central European "outs", could be successful both with and without the euro.
> (Darvas, 2018)

As argued by Bod et al. (2021) one would have assumed that particular domestic interests or political factors would gradually lose importance in the process of convergence within the EU, and the increasingly positive cost–benefit balance tilts the arguments in favour of a timely EA entry. Yet, the hoped-for convergence had been repeatedly disturbed by episodes of divergence, particularly at times of crises and turbulences, weakening the economic logic of euro adoption. The 2022 outbreak of war in Ukraine, following the brutal Russian invasion and subsequent exchange rate fluctuations on global financial markets leading to the depreciation of the Polish zloty, added a new argument of a geopolitical nature in favour of EZ membership.

The last available (pre-Covid-19) Convergence Report by EC (2020) indicates that, apart from the legal criterion, Poland does not fulfil all nominal convergence criteria, either. Specifically,

> the Act on the Narodowy Bank Polski (NBP) and the Constitution of the Republic of Poland – is not fully compatible with the compliance duty under Article 131 TFEU. In addition, the Act on the NBP also contains some imperfections relating to central bank independence and the NBP integration into the European System of Central Banks (ESCBs) at the time of euro adoption.

As inferred from the latest available Convergence Report (EC, 2020), Poland does not fulfil the criterion on price stability, as the average inflation rate in Poland in 2020 was 2.8%, above the reference value of 1.8%. Poland fulfils the criterion on public finances since the general government deficit declined to 0.2% in 2018. However, the general government debt-to-GDP ratio is forecasted to strongly increase from 46% in 2019 to over 58% in 2021. Poland does not fulfil the exchange rate criterion – Polish zloty is not participating in ERM II. Poland fulfils the criterion of the convergence of long-term interest rates. The average long-term interest rate was 2.2%, below the reference value of 2.9%. Obviously, the (post)Covid environment will drastically change the general price levels across economies, with inflation levels recording unprecedented values even in advanced economies.

As we can infer from the latest Convergence Report (2020), Poland's external balance stayed in surplus over the past two years, supported by an improvement in the services trade balance. The Polish economy is well integrated with the euro area through trade and investment linkages. Based on selected indicators relating to the business environment, Poland performs around the average of euro area MS. Poland's financial sector is well integrated into the EU financial sector.

Cieślik and Teresiński (2020) compare business cycles in the Eurozone and Poland using a dynamic stochastic general equilibrium (DSGE) approach. Although they do not find significant differences in structural parameter estimates, it turns out that the persistence and volatility of shocks differ between the two economies. Impulse response functions are comparable and output fluctuations are driven by similar demand shocks, but they observe a significant effect of the exogenous spending shock in the EZ and the price markup shock in Poland. Their analysis also shows that the euro adoption in Poland is currently not recommended unless relevant changes in macroeconomic and labour market policies are implemented. Dissimilarities between the Eurozone and Poland might be successfully overcome due to the implementation of relevant macroeconomic and labour market policies, and therefore, despite the existing differences, the euro adoption could still be justified.

The results obtained by Heller and Warzala (2019) demonstrate that the position of countries after joining the Eurozone varies from nation to nation. Latvia and Lithuania joined the Eurozone only a few years ago (2014 and 2015, respectively), and thus the long-term effects are not yet clear. In the other countries researched, however, macroeconomic indicators of stabilisation can be observed after their entrance into the Eurozone. In this context, Poland's economy also seems to be stable, although it remains out of the Eurozone. All the countries researched appear to have experienced growing β- and σ-convergence with the European Union core (EU 12). Adopting the common currency cannot be considered a remedy for all national economic difficulties. Entering the common currency area can be regarded as one of several essential factors that may support economic growth, but for this development to take place, a series of other economic conditions must be met. Progressing convergence associated with Eurozone membership can be identified; nevertheless, in the case of Poland, the decision to join the EZ should be preceded by systematic and comprehensive analysis, i.e., one that embraces both short-term as well as long-term changes to jumpstart euro adoption instead of becoming a stalling point requiring difficult structural adjustments.

Casagrande and Dallago (2021) claim that European institutional variety means that each MS reacts differently to shocks and policies, follows a different path of recovery, and adapts to common institutions, including the common currency, in different ways. As noted by the varieties of capitalism (VoC) theory, proponents of economic convergence have underestimated the potential for advanced capitalist economies not to converge toward a single liberal market because of the comparative institutional advantage of different socioeconomic models (Hall & Soskice, 2001). VoC theory seems to conclude that economic convergence based on institutional convergence is undesirable or simply impossible for the Eurozone. However, there are no reasons to believe that a similar type of convergence is necessary for the success of the Eurozone: "there is increasing recognition in the economics literature that high-quality institutions can take a multitude of forms and that economic convergence need not necessarily entail convergence in institutional forms" (Rodrik, 2007, p. 52). The solidity of the Eurozone depends on "high-quality institutions", that is, the ability of the member countries to enable their institutional frameworks to coexist. The European benchmark aims to demonstrate that this coexistence is possible, and that each MS can reach similar sustainable outcomes, although in idiosyncratic ways. Institutional variety is not an obstacle; rather, it is the tool that enables understanding of how to calibrate the various national policies so that each country converges toward a situation capable of guaranteeing economic stability and development.

In conclusion, it should be stressed that convergence in the context of the process of joining the euro area is a multidimensional category. It is both the synchronisation of business cycles and reactions to external shocks; it is the most popular nominal convergence, i.e., fulfilment of the Maastricht criteria; it is structural convergence indicating the similarity of economic structures; and, finally, it is institutional convergence related to the adopted model of capitalism (VoC).

What does this mean for the future?

EZ membership is one of Poland's obligations laid out in the Accession Treaty of 2003, and thus in legal terms, it ought to be the question of "when" and not "whether" to adopt the euro. However, the whole situation becomes more complicated due to several factors (Götz et al., 2018). After the crisis, EZ accession seems to be governed by multiple rules and regulations, such as fiscal compact, ESM rules, and Banking Union, and requires considering the issue of meeting the Maastricht criteria, the convergence level, the cost–benefit analysis of having common currency as well as the new governance and architecture in post-crisis EZ (Götz, 2020). One must bear in mind that even if the current "outs" decide to join the euro, it will not happen overnight. Given the obligatory two-year membership of ERMII, three years might be the minimum transition period. Besides, it is not only about meeting the five Maastricht nominal convergence criteria or adjusting domestic legislation. Candidates will have to adhere to an increasing number of new regulations, which requires a lot of work that can be reasonably done only over a couple of years' time horizon.

The current discussion concerning EZ membership by Poland is subject to extremely high uncertainty caused by the recently dynamically changing international context. As argued by Götz et al. (2019), precise analysis could only take the form of exploration of possible scenarios: (1) definitive resignation from single currency in Poland, (2) rapid accession to EZ, and (3) further unclear postponement of Poland's EZ membership. Each of the variants gives rise to different political and economic effects, hence paving alternative paths for the long-term development of the Polish economy.

The discussion on joining the euro area must not ignore recent EZ reforms (Götz, 2020). Nominal criteria do not seem to be a major problem, as the example of the south EU countries showed – their literal fulfilment does not always reflect the actual condition of the economy in the long run. Resilience to possible crises resulting from, for instance, the state of public finances or competitiveness of the economy (market freedom – new entries, legal and economic solutions – e.g., labour market – but also export offer and its competitive advantages) seems much more important. This is because the elements of possible EZ risk-sharing seem to give way to financial market discipline and responsible fiscal policy.

There is a growing recognition that euro adoption in Poland is more a matter of willingness than overcoming real obstacles (Siemonczyk, 2018). For the moment, the priority of Polish economic policy is to increase the potential and competitiveness of the economy. New entrants must adhere to the guidelines of the Banking Union but also come to terms with problems of the financial system and its supervision, and non-banking sectors – insurance, pension funds – need to govern properly the functioning of SOEs as well as to put in order the insolvency framework (Götz, 2019). Poland would at the end of the day join a much different Eurozone from what one might have expected some years ago. EZ is now rather a "complex integration project" (Götz et al., 2018). Becoming an EZ member would require most likely meeting a set of new criteria and fulfilling extra conditions – as the case of Bulgaria shows (Götz, 2020). It illuminates that in the future EA membership would imply not only the necessity of meeting new ad hoc conditions but also the importance of real convergence (raised by the EU bodies) and the quality of institutions (often questioned) as well as the acceptance and readiness to welcome a new EZ member by the indigenous countries (Pieńkowski, 2018). Adhering to the rules of the Banking Union, participating in ESM would be the conditions sine qua non. This suggests that the old narrative concentrating on Maastricht criteria would not suffice. In addition, once an EZ member, the country's economy would be permanently and constantly exposed to market discipline.

In the discussion on the introduction of the euro in Poland, two tipping points can be identified. First, an earlier, popular argument was that in the long term, the benefits of adopting the euro in Poland outweigh the costs and that single currency can be a driver of real convergence, ensuring a faster reduction of the income gap, but the outbreak of the crisis in 2008 triggered a new wave of research on the effectiveness of the floating exchange rate as a tool mitigating the impact of negative demand shocks on the economy (Borowski, 2021). The tentative conclusion showed that higher GVC participation in Poland diminished the effectiveness of the exchange rate adjustment mechanism. In other words, the shield provided to the Polish economy by the floating zloty exchange rate is less effective today than it was two decades ago. The second turning point was the outbreak of the Covid-19 pandemic. To limit the negative economic effects of the pandemic, the NBP started to purchase government securities. International experience suggests that the effectiveness of central bank asset purchases may decline along with an increase in the central bank's balance sheet. This implies uncertainty about the effectiveness of unconventional monetary policy in small open economies, which needs to be factored into the debate on the long-term macroeconomic effects of adopting the euro in Poland. If further research validates the decreasing marginal effectiveness of asset purchases, this would be another argument – apart from the less powerful exchange rate adjustment mechanism – pointing to the diminishing cost of monetary integration. This, in turn, would suggest that the welfare effects of the adoption of the euro in Poland could still be unequivocally positive.

However, some experts believe that after 2010 the crisis in the euro area caused a rather radical re-evaluation of views. From the serious problems of some of the euro area member states (Greece, Ireland, Portugal, Spain, Cyprus, Slovenia, and, to some extent, Italy), the conclusion was drawn that the loss of autonomous exchange rate and monetary policy poses such a serious threat to the loss of international competitiveness by the economy that not only can no acceleration of economic growth be expected, but rather a crisis and chronic stagnation must be reckoned with. In the absence of a sovereign exchange rate policy, restoring the competitiveness of the economy is possible only through so-called internal devaluation, i.e., a reduction in wages and prices, which must be associated with a chronic recession with all the social and political consequences that this entails. Under these circumstances, giving up one's own currency is not advisable at all or at least in the not-too-distant future (Małecki, 2018). Special requirements must be placed on fiscal policy. In the absence of autonomous monetary and exchange rate policies, it may be the only macroeconomic instrument available in crises. However, this will only be possible if, in good times, an adequate fiscal buffer is built up to enable a strongly expansionary fiscal policy to be undertaken if necessary. The medium-term objective of fiscal policy should therefore not be a deficit below 3% of GDP, but at least a balanced budget, and in good times a budget surplus. In the case of Poland, this would therefore require a fundamental change of priorities in fiscal policy. Appropriate infrastructure for conducting macro-prudential policy should be prepared in advance. For this purpose, a specific institution must be appointed, characterised by the greatest possible degree of independence, and equipped with the broadest possible range of instruments, which will effectively prevent unstable credit booms and the emergence of speculative bubbles in the markets for real estate and financial assets.

Czerniak and Smoleńska (2019) focus on the implications of Poland's decision to delay its adoption of the common currency and, in contrast to previous studies, distinguish between different types of costs and benefits – i.e., consequences of monetary integration that are certain and easily measurable (e.g., the reduction of transaction costs) and those that are less certain and can only be roughly estimated (e.g., the increase in investment activity or reduction in the cost competitiveness of exports). While the ratio of measurable costs and benefits suggests that adopting the euro could give Poland an additional growth stimulus, such an effect would be small or within the margin of growth forecast error. Most significant costs and benefits are contingent on the institutional framework. Premature and badly prepared monetary integration could result in economic losses significantly exceeding the measurable benefits – estimates suggest long-term GDP loss of even 7.5%. On the other hand, monetary integration preceded by sound institutional preparation would bring Poland an additional growth stimulus for the next decades – GDP could be higher by as much as 7.8%. This would be the case in particular with improved regulations of labour and financial markets and a relatively weak conversion rate of zloty to euro, additionally supported by a responsible and non-populist fiscal policy, i.e., budgetary discipline also at the peak of the economic cycle. Czerniak and Smoleńska's (2019) analysis demonstrated that delaying euro adoption does not provide a clear-cut answer to the questions of "whether" and "for how long" Poland should refrain from pursuing monetary integration with the EZ. Although the balance of measurable costs and benefits indicates that adopting the euro early would give some boost to economic development, the effect would be negligible, whereas with delayed monetary integration, the measurable costs will fall in real terms. On the other hand, the benefits will grow in time, suggesting that postponing EZ will not be too expensive for Poland.

Also, ongoing EZ reform will impact the costs and benefits. Emerging EMU institutions and new risk-sharing mechanisms provide a new framework for economic governance and crisis management. Thus, the growing cost of delaying euro adoption is a limited impact on the future EMU architecture and whether it will be conducive to the Eurozone as a whole, and Poland in particular. The ongoing discussion among experts (Bruegel, A debate on fiscal rules and the new monetary strategy, Presentation of the Yearbook of the Euro 2022, 17.02.2022) points out the future reorientation from purely monitoring fiscal national policies towards more central coordination of thereof and focus on expenditures but not at the expense of key (green, digital) investments, as such are critical for the provision of European public goods and can be justified to be financed by debt (whereas consumption from current revenues taxes). All these upcoming challenges must be factored into the proper debate on euro adoption.

Conclusions

The upcoming twentieth anniversary of the unprecedented enlargement of the EU by ten new countries in 2024 provides an opportunity to reflect on the problem of joining the euro area. This chapter is an attempt to analyse and evaluate the process of joining the euro area by Poland (the enlargement of the euro area in the example of Poland) conducted against the background of the changes taking place in the area itself – i.e., in the context of the introduced reforms leading to deepening of monetary integration. It tries to identify the most important challenges connected with this process – to determine the scope of benefits, but also potential threats connected with the adoption of the common currency.

Comprehensive research regarding EZ accession by new MS in a post-crisis environment indicates the multidimensionality of the context and the variety of variables that are necessary for a reliable evaluation. At the same time, it seems to become extremely important not only to get into the Eurozone but to be able to stay within it for good. Quickly changing surroundings – transformations of the euro area and planned modifications of the EU itself – cause any estimates of profits and losses to be subject to multiple additional conditions.

Planned and implemented reforms of the Eurozone also reveal that there is no single right recipe so far; the implemented changes are assessed very differently, but they show a clear direction of change as they emphasise market discipline while introducing risk-sharing.

The euro is not a guarantee of success, but it is an opportunity for the well prepared. Member states must be reminded to build their own fiscal space, to create cushions in the good times to respond to the bad times without expecting European rescue (Fernández Méndez de Andés, 2022). There is not yet a fiscal stabilisation facility EZ, and when there is one, it would most certainly be subsidiary in nature.

The case of Croatia, which had a euro adoption strategy back in 2017 and is joining only in January 2023 after six years, illuminates the complexity and the length of this process, which even more justifies the need of starting a discussion on preparation now. The necessary arrangement now also encompasses participation in BU pillars, especially the second – supervision mechanism – but also in the pre-entry committee and subsequent commitments in areas such as anti-laundering money or regulations of SOE.

It is time to initiate a debate on the current complex project that is the Eurozone and raise awareness of what the Eurozone is becoming. It is illusory to think that we will enter when the EU zone is healthy, and Poland is 100% ready. It is necessary to be well prepared, to take care of stable finances, as the budget policy will remain the only instrument in the policy mix, to boost competitiveness (other than cost competitiveness), and to remain aware of unequal distribution of effects.

The current EU framework needs revision as it is not good enough in anticipating future problems, and previous experience and dealing with crises 2008+ or Covid-19 have showed it actually reaches its political and legal limits (Maduro et al., 2021). Recent developments revealed the tweaking possibilities have been mostly exhausted and, in the current environment ultra-low interest rates, monetary policy is becoming ineffective, which requires more European fiscal stance and coordination across dimensions – fiscal and monetary policies but also national and EU levels. Accommodating for growing EZ heterogeneity requires more flexibility and new rules as the old ones are no longer fit for the purpose; new ones should focus on externalities and sustainability of EMU. Even if certain actions still from a legal perspective can be handled within existing treaties, they will require enormous political will and cooperation.

To sum up, one can risk a statement that just as for the EU the situation of a common monetary policy with no fiscal policy is unstable, so too for Poland; it is unstable in the long run to be a member of the EU but to remain outside the EZ. This can be described as certain parallel dilemmas: "EZ & PL facing twin challenges". This often-expressed temptation for quick and easy answers concerning EZ membership – binary decisions and absolute opinions based on definite cost–benefits analysis – should be certainly avoided and replaced by balanced and broader discussion with arguments being substantiated rather than ascertained.

Note

1 ECB approved its new monetary policy strategy in July 2021. The revision was justified by trends such as globalisation, digitalisation, population ageing, and climate change, all of which affect the structure and functioning of financial systems: for instance, the rise of non-bank financial intermediaries and the rapid emergence of digital and decentralised finances, and in light of a long period of very low interest rates and expansion of monetary instruments that can no longer be considered nonconventional after continuous use for over ten years. The new strategy includes two fundamental revisions: a symmetric inflation target of 2%, and a requirement for forceful monetary policy action when the economy is close to the lower bound. The ECB has broadened its toolkit to encompass "forward guidance, asset purchases and longer-term refinancing operations, or any other instrument, as appropriate". Financial stability is a precondition for price stability, and ECB, within its mandate, recognises the need to incorporate climate considerations into its monetary policy framework (Fernández Méndez de Andés, 2022).

References

Beetsma, R.M., Cimadomo, J. & Van Spronsen, J. (2021). One scheme fits all: A central fiscal capacity for the EMU targeting Eurozone, national and regional shocks. *European Central Bank Working Papers*. Retrieved from: http://www.ecb.europa.eu/pub/pdf/scpwps/ecb.wp2666~170f00add8.en.pdf

Bod, P.Á., Pócsik, O. & Neszmélyi, G.I. (2021). Varieties of euro adoption strategies in Visegrad countries before the pandemic crisis. *Acta Oeconomica*, *71*(4), 519–550.

Borowski, J. (2021). Poland and euro adoption: From integration-driven enthusiasm to post-pandemic uncertainty. In K. Arató, B. Koller, & A. Pelle (Eds.), *The Political Economy of the Eurozone in Central and Eastern Europe* (pp. 184–197). London: Routledge.

Casagrande, S. & Dallago, B. (2021). Benchmarking institutional variety in the eurozone: An empirical investigation. *Economic Systems*, *45*(1).

Cieślik, A. & Teresiński, J. (2020). Comparing business cycles in the Eurozone and in Poland: A Bayesian DSGE approach. *Bank i Kredyt*, *51*(4), 317–366.

Codogno L. & van den Noord, P. (2020). Going fiscal? A stylised model with fiscal capacity and a Eurobond in the Eurozone. *Luiss SEP Working Paper*, 4. Retrieved from: https://sep.luiss.it/sites/sep.luiss.it/files/Going%20fiscal.%20A%20stylised%20model%20with%20fiscal%20capacity%20and%20a%20Eurobond%20in%20the%20Eurozone.pdf

Czerniak, A. & Smoleńska, A. (2019). Poland without the euro: A cost benefit analysis. *EUI Research Repository*. Retrieved from: https://cadmus.eui.eu/handle/1814/65788

Darvas, Z. (2018). Should central European EU members join the euro zone? *Bruegel*. Retrieved from: http://bruegel.org/2018/09/should-central-european-eu-members-join-the-euro-zone/

De Grauwe, P. & Ji, Y. (2022). The fragility of the Eurozone: Has it disappeared? *Journal of International Money and Finance*, *120*.

Demertzis, M. (2022). The euro comes of age. *Bruegel*. Retrieved from: http://www.bruegel.org/2022/01/the-euro-comes-of-age/

Dorn, F., Fuest, C., Heinemann, F., Schratzenstaller, M., Thöne, M., Becker, P., Waldhoff, Ch., Neumeier, Ch., Barley, K. & Freund, D. (2021). Corona-Aufbauplan: Bewährungsprobe für den Zusammenhalt in der EU? *ifo Schnelldienst*, *74*(2), 3–30. Retrieved from: http://www.ifo.de/publikationen/2021/aufsatz-zeitschrift/corona-aufbauplan-bewaehrungsprobe-fuer-den-zusammenhalt-der

European Commission. (2020). *Convergence Report 2020*. Retrieved from: https://ec.europa.eu/info/publications/convergence-report-2020_en

Fernández Méndez de Andés, F. (2022). *Good Policies, A Gap Year on Reforms. A Yearbook on the Euro 2022*. Retrieved from: http://www.fundacionico.es/documents/137403/0/EURO+IN+2022+INT_Definitivo.pdf/ed9bbb86-c582-5fa5-e9de-ee2f2c495b9e?t=1645024248072

Forsal (2021). *Emisja koronaobligacji wzmocni euro i nie zagrozi dolarowi* (*The issue of corona bonds will strengthen the euro and will not threaten the dollar*). Retrieved from: https://forsal.pl/gospodarka/artykuly/8222811,emisja-koronaobligacji-wzmocni-euro-i-nie-zagrozi-dolarowi.html

Georgiou, A.V. (2020). Is the European Union failing the viability tests? *World Economics*, *21*(2), 105–108. Retrieved from: https://cepr.org/voxeu/blogs-and-reviews/european-union-failing-viability-tests

Götz, M. (2012). *Kryzys i przyszłość strefy euro* (*The crisis and the future of the Eurozone*). Warsaw: Difin.

Götz, M. (2019). Analysing Poland's Eurozone accession through lenses of policy arrangement approach. *Przegląd Zachodni*, *371*(2), 189–209.

Götz, M. (2020). Euro area reforms and Poland – The state of the game. In A. Visvizi, A. Matysek-Jedrych, & K. Mroczek-Dąbrowska (Eds.), *Poland in the Single Market, Politics, Economics, the Euro* (pp. 166–182). London: Routledge.

Götz, M. & Jankowska, B. (2021). Companies in central and Eastern Europe and Eurozone membership: An attempt at a microeconomic analysis. In K. Arató, B. Koller, & A. Pelle (Eds.), *The Political Economy of the Eurozone in East Central Europe "Why In – Why Out?"* (pp. 99–115). London: Routledge.

Götz, M., Nowak, B.E. & Orłowski, W.M. (2018). Poland and the Euro zone. Three possible scenarios and their consequences. *Studia Europejskie-Studies in European Affairs*, *3*, 203–219.

Götz, M., Nowak, B.E. & Orłowski, W.M. (2019). Polska w strefie euro? Trzy scenariusze i ich prawdopodobne konsekwencje ogólnoekonomiczne (Poland in the eurozone? Three scenarios and their probable general economic consequences). *Środkowoeuropejskie Studia Polityczne*, *1*(1), 123–154.

Hall, P.A. & Soskice, D. (2001). *Varieties of Capitalism: The Institutional Foundations of Comparative Advantage*. Oxford: Oxford University Press.

Heimberger, P. (2021). EU bonds are a model for the future of Europe. *The Vienna Institute for International Economic Studies*. Retrieved from: https://wiiw.ac.at/eu-bonds-are-a-model-for-the-future-of-europe-n-480.html

Heinemann, F. (2021). The political economy of euro area sovereign debt restructuring. *Constitutional Political Economy*, *32*(4), 502–522.

Heller, J. & Warzala, R. (2019). The effects of entering the Eurozone on other central and Eastern European countries in relation to Poland. *Journal of Competitiveness*, *11*(1), 5–21.

Howarth, D. & Quaglia, L. (2021). Failing forward in economic and monetary union: Explaining weak Eurozone financial support mechanisms. *Journal of European Public Policy*, *28*(10), 1555–1572.

Jones, E., Kelemen, R. & Meunier, S. (2021). Failing forward? Crises and patterns of European integration. *Journal of European Public Policy, 28*(10), 1519–1536.

Maduro, M., Martin, P., Pisani-Ferry, J., Piris, J.-C., Reichlin, L., Steinbach, A. & Weder di Mauro B. (2021). *Reforming the EU Macroeconomic Policy System: Economic Requirements and Legal Conditions*. Retrieved from: https://voxeu.org/article/reforming-eu-macroeconomic-policy-system-economic-requirements-and-legal-conditions (accessed date 16.12.2021).

Małecki, W. (2009). Globalny kryzys finansowo gospodarczy a przystąpienie Polski do Unii Gospodarczej i Walutowej (The global financial and economic crisis and Poland's accession to the Economic and Monetary Union). In W. Małecki (Ed.), *Globalny kryzys finansowy a polska gospodarka* (*The global financial crisis and the Polish economy*) (pp. 161–184). Warsaw: Vizja Press and IT.

Małecki, W. (2018). New political and economic circumstances surrounding polish accession to the eurozone. *Gospodarka Narodowa. The Polish Journal of Economics, 294*(2), 29–47.

Ministry of Finance (2021). *Convergence Monitor with the Economic and Monetary Union*. Retrieved from: http://www.gov.pl/web/finanse/monitor-konwergencji-z-ugw

Odendahl, Ch. & Springford, J. (2020). *CEPR Video with Philippe Martin, Lucrezia Reichlin, Revisiting the EU Framework. Economic Necessities and Legal Options*. Retrieved from: https://voxeu.org/content/revisiting-eu-framework-economic-necessities-and-legal-options

Pieńkowski, J. (2018). Aspiracje Bułgarii do członkostwa w strefie euro (Bulgaria's aspirations for membership in the Eurozone). *Biuletyn PISM, 1703*(130). Retrieved from: https://pism.pl/publikacje/Aspiracje_Bu_garii_do_cz_onkostwa_w_strefie_euro

Pisani-Ferry, J. (2014). *The Euro Crisis and Its Aftermath*. New York: Oxford University Press.

Rodrik, D. (2007). *One Economics, Many Recipes: Globalization, Institutions, and Economic Growth*. Princeton: Princeton University Press.

Sandbu, M. (2017). *Europe's Orphan: The Future of the Euro and the Politics of Debt*. Princeton and Oxford: Princeton University Press.

Siemonczyk, G. (2018). Euro w Polsce. Żeby euro mieć, trzeba tylko chcieć (Euro in Poland. To have euro, you just need to want euro). *Rzeczpospolita*. Retrieved from: http://www.rp.pl/Finanse/301019945-Euro-w-Polsce-Zeby-euro-miec-trzeba-tylko-chciec.html&cid=44&template=restricted

Szczurek, M. (2021). EU Emergency COVID-19 Instruments as an attempt to address deficiencies in the EMU design. *Gospodarka Narodowa. The Polish Journal of Economics, 308*(4), 83–102.

Vasiloiu, I.N. (2019). Expanding the eurozone. The stage of economic convergence for Bulgaria, Czech Republic, Croatia, Hungary, Poland and Romania. *Theoretical & Applied Economics, 26*(4), 5–18.

5 How the COVID-19 pandemic has affected the macroeconomic environment for doing business

A close look at the GDP fluctuations and public debt distress in CEE countries

Marta Wajda-Lichy, Łukasz Jabłoński, and Kamil Fijorek

Introduction

Before the COVID-19 pandemic, i.e., 2010–2019, the world increased its output at an average annual growth of approximately 3.3%, which was highly spatially diversified between regions and groups of countries. For example, the Central and Eastern European (CEE) countries grew at that period moderately, i.e., 3.1% annually, which indicates that this group of countries turned out to be more successful in terms of economic growth than high-income countries, including averages of the European Union (EU), EU-15, and the Organisation for Economic Co-operation and Development (OECD). Nevertheless, the economic performance of the CEE countries was diversified before the pandemic (Figure 5.1). Annual average GDP growth rate above 3% was recorded by Romania (3.8%), Poland (3.6%), and the Baltic states, e.g., Latvia (3.2%), Lithuania (3.7%), and Estonia (3.7%). The lowest economic growth in this group of countries was recorded in Croatia and Slovenia (below 2.0%). Other countries of this group, such as Czechia, Hungary, Bulgaria, and Slovakia, yielded a GDP growth rate that ranged between 2.0% and 3.0% annually. In turn, China and India increased their output at the highest rate of growth, averaging 7.15% annually, compared to the earlier mentioned group of countries. Due to the strong economic interdependence between them and other Asian economies, the Association of Southeast Asian Nations (ASEAN) group of countries also yielded a relatively high average growth rate in this period (5.0%) (WDI, 2022).

The economic performance of the global economy in 2020 was determined by the eruption of pandemic of COVID-19, and economic policy measures introduced to mitigate negative outcomes of COVID-19 crisis. Considering the negative health impact, high mortality, and spatial coverage of the Sars-Cov-2 virus, governments of a majority of countries introduced strict containment measures in the middle of March 2020. These measures aimed to limit social contact and travelling among and between countries. Consequently, between March and April, the Oxford stringency index reached a level of 80 points (Figure 5.2), where 0 points represents a lack of restrictions and 100 points represents complete restrictions on social contact and travelling (Lacey et al., 2021, p. 8).

DOI: 10.4324/9781003345428-5

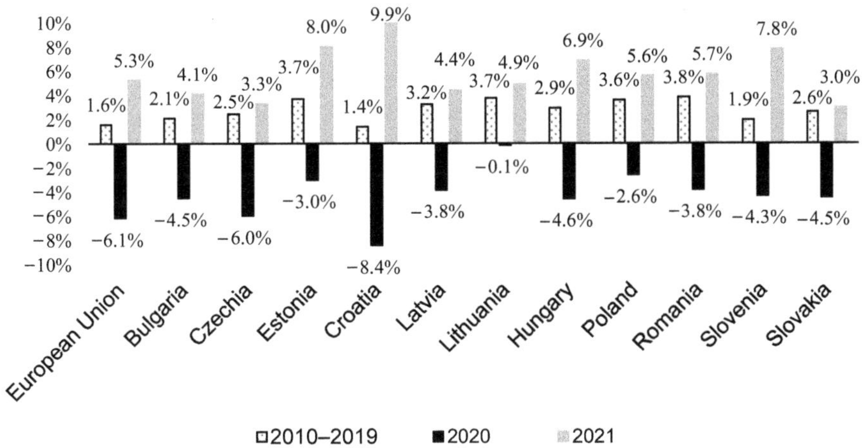

Figure 5.1 Annual average GDP growth rate

Source: own elaboration based on WDI (2022)

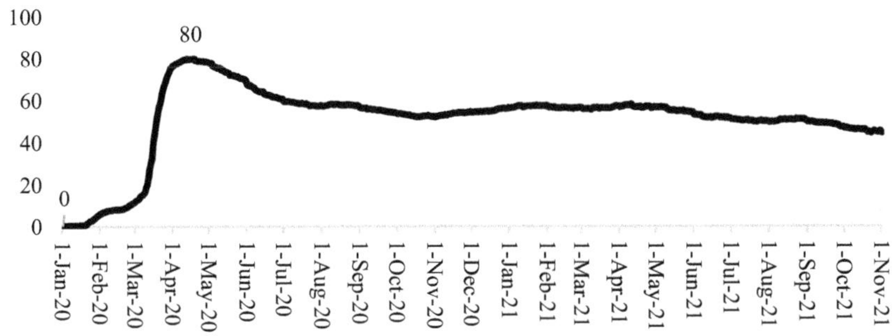

Figure 5.2 Global average Oxford Stringency Index by day

Source: own elaboration based on Hale et al. (2021)

The restrictions imposed to mitigate the negative health effects of the pandemic caused economic slowdown and then crises, which in turn varied between countries at different levels of economic development. High-income countries, such as Western European countries of the EU-15 or the OECD, together with Southern-American Mercosur countries, faced much steeper drops in GDP than the CEE countries. Although the GDP of all CEE countries in 2020 was on average 3.8% lower than in the previous year, the extent of the pandemic recession varied within this group of countries. The greatest declines were experienced by Croatia (−8.4%) and Czechia (−6.0%), with Lithuania experiencing the lowest (−0.1%). Other countries of this group faced a moderate recession that ranged between −2.6% and −4.5%, i.e., Poland (−2.6%), Estonia (−3.0%), Romania and Latvia (−3.8%), and Slovenia, Slovakia, Bulgaria, and Hungary (approximately −4.5%; see Figure 5.1).

The economic performance of 2021 turned out to be the most successful in almost 50 years. The global GDP rose then by approximately 6.0% annually. As a result of easing most remaining pandemic-related restrictions and due to well-tailored fiscal and monetary policies during the pandemic, the majority of emerging countries in South-East Asia and Latin America experienced rapid economic growth in 2021. The GDP of South-American and Latin American countries in 2021 was approximately 7.0% higher compared to 2020, while the CEE countries were approximately 5.4% higher (Figure 5.1). Post-pandemic economic recovery turned out to be most successful in Croatia, Slovenia, Estonia, and Hungary, which increased their GDP in 2021 by 9.9%, 7.8%, 8.0%, and 6.9%, respectively. Other countries of this group increased their output more moderately, i.e., Romania and Poland (5.6% and 5.7%, respectively), Bulgaria, Latvia, and Lithuania (4.1% to 4.9 %), and Slovakia and Czechia (3.0% and 3.3%, respectively; BIS, 2022, p. 2; IMF, 2022b). Most countries continue to face challenges with regard to growth in a post-pandemic environment, including fiscal burdens as well as inflationary pressures; as such, high growth rates should not be taken for granted.

Fiscal policy responses

The COVID-19 pandemic and its economic outcome posed some challenges to fiscal policy responses, among which at least two are worth emphasizing. The measures implemented to mitigate the negative health outcomes of COVID-19 caused deterioration in the fiscal outlooks of national economies. Budget revenues decreased since, on the one hand, the tax base narrowed (i.e., company profits), while income from capital and import of some taxpayers decreased; on the other hand, fiscal administration reduced the advanced tax payment (CIT, PIT) as a result of lowering both tax rates and tax exemptions. Simultaneously, national governments increased public spending to support (a) health care systems in limiting the epidemiological implications of COVID-19, (b) companies to limit threat of their bankruptcy, and (c) households that faced deterioration in their disposal income (Haroutunian et al., 2021).

To counteract negative implications of the COVID-19 pandemic, national governments commonly used fiscal policy measures, the usefulness of which in stabilizing an economy has been undermined since 1980 in favour of monetary actions. Early monetary policy responses to the pandemic crisis show, however, that monetary policy without implementing fiscal measures is unable to counter the devastating economic effects of COVID-19 on the real economy. In such conditions, policy makers gave a greater degree of prominence to fiscal policy measures, in particular those of a discretionary nature. It is worth emphasizing the new aspect of the pandemic crisis, that governments had to provide companies and individuals with financial relief while at the same time restricting running economic activity. As a result, discretionary fiscal policy measures became more important in counteracting the negative outcomes of the pandemic crisis (Devereux et al., 2020, p. 228; Mazzucato & Kattel, 2020).

Since all countries were hit by an economic shock determined by similar epidemiological and health issues, governments took similar actions to respond the pandemic crisis. In the initial phase, i.e., March 2020, governments launched emergency packages that covered both liquidity support and budgetary measures. National governments introduced mainly fiscal measures to improve the capacity of the health care system to mitigate the devastating implications of the virus and to hospitalize infected individuals, along with measures tailored to provide loans and tax credits for companies and direct cash transfers and other supplementary ad hoc programmes for households. They were targeted to support the companies and individuals affected by the pandemic. These measures were renewed in narrowed scope at the end of 2020, when a majority of European countries introduced lighter lockdowns to counteract the second wave of rising infections. Additional measures were partially introduced between the broad and lighter lockdowns to enhance recovery. In this phase, the majority of companies reopened, but some sectors were still covered by health measures and related restrictions on social contact (Haroutunian et al., 2021).

Thus, the fiscal interventions introduced during the pandemic by the majority of countries covered, firstly, budgetary measures aimed at supporting the health care system in counteracting health outcomes of pandemic; secondly, direct financial support for companies; and, thirdly, direct cash transfers for individuals. The fiscal administration also used liquidity measures, consisting of broadening tax deductibility and tax credits and other public payments suspension, along with preferential loans for companies (Haroutunian et al., 2021; Lacey et al., 2021, pp. 8–14).

The majority of countries used similar fiscal interventions to counteract the pandemic crisis, and they took these actions relatively rapidly. However, two issues are worth emphasizing given the context of the CEE countries. Firstly, highly developed countries introduced fiscal packages faster than those countries at a lower level of economic development. Nevertheless, the majority of countries watched actions taken by governments of those countries that were hit by the pandemic early (i.e., China, Hong Kong SAR, Singapore) and consequently took swifter counteracting action. Therefore, the EU- and OECD-member states implemented fiscal discretionary measures earlier comparing to emerging markets, which took fiscal action at the turn of March and April 2020 (Elgin et al., 2021; Haroutunian et al., 2021; World Bank, 2020, p. 8). Similarly, the CEE countries introduced stimulus fiscal packages in mid-March, i.e., during the initial phase of the pandemic. They used similar fiscal measures, such as alleviating the fiscal burden for business (lowering health care and social contributions, subsidizing wages for employees, tax credits, launching credit guarantees, loans for entrepreneurs, subsidized interest for working capital); supporting household income by, for example, providing a monthly basic income; and financial assistance to the self-employed, pensioners, and students, as well as subsidies to kindergarten and large families (IMF, 2022a).

Secondly, the sizes of fiscal packages were related to the level of a country's economic development (Aizenman et al., 2021; IMF, 2021b; Peters & Jandrić, 2021; World Bank, 2020). Therefore, countries with higher GDP per capita dedicated a greater percentage of their GDP to fiscal stimulus during the pandemic compared to those with lower per capita incomes. In 2020 and 2021, high-income countries' pandemic responses amounted to 16% of GDP (additional spending or foregone revenues). Another 11% of their GDP was dedicated to balance sheet measures, such as equity injections, loans, asset purchase or debt assumptions, and contingent liabilities. Middle-income countries responded to pandemic crisis more moderately, with approximately 4.2% of GDP dedicated to additional spending or foregone revenues, with another 2.5% of GDP for other fiscal measures. In turn, the least developed countries used a fiscal stimulus that amounted to 1.8% of GDP as additional spending and foregone revenues and 1.6% of GDP for other fiscal measures to counteract the COVID-19 pandemic (IMF, 2021b).

The CEE countries, like the rest of the EU, used affluent fiscal stimulus during the pandemic. Czechia (20.8% of GDP) and Slovenia, Hungary, and Poland (approximately 13% of GDP) dedicated the greatest proportion of GDP to counteracting the devastating implications of the pandemic. Estonia (8.6% of GDP), Slovakia (8.8% of GDP), and Lithuania (9.2%) used relatively smaller stimulus packages (IMF, 2021b). Regardless, the differences among the CEE countries in size of fiscal packages were larger in relation to GDP than those used by emerging and developing countries. Moreover, a large proportion of fiscal packages in these countries, as in other EU and OECD countries, was dedicated to protecting the incomes of and supporting households and employment, and then the fiscal stimulus was directed to the healthcare system.[1]

As a result, the governments of the CEE countries spent greater proportions of their GDP in 2020 compared to the pre-pandemic period. It is worth emphasizing that rapid increase of this spending in 2020 resulted from, firstly, affluent fiscal stimulus and, secondly, economic contraction due to the pandemic crisis. Simultaneously, post-pandemic recovery in 2021 lowered the governmental spending as reflected by percentage of GDP, although some pandemic fiscal measures were still operating at that time (Figure 5.3).

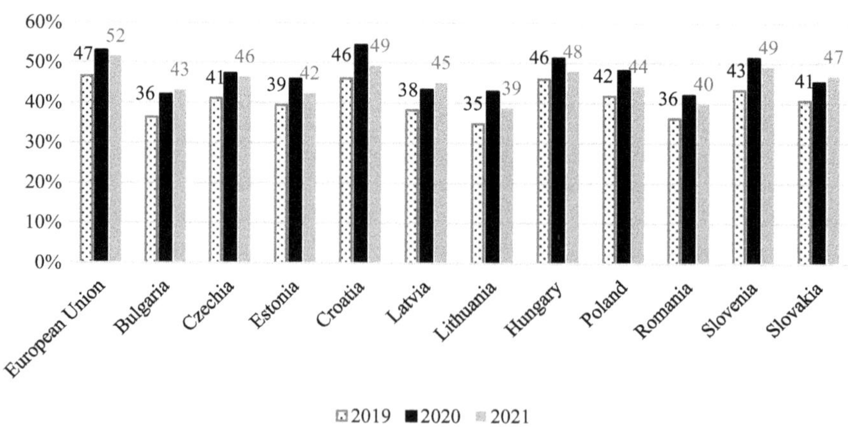

Figure 5.3 Total general government expenditure as a percentage of GDP

Source: own elaboration based on Eurostat (2022)

General government indebtedness

Unplanned government expenditures during the pandemic coincided with a sharp decline in public sector revenues as a result of a sudden collapse in economic activity. An obvious effect of these developments was the deterioration of public finance stability, recorded by many economies as substantial increases in public deficits and government indebtedness. Figure 5.4 shows public sector debt, defined as the total gross debt at face value outstanding at the end of each quarter for the general government sector, given as a percentage of GDP. The data on a quarterly basis allows us to check how quickly public debt spread across countries in the aftermath of the COVID-19 pandemic.

In just the first two quarters of 2020, public debt has increased by 10 p.p. on average in the EU economies. Among CEE countries, Slovenia, Croatia, Slovakia, and Estonia recorded higher increases in debt-to-GDP ratio than the EU average, by 12.3, 11.6, 11.5 and 10.2 p.p. respectively. Over the two first quarters of 2020, Poland and Czechia also increased their debt-to-GDP ratio substantially, by around 9 p.p. In the other CEE countries, debt-to-GDP increased in this period by 1.2 p.p. (Bulgaria) to 6 p.p. (Latvia).

According to the Stability and Growth Pact (SGP), agreed in 1997 (i.e., two years before the creation of the Economic and Monetary Union), the EU member states are required to keep sound public finance, i.e., government deficits below 3% of GDP and public debt levels below 60% of GDP. The EU fiscal governance rules were revised after the global financial crisis in 2008; however, the above-mentioned limits were maintained, specifying that member states are required to reduce the gap between the debt-to-GDP ratio and the 60% threshold on average by 1/20 per year. The SGP also provides a general escape clause that can suspend the enforcement

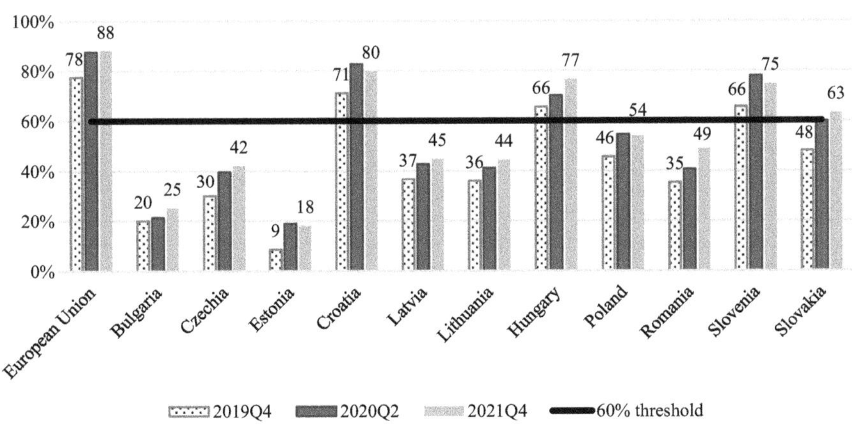

Figure 5.4 General government debt as a percentage of GDP

Source: own elaboration based on Eurostat (2022)

of fiscal rules in exceptional times. The COVID-19 pandemic was considered an exceptional circumstance, and thus in March 2020 the European Commission applied the above clause, suspending enforcement of the excessive deficit procedure. Otherwise, the procedure would have been applied against four CEE countries. In 2020, the 60% limit for debt-to-GDP ratio was exceeded by Croatia, Hungary, and Slovenia – each with excessive debt recorded prior the outbreak of the pandemic. Slovakia, whose public debt-to-GDP of 48% was well below the limit in 2019, exceeded it in 2021. Although the rest of the 11 CEE countries recorded a ratio of debt-to-GDP below the 60% limit, this does not mean there were no macro and microeconomic effects.

What does economics tell us about the consequences of public debt?

On the one hand, the debt incurred must be repaid with interest, which implies an overall macroeconomic burden. Its size depends on the scale and the method of debt financing, as well as the borrower's credibility and the depth of financial markets. The final cost of the public debt burden is uncertain, as the value of the outstanding liabilities fluctuates not only with the level of sovereign security yields but also due to the volatility of government spending and revenues. The latter are closely associated with a business cycle and fiscal policy preferences. As borrowing enables governments to smooth cyclical fluctuations and sustain economic growth, expansionary fiscal policy may generate future fiscal revenues. According to Keynesian economics, the effects of fiscal policy are amplified by the mechanism of the expenditure multiplier. Hence, public debt managers should account for the dynamics of the debt burden. Moreover, the lagged effects of fiscal policy should be considered. Since repayment of the current debt is staggered over time, the cost of the debt may often burden future generations (Diamond, 1965).

On the other hand, by borrowing from the financial market, governments compete with the private sector for funds. As the public sector increases its indebtedness, it absorbs savings, leaving fewer funds available for the private sector. Thus, additional government debt usually raises interest rates, making investment returns lower and reducing a number of business projects. Diamond (1965) also points to the effect of reduction of capital stock, arising from the substitution of government debt for the physical capital in individual portfolios. Moreover, higher indebtedness increases the risk perception of creditors, who begin to perceive the debtor as less reliable, demanding a higher risk premium. In macroeconomics, this negative effect of public debt on private investment is called crowding-out. It may be amplified by consumers' behaviour, whose purchases of houses, as well as spending on durable goods, are usually financed by credits, and thus are interest-sensitive. Since the key factor that discourages private sector demand is the increased interest rate, monetary policy can influence the magnitude of the crowding-out effect. For instance, the provision of additional money by the central bank might inhibit an upward pressure on interest rates, reducing the crowding-out. However, given that most central banks focusing their strategies on maintaining price stability are prohibited from directly financing the budget deficits, an increase in the money supply coexisting with an expansionary fiscal policy is hardly uncertain (Aiyagari & McGrattan, 1998; Battaglini & Coate, 2008).

The theory of macroeconomics identifies also another channel, through which additional public sector debt affects private sector behaviour. It is related to the Ricardian equivalence theorem. This approach to the economic effects of expansionary fiscal policy points to the forward-looking perspective of consumers' behaviour. As looking-ahead households expect that a debt-financed tax cut will be financed by tax increases, more of their current income is saved to pay future fiscal levies. In other words, higher public debt induces consumers to spend less, dampening the expansionary effects of fiscal policy. Moreover, accounting for the long-term perspective of public debt servicing, Robert Barro argued that the current generation's greater propensity to save may be due to solidarity between generations (Buchanan, 1976). Therefore, the current generation cares about future generations, paying off the outstanding public debt. Thus, the substitution of debt with tax finance will exert no effect of expansionary policy on total spending. The logic behind the Ricardo–Barro concept is that if consumers are sufficiently forward-looking, they will perceive public debt as an indicator of economic uncertainty (Buchanan, 1976; Diamond, 1965).

When considering economic consequences of public debt, its influence on price level cannot be neglected. The theory of economics classifies expansionary fiscal policy as one of the classical sources of demand–pull inflation. The inflationary effects of public debt depend not only on its size, but also on the method of deficit financing. For instance, debt monetization – i.e., when the central bank increases money supply to finance the budget deficit – drives prices up. According to the quantity theory of money, the effect of a proportional increase in prices to changes in money supply is apparent over a long period. Nevertheless, new classical economics points to rational expectations, which accelerate inflationary pressure, especially in the aftermath of implementing expansionary policy-mix. Besides monetization, other forms of public debt financing, such as the issuing of sovereign bonds without increasing money supply, can also increase prices, especially when the economy is operating at its full potential. Nevertheless, this way of debt financing entails less in inflationary pressure than monetization (Blanchard et al., 2010).

Eventually, the economic consequences of public debt have an international dimension. In an open economy, if government deficit absorbs national saving, foreign markets can compensate for a shortfall of domestic funds. National income identity, which presents one of the fundamental relationships between household saving, investment, public sector saving, and trade balance, shows that if domestic saving, both private and public, are negative, the economy runs with a trade deficit, which implies borrowing from abroad. On the one hand, since public debt held by non-residents is often denominated in foreign currency, yields on sovereign bonds as well as interest on loans denominated in foreign currency are generally lower, making foreign financing attractive. On the other hand, exchange rate volatility generates the risk of higher costs of debt servicing. Moreover, foreign investors are perceived as more volatile than domestic debt holders. In times of crises, they quickly sell their assets and withdraw capital from the domestic economy, reducing the supply of loan funds. The next section discusses the economic consequences of public debt in CEE countries from the perspective of doing business.

The public debt structure in CEE countries – challenges for doing business

The costs of debt servicing and other economic consequences of public indebtedness depend on not only the size but also the structure of the debt, which indicates the sources and instruments of debt financing. Hence, additional data related to the origin of the lenders and the type of debt instruments, as well as their maturity and the currency in which the debt is denominated, can deliver information for the detailed assessment of the condition of public finance. Additionally, potential government liabilities such as government guarantees or non-performing loans may give also a more comprehensive picture of government indebtedness.

Figure 5.5 shows the structure of general government debt by instruments such as currency and deposits, debt securities, and loans. This breakdown applies to the outstanding government debts of CEE countries at the end of 2021.

As can be easily seen, debt securities are the main instruments of financing public sector debt in EU economies. At the end of 2021, they accounted on average for 78.3% of CEE economies and for 82.5% of total EU member states' government debt. Loans made up 20.4% and 14.5%, respectively. The rest of public debt was covered by currency and deposits, amounting to around 1.5% of CEE economies and 3.0% of EU government debt. In terms of the maturity, long-term loans as well as bonds with long-term maturity account for more than 95% of CEE government public debt (Eurostat, 2022), implying that repayments are spread out over time and may burden future generations.

In general, the CEE countries' debt structure by instruments and by maturity seems similar to the EU average. Only Estonia appears to be an outlier, with 62% of its public debt financed by loans, and 36% by sovereign bonds, of which 20% have

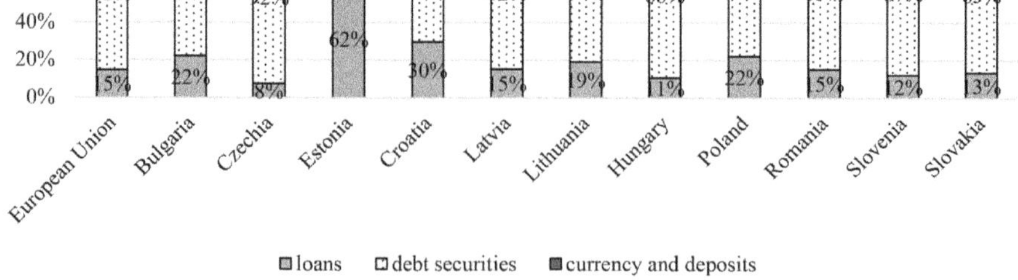

Figure 5.5 The breakdown of general government debt by instruments

Source: own elaboration based on Eurostat (2022)

short-term maturity. Apparently, such a structure implies a substantial increase in debt servicing costs over a short term. Moreover, in the context of the successive waves of the pandemics and Russia's aggression of Ukraine in 2022, the deterioration of Estonia's fiscal sustainability may seem very likely. However, accounting for a very low debt-to-GDP ratio of 18%, which has been the lowest in the EU, Estonia's public finances are not at risk. In contrast, Croatia may be strongly affected by the increase in debt burden, as both a debt-to-GDP ratio (almost 80% GDP in 2021) and a share of loans in debt financing (30%, including short-term loans) are high. Moreover, after the adoption of the euro in 2023, Croatia's debt was converted to the common currency, and as a euro member, Croatia is required to comply with stricter fiscal discipline rules.

It is worth noting that the CEE countries substantially differ in terms of the currency in which their public debt is denominated, as well as the origin of debt holders. Table 5.1 presents the breakdown of government debt by debt holder and by currency. In Estonia, Lithuania, Latvia, and Slovenia, public debt is mainly hold by non-residents. In Slovakia, Romania, and Bulgaria the share of foreign debt holders is also high, as they are close to 50%. As foreign investors are inclined to sell assets quickly in uncertain times, these countries are exposed to a higher risk of capital outflows than Czechia, Hungary, and Poland, whose shares of non-resident debt holders vary from 29% to 34%. Generally, across the CEE countries, as well as in the whole EU, most of the public debt financed by domestic entities is held by financial corporations. The role of domestic households as a lender to the government is very small, only about 3% on average, with the exception of Hungary, whose public debt at 24% is held by domestic households.

Domestic debt holders are generally considered as a more stable source of funding in times of crises. Nevertheless, what matters for public finance sustainability is also

Table 5.1 The breakdown of general government debt by debt holder, and by currency (% of total government debt)

	Domestic financial corporations	*Domestic non-financial corporations*	*Households; non-profit institutions serving households*	*Non-residents*	*Debt denominated in national currency*
Bulgaria	53.3	0.2	0.4	46.1	25.4
Czechia	67.1	1.3	1.8	29.7	92.3
Estonia	28.3	1.9	0.0	69.7	100
Croatia	65.2	0.2	0.6	34.0	29.3
Latvia	32.6	2.5	1.0	63.9	100
Lithuania	35.0	0.2	0.1	64.7	100
Hungary	42.8	1.5	24.0	31.7	77.4
Poland	60.4	2.4	4.1	33.1	77.3
Romania	45.6	2.1	3.0	49.2	46.7
Slovenia	44.5	0.2	1.1	55.2	99.9
Slovakia	46.5	3.9	0.0	49.6	100
EU	49.3	1.4	3.3	46.0	–

Source: own elaboration based on Eurostat (2022), data applied to the outstanding debt at the end of 2021

the currency of borrowing. Thus, in an open economy, an additional foreign-related factor influencing the debt burden is the exchange rate volatility. As the ability to raise funds in the integrated financial market has greatly increased after joining the EU, a part of the CEE countries' debt is denominated in foreign currency, mainly the euro. In the case of the eurozone member states (Estonia, Lithuania, Latvia, Slovakia, and Slovenia), all or almost all (99.9% in Slovenia) of their government debt is denominated in the euro, which is their legal tender. Although in the eurozone the exchange rate risk vis-à-vis other participants in the monetary union has been eliminated, the risk of public finance distress remains. The problem emerges from the financial dilemma, which indicates the financial instability under conditions of free capital transfer and fiscal autonomy. The example of Greece in 2010 showed that a euro member state can be at serious risk of insolvency due to the excessive public sector indebtedness.

As for the non-eurozone countries, the structures of their debt by currency of denomination differ noticeable. National currencies preponderate in government debt financing of Czechia (92.3%), Hungary (77.4%), and Poland (77.3%). In Bulgaria, Croatia, and Romania, which were also outside the euro area in 2022, the euro was primarily the currency of public debt denomination, respectively 75%, 70%, and 54%. The dominance of euro-denominated debt, without participation in the euro area, i.e., without having irrevocable conversion of the national currency into the euro, implies volatility of debt servicing costs due to exchange rate fluctuations. While Croatia got an official confirmation of abrogation of the derogation from 1 January 2023, the ECB and the European Commission assessed Bulgaria and Romania as not ready for joining the eurozone (European Commission, 2022). Bulgaria, however, which adopted a currency board as its exchange rate regime in 1997, successively eliminated the fluctuations of leva vs euro and expressed its will to join the eurozone by entering to the Exchange Rate Mechanism (ERM II), committing unilaterally to continue pegging its currency to the euro within the existing currency board arrangement. In contrast, Romania, with an exchange rate system classified as managed floating or crawl-like arrangement (IMF, 2021a), is much more prone to exchange rate changes. Thus, its path to the eurozone membership seems more distant, as in 2022, it did not fulfil any of the convergence criteria, neither fiscal nor monetary ones.

Since the government may be also a creditor, or guarantor to other entities, the unpaid loans result in government losses. In times of economic disruption, the amount of defaulted loans increases, so guarantee liabilities can become a significant source of public finance distress. Figure 5.6 shows government contingent liabilities, which arose in 2020 as a consequence of the provision of the COVID-19-related state guarantee programmes to public and private agents. Guarantees are defined as arrangements whereby the guarantor undertakes to a lender that if a borrower defaults, the guarantor will make good the loss the lender would otherwise suffer. In practice, it means that the guarantor repays the debt of the insolvent or bankrupt borrower.

In 2020, the highest values of the cumulative government guarantees, measured in relation to GDP, were recorded in Hungary and Slovenia, respectively of 8.17% and 6.25%. In the case of debtor default, the guarantees would make the total public debt of these countries close to 90% of GDP. If guarantees granted by governments

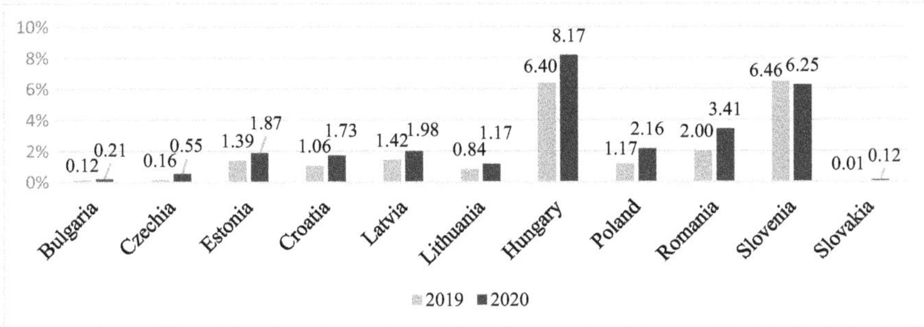

Figure 5.6 Total stock of government guarantees as percentage of GDP

Source: own elaboration based on Eurostat (2022)

Table 5.2 Fiscal sustainability assessment

	Excessive budget deficit/ GDP ratio in 2021 (over 3%)	*Excessive debt/GDP ratio in 2021 (over 60%)*	*Sensitivity to interest rate changes**	*Sensitivity to exchange rate changes**	*Risk exposure to external debt holders*	*Risk of fiscal sustainability over medium term**	*Risk of fiscal sustainability over the long term**
Bulgaria	yes	no	medium	no	high	medium	medium
Czechia	yes	no	medium	no	medium	medium	high
Estonia	no	no	low	no	high	low	low
Croatia	no	yes	medium	yes	medium	high	medium
Latvia	yes	no	medium	no	high	low	low
Lithuania	no	no	medium	no	high	low	low
Hungary	yes	yes	medium	yes	medium	medium	high
Poland	no	no	medium	yes	medium	low	medium
Romania	yes	no	medium	yes	high	high	medium
Slovenia	yes	yes	medium	no	high	high	high
Slovakia	yes	yes	medium	no	high	high	high

Note: * Assessment based on stochastic simulations and financial stress test scenarios for EU countries published in Fiscal Sustainability Report 2021 (European Commission, 2022).

Source: own elaboration

materialize, the debt-to-GDP ratio of 90% would be also hit by Croatia, and the 60% threshold would be exceeded by Poland and Slovakia. Regarding the non-performing loans as the additional indicator of potential loss for government, their size is much smaller compared to government guarantees.[2] On average, the value of non-performing loans in relation to GDP amounted in CEE countries to 0.5%. Croatia and Slovenia, whose debt-to-GDP in 2020 was well above the 60% limit, respectively 87% and 80%, recorded the highest ratios of non-performing loans to GDP (1.4% and 2.2%). Table 5.2 summarizes the fiscal condition of CEE countries, taking into account the risks of unsustainability in the medium and long term.

Crowding-out effect – evidence from CEE economies

To explore how public debt affects private sector investments in CEE countries, a linear fixed effects panel regression model (log-log specification) with country-specific fixed effects and with DK standard errors (Driscoll & Kraay, 1998) has been applied. By employing country-level yearly data on fixed capital formation as a dependent variable (I), we related them to the potential determinants, such as public debt (PDEBT), GDP, and foreign direct investment (FDI). Fixed capital formation and GDP are given in millions of euros as chain-linked volumes, i.e., data calculated at the previous year's prices, whereas the general government debt and the stock of foreign investment inflows are taken as a percentage of GDP. All the data has been derived from the Eurostat database, with the exception of FDI, which comes from UNCTAD and the central bank balance sheets of the panel countries. The model specified in equation (1) has been estimated for a set of 11 CEE countries over the period 1995–2021 in the following form:

$$\ln I_{jt} = \gamma_{j0} + \gamma_1 \ln PDEBT_{jt} + \gamma_2 \ln GDP_{jt} + \gamma_3 \ln FDI_{jt} + \varepsilon_{jt}, \quad (1)$$

where j stands for a country and t refers to the year.

The results presented in Table 5.3 show that all the explanatory variables appear to be significant (at 1% level) determinants of private sector investments.

A negative regression coefficient for debt-to-GDP ratio implies that government indebtedness negatively affects private investments. Specifically, a 1% increase in the debt-to-GDP ratio results, on average, in a 0.23% crowding-out of gross fixed capital formation in the panel countries. The detected dependencies also show that a 1% increase in GDP entails on average a 1.19% higher level of gross fixed capital formation. This relation may operate through the mechanism of investment-accelerator, i.e., when economic growth drives investments. Moreover, the finding that a 1% accumulation of FDI enhances national capital formation by 0.16%, on average in the panel countries, implies positive effects of functioning in the common market. Since foreign investors can compete with domestic ones, there is a concern about the erosion of domestic shares in national projects. The results obtained for 11 CEE countries imply, however, a positive role of the stock of foreign capital inflow in enhancing national investments. This relation may occur through spill-over effects and offshoring with domestic enterprises. In sum, the detected dependencies imply that, when pursuing an expansionary fiscal policy, economic policy makers in CEE countries should account for a crowding-out effect. Therefore, the level of debt-to-GDP ratio should be of particular concern, especially in the countries with excessive and deteriorating public indebtedness.

Table 5.3 Model estimation results for private sector investment

Symbol	*Regression coefficient*	*SE*	*t value*	*p value*
PDEBT	−0.23	0.05	−5.09	0.0000***
GDP	1.19	0.05	21.76	0.0000***
FDI	0.16	0.04	4.34	0.0000***

Notes: R^2 = 0.977, n = 11, T = 27, N = 297. Driscoll-Kraay robust standard errors (SE). Asterisks *** denote statistical significance at 0.01.

Source: own elaboration

Conclusions

The consequences of the COVID-19 pandemic received particular attention in the economic literature and political debate. Concerns over the effects of expansionary fiscal policy aiming at providing health care and economic stimulus packages have been particularly acute, as it was associated with increasing levels of public debt. The theory of economics explains the consequences of fiscal expansion, both positive and negative. One that diminishes expansionary fiscal effects is related to the crowding-out of private sector spending, mainly investments, by public sector spending. This study explored the relationship between public debt and investment in CEE countries. The findings show that, on average, a 1% increase in the debt-to-GDP ratio leads to a crowding-out of domestic fixed capital formation of 0.23%. The magnitude of the crowding-out may differ among the countries due to different factors, for example, the public debt structure, the sensitivity of investment to interest rate, or the level of economic openness and monetary policy framework. Nevertheless, increasing government debt amplifies the risk of private sector crowding-out, so it is necessary to monitor the levels of debt-to-GDP ratio.

Although in 2021 the ratio of debt-to-GDP in the CEE countries was, on average, below the 60% threshold, and also well below the EU average, some countries recorded excessive indebtedness or were at high risk of fiscal unsustainability. Ensuring long-term sound fiscal policy faced new challenges that emerged from the Russian invasion on Ukraine in 2022, which gave rise to new needs for government tasks. Accounting for a high level of economic and political uncertainty, the phasing-out of fiscal measures implemented during the COVID-19 crisis and transition towards prudent levels of public debt should be gradual, as too abrupt consolidation could have detrimental effects on post-pandemic recovery.

Notes

1 It is worth emphasizing that in this aspect there is a great difference between the high-income countries (EU) and the emerging markets of Asia and the Pacific. The latter spent the predominant part of pandemic fiscal measures on health care systems, and then on actions supporting households and families. Simultaneously, credit guarantees, loans for entrepreneurs, and subsidized interest for working capital were less popular in this group of countries than in Europe (IMF, 2021b, p. 10; Lacey et al., 2021, p. 14).

2 According to the Eurostat definition, "a loan is non-performing when payments of interest or principal are past due by 90 days or more, or interest payments equal to 90 days or more have been capitalized, refinanced, or delayed by agreement, or payments are less than 90 days overdue, but there are other good reasons (such as a debtor filing for bankruptcy) to doubt that payments will be made in full" (Eurostat, *Statistics Explained*).

References

Aiyagari, S.R. & McGrattan, E.R. (1998). The optimum quantity of debt. *Journal of Monetary Economics*, *42*(3), 447–469.

Aizenman, J., Jinjarak, Y., Nguyen, H. & Noy, I. (2021). The political economy of the COVID-19 fiscal stimulus packages of 2020. *NBER Paper no. 29360*.

Battaglini, M. & Coate, S. (2008). A dynamic theory of public spending, taxation, and debt. *The American Economic Review, 98*(1), 201–236.

BIS. (2022). BIS annual economic report 2022. Promoting global monetary and financial stability. *Bank for International Settlements*. Retrieved from: http://www.bis.org/publ/arpdf/ar2022e.htm

Blanchard, O.J., Amighini, A. & Giavazzi, F. (2010). *Macroeconomics A European Perspective*. London: Pearson Education Limited.

Buchanan, J.M. (1976). Barro on the Ricardian equivalence theorem. *Journal of Political Economy, 84*(2), 337–342.

Devereux, M.P., Güçeri, İ., Simmler, M. & Tam, E.H.F. (2020). Discretionary fiscal responses to the COVID-19 pandemic. *Oxford Review of Economic Policy, 36*, 225–241.

Diamond, P.A. (1965). National debt in a neoclassical growth model. *The American Economic Review, 55*(5), 1126–1150.

Driscoll, J.C. & Kraay, A.C. (1998). Consistent covariance matrix estimation with spatially dependent panel data. *The Review of Economics and Statistics, 80*(4), 549–560.

Elgin, C., Yalaman, A. & Sezer, Y. (2021). *Democracy and Fiscal-Policy Responses to COVID-19* (No. 62/2021; CAMA Working Paper). Canberra: Centre for Applied Macroeconomic Analysis, National Australian University.

European Commission. (2022). Convergence report 2022. *Directorate-General for Economic and Financial Affairs*. Retrieved from: https://economy-finance.ec.europa.eu/publications/convergence-report-2022_en

Eurostat. (2022). *Eurostat Database*. Retrieved from: https://ec.europa.eu/eurostat/databrowser/explore/all/all_themes?lang=en&display=list&sort=category

Hale, T., Angrist, N., Goldszmidt, R., Kira, B., Petherick, A., Phillips, T., Webster, S., Cameron-Blake, E., Hallas, L., Majumdar, S. & Tatlow, H. (2021). A global panel database of pandemic policies (Oxford COVID-19 Government Response Tracker). *Nature Human Behaviour, 5*(4), 529–538.

Haroutunian, S., Osterloh, S. & Sławińska, K. (2021). The initial fiscal policy responses of euro area countries to the COVID-19 crisis. *Economic Bulletin Articles, 1*. Retrieved from: https://EconPapers.repec.org/RePEc:ecb:ecbart:2021:0001:3

IMF. (2021a). Annual report on exchange arrangements and exchange restrictions 2020. *International Monetary Fund*. Retrieved from: https://doi.org/10.5089/9781513556567.012

IMF. (2021b). Fiscal monitor. A fair shot. *International Monetary Fund*, Washington, D.C.

IMF. (2022a). Policy responses to COVID19. *IMF*. Retrieved from: http://www.imf.org/en/Topics/imf-and-covid19/Policy-Responses-to-COVID-19

IMF. (2022b). World economic outlook update, July 2022: Gloomy and more uncertain. *International Monetary Fund*. Retrieved from: http://www.imf.org/en/Publications/WEO/Issues/2022/07/26/world-economic-outlook-update-july-2022

Lacey, E., Massad, J. & Utz, R. (2021). *A Review of Fiscal Policy Responses to COVID-19*. Washington: The World Bank.

Mazzucato, M. & Kattel, R. (2020). COVID-19 and public-sector capacity. *Oxford Review of Economic Policy, 36*, 256–269.

Peters, M.A. & Jandrić, P. (2021). Surreal economics, fiscal stimulus, and the financialization of public health: Politics of the Covid-19 narrative. *Educational Philosophy and Theory*, 1–6.

WDI. (2022). *World Development Indicators Database*. Retrieved from: http://www.worldbank.org

World Bank. (2020). The fiscal impact and policy response to COVID-19 (p. 49) (Working Paper). *World Bank*. Retrieved from: https://openknowledge.worldbank.org/handle/10986/35424

6 Trade openness and trade dependence

How did the COVID-19 pandemic reshape trade flows and trade policies in Central and Eastern European countries?

Marta Wajda-Lichy

Introduction

Many modern economies owe much of their success to comparative advantages and economies of scale, materializing through foreign trade. Gaining benefits from the international exchange of goods and services was also the driving force behind the intensification of globalization and regional integration processes, including the EU enlargement in 2004 and after, when most of the Central and Eastern European (CEE) countries acceded to the common market. By becoming members of the EU, the CEE countries joined a single trading block, which has been the most important player in the world trade. Free trade within the single market, as well as the low level of common external tariffs, and the increasing number of preferential trade and trade-investment partnership agreements signed with third countries have encouraged the EU companies to exchange goods and services internationally, both within and outside of the single market.

The combined shares of all the EU member states, covering both intra and extra-EU trade, has made the EU the world's leading exporter of goods and services. Before the COVID-19 pandemic, in 2019, the EU's share in the global exports of goods amounted to 30.6%. However, when considering the ranking of individual countries, the first global exporter of goods was China, providing 13.1% of global merchandise exports in 2019, followed by the USA, whose share was 8.6%. In 2021, the second year of the COVID-19 pandemic, the global export shares of the EU and the USA declined to 29% and 7.8%, respectively, whereas China's share strengthened to 15.1%. It is worth adding that before the previous worldwide turmoil in 2008, i.e., the global financial crisis (GFC), the shares of the EU in the world exports of goods amounted to 35%, of which Germany contributed 9%, which ranked ahead of China. Since the GFC affected more developed rather than developing economies, China continued its trade expansion, largely within the Asian region, overtaking Germany, as well as the USA, in their shares of global merchandise exports. In service exports, the EU was also ranked first, with a 37% share recorded in 2019. Within two years of the outbreak of the COVID-19 pandemic, the EU increased its share to almost 40%, remaining the leader in global services exports. The categories of services whose exports have been growing consequently even during pandemic times have been telecommunication, computers, and information.

DOI: 10.4324/9781003345428-6

The EU increased its share in global ICT services exports from 48.5% in 2019 to 49.7% in 2021.

On the import side, the COVID-19 pandemic changed little in the ranking of the top three global traders. The EU has continued to lead in the world's goods imports with a share of around 28%; however, similarly to goods exports, the EU's share of goods imports has been declining over past decades, while China's has been steadily rising. The US, as a single country, with a 13% share, was ranked first as the world's largest purchaser of goods in 2021, followed by China (12%). Concerning service imports, the EU remained a global leader, covering 35% of the world's commercial services imports in 2021.

A distinctive feature of the EU trade is that its high ranking in world trade engagement has been associated with the surpluses in the overall trade balance, implying the existence of the sustainable comparative advantages of the EU economies. However, neither comparative advantages nor high ranking in world trade can be taken for granted, since developing countries have been steadily penetrating foreign markets since the last decade of the 20th century, resulting in erosion of developed countries from many areas of international trade.

CEE countries as the EU traders

The EU's high ranking in world trade has been possible by adding up intra- and extra-EU trade of all member states, including Germany, the leader economy, which accounts for around 25% of the EU's goods trade and 15% of the EU's service trade, in both exports and imports. It is obvious that the contributions of each of the EU member states to the EU total exports and imports vary due to many factors, such as their economic potential, revealed comparative advantages, or geographical location determining, for example, whether a country has access to seaports or transit routes. The overall export shares of the eleven CEE countries (Bulgaria, Croatia, Czechia, Estonia, Hungary, Latvia, Lithuania, Poland, Romania, Slovakia, and Slovenia) amount to around 20% of EU total exports, which is below that of Germany. However, it is worth noting that the share of CEE countries in the EU trade is twice as large as their contribution to the EU's GDP, implying a high level of economic openness.

Figure 6.1 compares the contribution of CEE countries to the EU's GDP with their shares in the EU's trade, in both exports and imports. Two regularities can be easily discerned. The first confirms that the larger the economy, i.e., the higher the GDP, the larger the share in EU trade. The second indicates that a country's share in EU exports is proportional to its share in EU imports. For instance, Poland, Hungary, Czechia, and Romania – the biggest CEE economies – cover together 14% of EU imports and 15.5% of EU exports, while the shares of the rest of the CEE countries, which are relatively tiny economies, sum up to 4% and 5.5%, respectively. Slovakia seems to stand out, providing 2.1% of EU exports and 2% of EU imports, whereas its contribution of 0.7% to the EU's GDP is relatively small (half of Romania's GDP). In Figure 6.1, the size of the bubbles refers to the country's share in the EU's GDP.

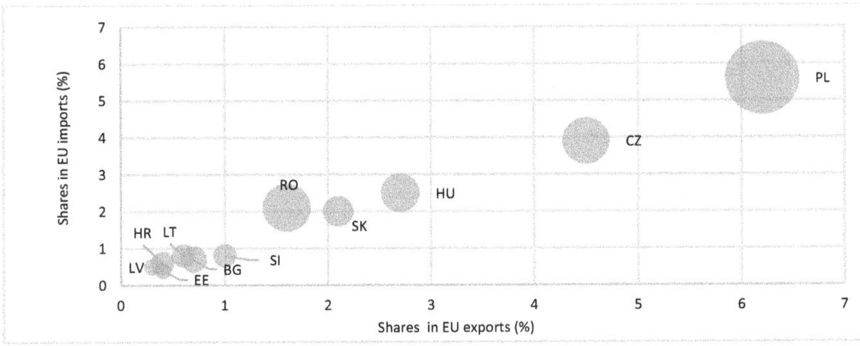

Figure 6.1 Shares of CEE countries in total EU exports, imports, and GDP (as a percentage)

Source: own elaboration based on the data for 2021 derived from the Eurostat database

The evidence that the shares in the EU trade are much larger than the shares in the EU's GDP indicates the high level of openness of CEE economies and therefore their strong reliance on foreign markets. Indeed, the sum of exports and imports of goods and services related to GDP, which is typically used to measure countries' economic openness, amounted on average to 134% in CEE countries in 2019, i.e., before the COVID-19 pandemic outbreak, exceeding the average of 92% recorded for the EU as a whole (Figure 6.2). Generally, small economies tend to be more open because they are less self-sufficient and have limited capacity for gaining economies of scale within their domestic territories. Apart from Poland, which contributes around 4% to the EU's GDP, the share of none of the other CEE economies exceeds 2% of the EU production. For example, Romania's share of the EU's GDP is 1.7%, Czechia's 1.6%, and Hungary's 1.1%. The shares of the rest of the CEE countries range from 0.7% for Slovakia to 0.2% for Estonia and Latvia. Thus, the level of Poland's economic openness of 106% of GDP (in 2019) was lower than that of Slovakia, Hungary, Slovenia, or Lithuania, whose levels of trade openness of 184%, 161%, 159%, and 149%, respectively, were the highest among the CEE economies. It is worth noting that Germany, with the largest GDP and the highest volume of both exports and imports among the EU economies, has a trade-to-GDP ratio close to but below the EU average (cf. Figure 6.2).

In 2020, which was the first year of the COVID-19 pandemic, the average trade-to-GDP ratio in CEE countries shrank to 126.5%, and to 85.6% in the EU as a whole. Germany's trade was also negatively affected by the pandemic shock, which reduced the level of German economy openness by 6.5 percentage points, i.e., to 81.1%. In 2021, trade openness rebounded in CEE countries, in Germany, and in the EU as a whole, to 139.6%, 89.4%, and 93.3%, respectively (Figure 6.2).

Since total trade-to-GDP is a general measure of the scale of economic openness, it does not give information on the nature of dependence on foreign trade. Therefore, the decomposition of exports and imports by category of product, as

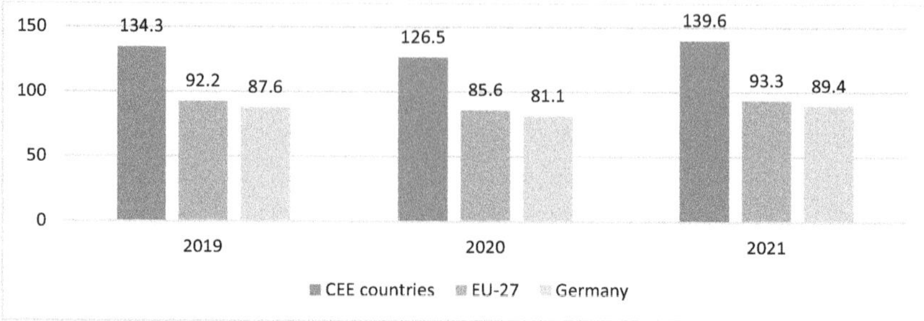

Figure 6.2 Trade openness as a percent of GDP in 2019, 2020, and 2021

Source: own elaboration based on data from the WDI database. CEE countries comprise 11 EU economies (Bulgaria, Croatia, Czechia, Estonia, Hungary, Latvia, Lithuania, Poland, Romania, Slovakia, and Slovenia), for which a simple average was calculated

well as by trading partner, provides more detailed information about the countries' interdependencies and the sources of their vulnerability to external shocks. The next part of this chapter discusses the openness of CEE economies by product, direction, and interlinkages of trade flows.

CEE economies' openness by product, direction, and interlinkages of trade flows

To assess the importance of trade to a country's economy, as well as the nature of a country's linkages with foreign markets, it is useful to divide trade flows into exports and imports and relate each of them to GDP. The export-to-GDP ratio allows for assessing country's dependence on foreign demand, whereas the relation of import-to-GDP reflects the reliance of the supply side of the economy on foreign partners, indicating the need to meet the residents' demand with final goods, intermediaries, and services delivered from abroad.

Figure 6.3 depicts trade openness by exports and imports of goods and services related to the GDP of CEE countries and the EU. The imports-to-GDP ratio and the exports-to-GDP ratio, presented as bars, are given as five-year averages covering 2015–2019, which allows capturing structural patterns of trade openness over the medium period preceding the outbreak of the COVID-19 pandemic. Two distinctive features emerge from these data. First, all the CEE countries recorded higher import intensity than the EU average, indicating a relatively greater dependence of their markets on purchases from abroad. Apart from Romania and Croatia, the degree of openness in exports of goods was also above the EU average, implying higher vulnerability of CEE economies to the business cycles of their trading partners. Second, in services trade, eight of the eleven CEE countries recorded exports-to-GDP ratios above the EU average. In Croatia, for example, more than 50% of overall exports relied on services. The share of services in total exports was also high in Estonia, Latvia, Lithuania, and Romania, amounting to around 30%. In contrast to services

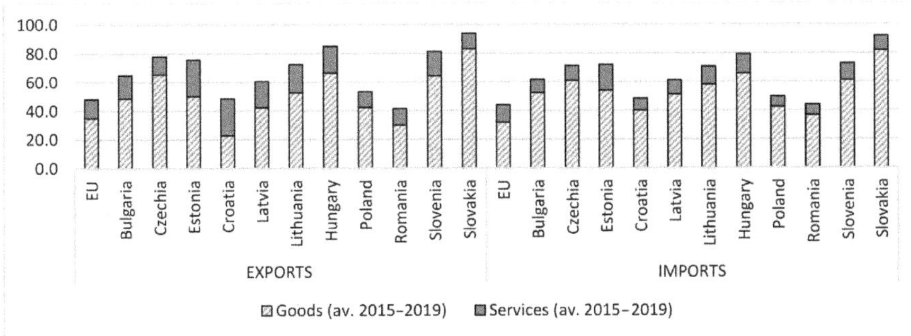

Figure 6.3 Breakdown of trade openness by export and import flows of goods and services (as a percent of GDP)

Source: own elaboration based on data from the Eurostat database

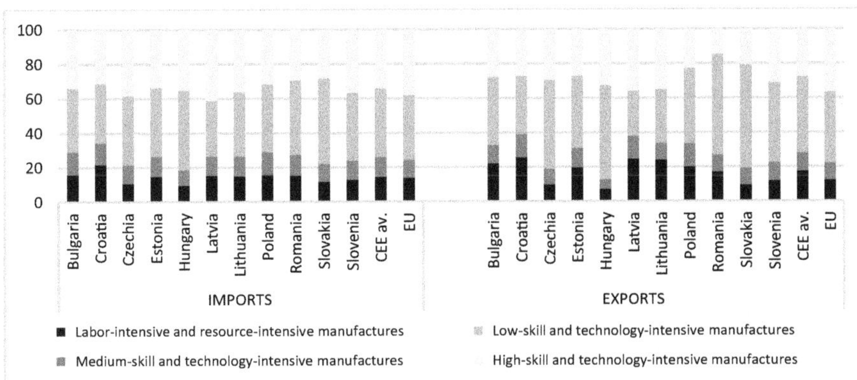

Figure 6.4 The breakdown of goods exports and imports by labor skills and technology involvement

Source: data for 2019 derived from the UNCTAD database

exports, the shares of services in imports of most CEE countries were below the EU average of 12.2%, except for Estonia, Hungary, and Lithuania, whose services imports-to-GDP ratio ranged from 12.5 to 18%.

A more detailed breakdown of the merchandise trade may provide additional data for assessing the nature of CEE economies' openness. For instance, the classification of exported goods by the level of labor and technology engagement indicates that CEE countries specialize in exporting medium-skill and technology-intensive manufactures and in labor-intensive and resource-intensive products (UNCTAD database). The former, which include electronic motor vehicles, electrical machinery, and apparatus, cover on average 44% and 40% of CEE countries' exports and imports, respectively (Figure 6.4). The latter comprises, for example, textiles, footwear, and furniture, and takes on average 17% of CEE countries' goods exports and

14% of their imports. The evidence that the sum of shares of these two product groups and low-skill products accounts for most of the exports from CEE countries implies that the important source of CEE countries' advantages is low labor costs.

Indeed, the index of revealed comparative advantages (RCA) calculated for the CEE countries takes values above one for many exported products classified as labor-intensive and resource-intensive or medium-skill and technology-intensive. The concept of the RCA is based on Ricardian trade theory, which assumes that trade patterns among countries are governed by their relative differences in productivity. A country has a revealed comparative advantage in a given product when its ratio of exports of this product to its total exports of all goods exceeds the same ratio for the world as a whole, i.e., when RCA is above one. The higher the value of a country's RCA for a given product, the higher its export strength in this product. For example, in 2022 all the analyzed CEE countries record an RCA ratio above one in wood manufacturers, with the highest values of up to 17 in Estonia, 13 in Latvia, and 9 in Lithuania (UNCTAD database). High values of RCA have been also recorded in motor vehicles, and in parts and accessories for vehicles, as well as in the production of parts and components for other machines. Among the CEE countries, Slovakia revealed the leading export strength in motor vehicles. Its RCA was of 7, whereas in parts and accessories for vehicles the greatest competitive exporter was Romania (RCA of 4.3). Czechia, Hungary, and Poland also recorded a high RCA of about 2.5–3.6 in both categories of products related to the automotive industry. It is worth noting that high-skill and technology-intensive products, including automatic data processing machines, office machines, parts and accessories for telecommunication equipment, take on average 27% of CEE countries' exports and 34% of their imports, but in contrast to the medium-skill products these shares are below the EU average and fewer CEE countries reveal comparative advantages in this category of merchandise.

In addition to the comparative advantages revealed in the exports of labor-intensive products and medium- and low-skill products, a noticeable feature of CEE countries' trade is the large share of intermediate goods in both exports and imports. Figure 6.5 shows that the share of intermediate goods averages around 50% in CEE countries' exports and 56% in their imports. This evidence reflects strong linkages of CEE producers with foreign suppliers of raw materials and parts and semi-products, used as inputs to produce for the domestic market, as well as for exports.

The input–output data confirms strong backward and forward international linkages of CEE countries (OECD, 2022). In 2019, the share of foreign value added in CEE countries' exports (backward linkages) amounted on average to 34.6%, whereas forward linkages, which represent the domestic value added embodied in the exports of foreign partners, averaged 19.5%. Both measures, which are commonly used to assess an economy's participation in global value chains, are given as a percentage of domestic gross exports. As shown in Figure 6.6, the bars representing backward linkages clearly exceed those representing forward linkages. Greater participation as the recipients rather than the suppliers of parts and components used in manufacturing for exports makes the CEE economies more dependent on foreign

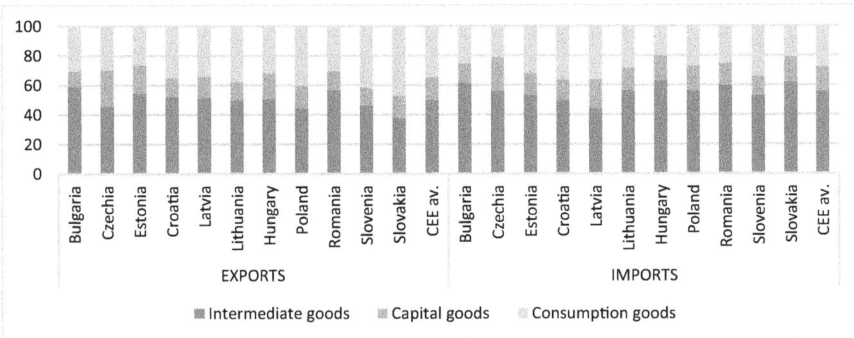

Figure 6.5 Trade structure of goods trade by product purpose and stage of manufacturing

Source: data for 2019 derived from the Eurostat database

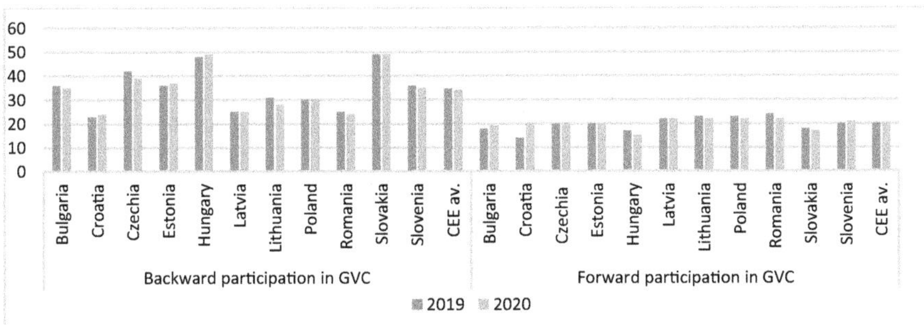

Figure 6.6 Forward and backward participation in GVC in 2019 and in 2020 (as percent of exports)

Source: own elaboration based on OECD (2022), database on TiVA

providers than foreign purchasers operating through global value chains. This observation applies to each of the analyzed CEE countries.

As noted earlier, the large share of intermediate goods in trade suggests active participation in GVCs, which involves interdependencies between domestic and foreign producers, often operating through outsourcing or offshoring. The former means transferring part of the business activities to an external entity, either domestic or foreign, while the latter involves relocating part of the production processing to another geographical location, often within the same company. Both activities aim to increase efficiency by cutting costs or gaining access to new inputs, including physical and human capital. Since offshoring and often outsourcing operate across borders, both strategies entail an increase in foreign trade (Khorana et al., 2022; McIvor & Bals, 2021). The enterprises from CEE engage in mainly international sourcing as the providers of products and services to the foreign firms that have outsourced part of their business activities to CEE markets.

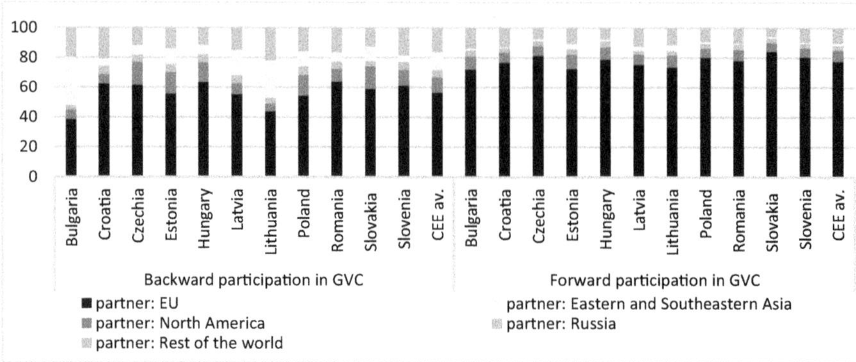

Figure 6.7 Breakdown of backward and forward linkages of CEE economies by trade partner

Source: own elaboration based on data for 2018 derived from OECD (2022) database on TiVA

Moreover, the CEE countries' participation in production fragmentation tends to be regional in nature and driven mainly by manufacturing enterprises from such branches as machinery and transport equipment (Szymczak et al., 2022). Figure 6.7 shows the backward and forward linkages of CEE countries by their foreign partners. The largest share of foreign value added into the CEE exports comes from other EU countries, on average 56%. Five CEE economies (Croatia, Czechia, Hungary, Romania, and Slovenia) record backward linkages with the EU partners above 60%. Russia and Asian countries are also important regions of origin of the foreign value added inserted into the CEE exports. Their inputs account, respectively, for 12% and 11% of foreign value added embedded in the CEE countries exports.

The predominance of the EU economies as partners in GVC is even more pronounced in forward linkages, implying that parts and components manufactured in CEE countries and then used by foreign manufacturers as inputs for their export production go mainly to the EU partners (on average 78%). The largest shares of the EU as a purchaser of parts and components exported by the CEE countries were found for Poland, Slovakia, the Czech Republic, and Slovenia (above 80%). Besides the single market, 7.2% of parts produced by CEE countries for further export processing were directly exported to Eastern and Southeastern Asia, 3% to North America, 1.8% to Russia, and 10% to the rest of the world. It should be noted, however, that besides the direct backward and forward linkages, relationships with non-EU partners may have an indirect form, as the exchange of inputs between two EU member states supplying inputs to the production of goods and services to be exported by other country outside the EU intertwines all the entities involved in value-added chains. It means, that the CEE economies are involved in GVC and exposed to external shocks both directly and indirectly. The latter, operating through EU trade partners, often runs through Germany as one of the greatest hubs of regional and global supply chains.

CEE countries' trade response to the COVID-19 pandemic

The COVID-19 pandemic severely hit the trade of all CEE countries, but not to the same extent. As shown in Figure 6.8, the largest reductions in exports of goods and services were in Croatia and Bulgaria, respectively, by 22.7% and 12.1%. In 2020, substantial collapses in exports were also recorded in Romania, Slovenia Slovakia, Czechia, and Hungary, whose negative rates of exports growth ranged from −9.4% to −6.1%. In Estonia and Latvia exports fell by less than 5%, whereas in Lithuania and Poland the overall exports slightly increased, by 0.4% and 0.1%, respectively. Regarding the changes in imports of goods and services in 2020, the largest declines were in the countries whose exports also responded abruptly to the pandemic crisis, i.e., in Croatia (−12.3%), Slovenia (−9.6%), Slovakia (−8.2%), Czechia (−6.9%), Bulgaria (−5.4%), and Romania (−5.2). In Lithuania and Hungary imports fell by around −4%, and in Latvia and Poland the declines in imports were by −2.5% and −1.1, respectively. Estonia was the only country, among the analyzed CEE's economies, that recorded an increase in imports, but by less than 1%.

A breakdown of trade growth by product and type of trade linkages helps to explain the differences in the CEE countries' trade responses to the COVID-19 pandemic in 2020. Generally, as Figure 6.9 shows, the pandemic crisis hit the services sector more severely than the manufactures sector. This reaction can be explained by the fact that the increasing spread of the COVID-19 virus forced governments across the world to implement lockdown measures, which restricted the movement of people and shut down businesses temporarily, especially those requiring direct contact with customers. These counter-pandemic measures led to unprecedented contractions in services such as travel, transport, or cultural and recreational services.

Generally, services account for about one-fifth of global trade; however, in some economies, such as Croatia, they constitute an essential part of their overall exports (54%), as well as a significant contribution to GDP (27%). In Bulgaria, Romania,

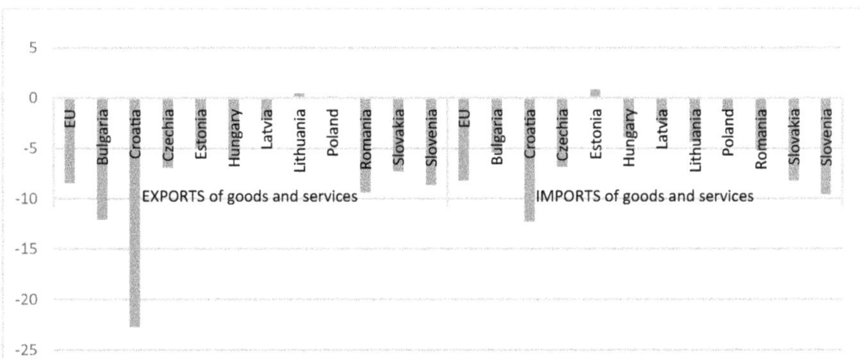

Figure 6.8 Growth rates of trade in goods and services in 2020

Source: own elaboration based on WDI database

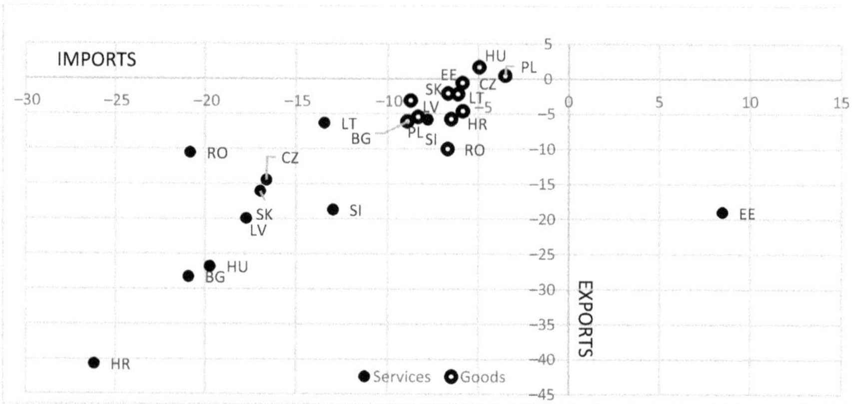

Figure 6.9 Growth rates of trade in goods and trade in services in 2020 (as a percentage)

Source: own elaboration based on data for 2020 derived from the WDI database

Estonia, Lithuania, and Latvia, services exports also account for a significant proportion of total exports, ranging from 27% to 35% of GDP in 2019. Considering that services, especially in an era of globalization, represent a major potential for high value-added trade (Durand & Milberg, 2020; Mayer, 2018; Nath & Liu, 2017), it is worth looking at the structure of the CEE countries' services exports. When breaking down services trade by main categories, i.e., travel, transport, goods-related services, and 'others', it turns out that the CEE countries largely export traditional services, such as travel and transport, which amount on average to 55% of their overall services exports, whereas the average for the EU is 35%. Another striking difference is that the share of services classified as 'other', accounts on average for almost 60% of EU services exports, but only 38% of the CEE countries' services exports. As the category 'other' encompasses labor-intensive services like construction as well as high value-added services, e.g., business services, financial, and ICT-related services, the lower export shares of this category indicate that the CEE countries do not specialize in modern services. It is worth mentioning that trade in traditional services was strongly reduced during the pandemic, whereas trade in modern services, especially in ICT, increased substantially.

Besides the services sector, sharp declines in trade were characteristic of intermediate goods. Figure 6.10 shows how the exports and the imports of three different product categories responded in 2020 to the COVID-19 crisis. As can be seen, three clusters emerged from the scatter plot, indicating larger declines in trade (both imports and exports) in intermediate goods (marked as filled circles) and capital goods (marked as empty circles) rather than in consumer goods (marked as triangles). Given that intermediate goods account for the bulk of CEE countries' exports and imports, respectively 50% and 56%, falls in this category substantially contributed to the overall slump in trade in 2020. Furthermore, sharp declines in exports and import of intermediate goods also imply severe disruptions in global supply chains,

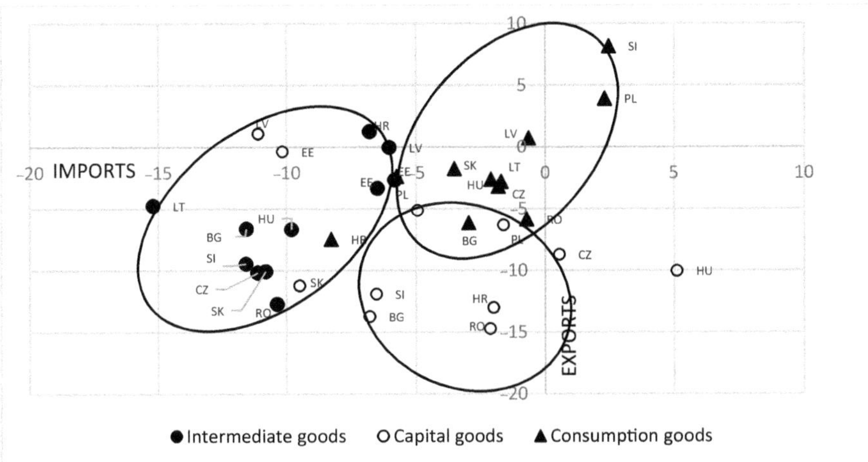

Figure 6.10 Export and import growth rates by three product categories: intermediate goods, capital goods, and consumption goods (as a percentage)

Source: own elaboration based on data for 2020 derived from the Eurostat database

as the CEE economies are both active purchasers and providers of parts and semi-products used as inputs to export manufacturing.

Indeed, when trade in value added is taken into account, the shifts recorded in the forward and backward linkages of the CEE economies suggest the dynamic adjustments in GVCs during the first year of the COVID-19 pandemic. In 2020, the share of foreign value added in exports fell in Bulgaria, Czechia, Lithuania, Romania, and Slovenia (Figure 6.6). Three CEE countries increased the share of foreign value in their exports (Croatia, Hungary, and Estonia), whereas the other three EEC countries (Latvia, Poland, and Slovakia) maintained their pre-pandemic proportions of foreign inputs in exports.

As for the forward linkages, the shares of domestic value added to foreign economies' exports decreased for Hungary, Lithuania, Poland, Romania, and Slovakia. Bulgaria, Croatia, and Slovenia strengthened their forward linkages, while Czechia, Estonia, and Latvia remained at their shares recorded in 2019. The shifts in value-added trade undoubtedly stemmed from pandemic austerity measures, which involved both supply-side and demand-side constraints. For example, the restrictions on access to intermediate goods and services, such as transportation, as well as shortages of specialized labor, reduced production capacity, whereas the cancellation of orders or declines in incoming orders for goods and services were demand-related reasons behind the trade collapse in 2020.

An interesting thread of the discussion on the causes and the nature of changes in value-added trade points to protectionism as a reason for the shifts in global trade linkages (European Commission, 2021; Evenett & Fritz, 2021; Khorana et al., 2022; Mayer, 2018; Petri & Plummer, 2020). While the intensive government subsidies to firms stopped mass layoffs, it also raised concern about the deteriorating of public finance and over-reliance on foreign markets (Evenett, 2020). The latter became a viral topic of the discussion in the post-pandemic era, when some European car manufacturers, e.g. Renault, announced they would reshore some parts of their production from foreign markets, including CEE countries, to their home countries. Indeed, many countries resorted to protectionism and inward-oriented strategies, aiming at shielding domestic jobs, reducing the dependence on foreign markets, and achieving higher value-added through upgrading in global supply chains. The increase in protectionism and the tendencies to transfer previously offshored activities back to domestic locations were already evidenced after the global financial crisis, but they intensified in the aftermath of the pandemic crisis (Aggarwal & Reddie, 2020; Verbeke, 2020).

Recent literature increasingly emphasizes that digitalization not only enhances international production fragmentation but may also reshape it by shortening the length of global value chains (Evenett & Fritz, 2021; Mayer, 2018, McIvor & Bals, 2021). Mayer (2018), for example, points to the modern technology that increases concentration of intangible assets in such activities as design, research, and development, as well as marketing, distribution and data analysis. On the one hand, it implies the increase in unequal distribution of value added between participants of different stages of the production chain. On the other hand, an increase in the use of digital technology, e.g., automation and robotics, in the assembly stages could increase efficiency and thus the value added at the middle stages of the manufacturing process. However, according to Mayer (2018), intellectual monopolization, which is especially acute in the digital sector, impedes the access of developing countries to state-of-the-art technology. It means that developing countries may be stuck in low value-added activities and unable to upgrade towards higher value-added activities (the problem of 'thin industrialization'). Moreover, the future value-added chains may be shortened, exacerbating unequal distribution of value added, when the owners of the modern technology begin applying it to the middle stages of production, having reshored them from abroad (Khorana et al., 2022; Verbeke, 2020). This scenario seems very likely, especially after the pandemic, when many companies began to lean toward inward strategies, reducing their dependence on external suppliers.

Conclusions

The theory of integration assumed that free trade is at the center of economic prosperity and competitiveness, contributing to the welfare effects of the trading partners. The EU, which is a common market, not only provides rules for free trade but also reduces barriers to the movement of capital and people, encouraging cooperation among companies from the member countries. By joining the EU, the CEE countries became a part of the common trading bloc that takes the largest shares of international trade, as both the exporter and the importer of goods and services. On the one hand, the common market has created conditions for the development of internal trade, and on the other hand, it has made it possible to benefit from the network effects resulting from the existing trade relationships of the EU countries with the rest of the world. The latter facilitated the involvement of the CEE countries into GVCs. Undoubtedly, by being a part of the single market, the CEE countries have become more open and intertwined with the EU, as well as to the global economy, through both direct and indirect trade linkages.

The COVID-19 pandemic, as well as the global financial crisis 2008, revealed that disruptions in foreign economies are quickly transmitted to the CEE markets via trade channels. There are some distinctive features of CEE countries' trade that explain their reactions to the COVID-19 pandemic. First, the level of CEE economies' openness, measured as a sum of exports and imports related to GDP is high (substantially higher than the UE average), which exposed them to external shocks. Second, given that major part of the CEE countries' trade is in intermediate goods, a high level of openness indicates the rapid transmission of external shocks to domestic production. Third, the CEE countries actively participate in international production fragmentation, as both suppliers and purchasers of parts and components used as inputs to the exports production. Accounting for the comparative advantages revealed in labor-intensive and resource-intensive products, as well as in middle-skill and technology-intensive products, the producers from the CEE countries tend to occupy the middle stages of the value chains, which generate relatively low value added. Since breaking the intellectual monopoly is unlikely, the way to upgrade is to apply new technology to a larger extent, so that the mid-chain activities in which CEE countries specialize bring them more added value.

As the CEE countries carry out most of their trade within the EU partners, which is a natural consequence of the functioning in the common market, it is crucial to know how the pandemic affected these trade relationships. Over two years of the pandemic, i.e., from 2020 to 2021, seven out of eleven CEE countries increased their shares of exports to the EU, which suggests a shift of the CEE dispatches from non-EU partners towards regional linkages. At the same time, purchases from the EU as the shares of the CEE countries total imports declined in ten countries, implying the increasing role of imports from non-EU partners. It is hard to say how much of this change was due to supply shortages from EU producers, and how much was due to the search for lower-cost suppliers. The shifts recorded in the forward and the backward linkages of the CEE economies suggested the dynamic adjustments in GVCs during the first year of the COVID-19 pandemic. In this context, one of the lively debated issues was to what extent the cause of these changes was due to temporary pandemic austerity, and to what extent the adjustments in trade linkages resulted from the strategic firms' decisions on moving business activities back into the domestic economy.

It can be concluded that the structural changes in production processing, including the decisions on reshoring or imports substitution, seem less likely to cause the abrupt trade changes in the CEE countries' trade in 2020, as the adjustments of this kind have far-reaching consequence and therefore require in-depth analysis of the new post-pandemic reality. In 2020, both the uncertainty of the duration of the pandemic and its final effects certainly held back strategic firms' decisions. Nevertheless, the pandemic has reinvigorated discussion about the level of economic openness and prompted greater protection of domestic markets. The new post-pandemic reality, as well as changes in the international geopolitical environment because of Russia's aggression against Ukraine in 2022, can be expected to cause a revision of company strategies and government trade policies. One of the biggest challenges for modern trade will undoubtedly be to maintain the current level of liberalization of the exchange of goods and services.

References

Aggarwal, V.K. & Reddie, A.W. (2020). New economic statecraft: Industrial policy in an era of strategic competition. *Issues & Studies, 56*(2), 1–29.

Durand, C. & Milberg, W. (2020). Intellectual monopoly in global value chains. *Review of International Political Economy, 27*(2), 404–429.

European Commission. (2021). Proposal for a regulation of the European parliament and of the council on the protection of the union and its member States from economic coercion by third countries. *Brussels, 775.*

Eurostat database. Retrieved from https://ec.europa.eu/eurostat/data/database

Evenett, S.J. (2020). Chinese whispers: COVID-19, global supply chains in essential goods, and public policy. *Journal of International Business Policy, 3*, 408–429. https://doi.org/10.1057/s42214-020-00075-5

Evenett, S.J. & Fritz, J. (2021). *Mapping Policies Affecting Digital Trade, University of St. Gallen Endowment for Prosperity through Trade and CEPR.* Retrieved from: http://www.rsis.edu.sg/wp-content/uploads/2021/06/Evenett-Fritz Mapping-Digital-Trade-rev-27-March-2021.pdf

Khorana, S., Escaith, H., Ali, S., Kumari, S. & Do, Q. (2022). The changing contours of global value chains post-COVID: Evidence from the Commonwealth. *Journal of Business Research, 153*, 75–86.

Mayer, J. (2018). Digitalization and industrialization: Friends or foes? In *UNCTAD Research Paper 25.* Geneva: UNCTAD.

McIvor, R. & Bals, L. (2021). A multi-theory framework for understanding the reshoring decision. *International Business Review, 30*(6).

Nath, H.K. & Liu, L. (2017). Information and communications technology (ICT) and services trade. *Information Economics and Policy, 41*, 81–87.

OECD. (2022). *Database on Trade in Value Added.* Retrieved from: https://stats.oecd.org//Index.aspx?DataSetCode=TIVA_2022_C1

Petri, P.A. & Plummer, M.G. (2020). East Asia decouples from the United States: Trade War, COVID-19, and East Asia's new trade blocs. *Peterson Institute Working Paper, 20–29.* Retrieved from: http://www.piie.com/system/files/documents/wp20-9.pdf

Szymczak, S., Parteka A. & Wolszczak-Derlacz J. (2022). Position in global value chains and wages in central and Eastern European countries. *European Journal of Industrial Relations, 28*, 211–230.

UNCTAD database, UNCTADstat. Retrieved from: https://unctadstat.unctad.org/EN/

Verbeke, A. (2020). Will the COVID-19 pandemic really change the governance of global value chains? *British Journal of Management, 31*(3), 444–446.

7 Geopolitical implications of reshoring in the pre- and post-pandemic period

Dawid Cherubin

Introduction

The chapter discusses geopolitical events related to international relations in light of the conflict between the US and China before and after the COVID-19 pandemic. The empirical analysis shows that the phenomenon of reshoring has become a new trend in international business, causing shifts from the previous trend of offshoring. In recent years, the new phenomenon has accelerated significantly due to two factors: the trade war between the US and China and the COVID-19 pandemic. Businesses are much more likely to relocate their production facilities from China to their home or nearby countries for two reasons. The first reason is a change in tax policy and subsidies to companies that will transfer capital to their home countries, as in the case of the US. The second reason is the shortening of supply chains to countries with high investment attractiveness reflected in cheap labor and more favorable tax regulations. The chapter consists of three parts. Part one describes the relations between China and the US from 2001 until the announcement of the COVID-19 pandemic. Part two outlines reshoring practices with indication of how countries are most likely to be chosen. Part three describes the situation of the reshoring phenomenon and its impact on Central and Eastern European (CEE) countries.

The US–China strain and global geopolitical consequences

To discuss the relationship between the pandemic and geopolitics it is vital to understand the terms properly. Nicholas Spykman (Furniss, 1952) states that geopolitics is closely related to economics, geography, and political factors as crucial elements of a behavior of a state in the international environment. Spykman mentions other conditioning factors, such as social, ethnic, political, racial and ideological ones. According to Spykman, geopolitics studies the influence of geographic location on political and economic events and shapes internal processes of the state, including its international affairs.

In order to understand the geopolitical impact of COVID-19 on organizations, it is worth presenting the big picture of international relationships, focusing on China and the United States. The ongoing difficulties – or even conflict – between those

DOI: 10.4324/9781003345428-7

two countries are crucial factors determining global trade, supply chain networks, and evolution of new technologies. The strained relationship between China and the US has heavily impacted the direction of the global politics of those countries before and during the pandemic.

The US and China geopolitical conflict started in 2001, but it grew to an open diplomatic conflict in 2011. On December 11, 2001, China joined the World Trade Organization (Manyin et al., 2012) with support of the United States, which had been the only superpower at that time. The beginning of the new century was geopolitically intensive for the US. The Middle East war and 9/11, as well as the 2008 Financial Crisis, have strained the US economy and weakened its international image, while the Chinese economy was flourishing. Between 2001 and 2012, the Chinese economy experienced one of the fastest growths in the world. For instance, the GDP growth rate of the People's Republic of China increased to an average rate of 10.5% in the first decade of a new century and the rate of Chinese GDP doubled from 7.5% to 15% between 2001 and 2012 (Wang, 2017). After the 2008 Financial Crisis, the US economy suffered from numerous issues starting with GDP, inflation, and social divisions, up to misalliance of geopolitical interests. During the Global Financial Crisis, the Chinese economy did not suffer in the least, and China seized the opportunity to become a major partner in global politics (Womack, 2017). China and its global politics posed threats to US hegemony and challenged the US during the 2008 Summer Olympics opening ceremony in Beijing. There were many symbolic messages to the world and particularly to the US at economic, geopolitical, and astropolitical levels that, given time, are very prominent now.

In 2011, Secretary of State Hillary Clinton gave a speech in Hawaii about the future of US politics toward the Asia and Pacific area (US Department of State, 2011). In diplomacy, symbolism plays a significant role, and Hawaii was chosen as a venue on purpose. This is the closest US state in proximity to Asia. Hillary Clinton's statement referred to the future geopolitical role of the Asia and Pacific area in relation to the US politics. The US influence on this particular region may be supported by the Secretary of State's exact words (US Department of State, 2011): "one of the most important tasks of American statecraft over the next decades will be to lock in a substantially increased investment – diplomatic, economic, strategic, and otherwise – in this region". The speech was directly addressed to Chinese government and their allies. The next step of the US government was signing the trade agreement Trans-Pacific-Partnership (TPP) with 11 other countries in Asia, and Canada and Mexico. The main goal of the TPP was to impose economic restrictions on China (Obama White House, 2011). Furthermore, US diplomacy showed its military presence in Australia and planned to deploy over 2500 Marines there (Compton, 2011).

The US challenge did not go unanswered. In 2013, Xi Jinping, General Secretary of Communist Party and Chairman of the Central Military Commission made his famous speech about the "Chinese dream". Xi Jinping (2013) pronounced that: "We will fulfill our international responsibilities and obligations and continue to work with the peoples of all other countries to advance the lofty cause of peace and development of mankind". The speech was directed primarily to Chinese society but also to US authorities.

In 2017, Donald Trump announced the strengthening of cooperation between the US and China. However, already in 2018 the Trump administration introduced sweeping tariffs on import from China worth 200 billion USD, which was in fact a response to the abuse of US technology and intellectual property (USTR, 2018). The open trade war between US and China reduced export of both countries. US export to China fell by 26.3%, while exports to the rest of the world increased by 2.2%. Chinese export to USA dropped by 8.5% but at the same time increased by 5.5% to the rest of the world. The countries that benefited the most were those with high international integration with global agreements and foreign direct investment (Gorman, 2022). Ironically, the US and China trade war has made European economies, like France and Spain, stronger. From economic perspective, it can be concluded that US has lost more than China. In 2019 Huawei filed a lawsuit against the US for banning their federal agencies from using Huawei's equipment. In response, the Trump administration warned their partners not to use Huawei hardware to build 5G networks, claiming that Chinese government might use it for spying. The culmination of geopolitical pushes between US and China was in 2018 and forced change of behavior and digitalization. Economics restrictions, like tariffs, hit the biggest companies belonging to Chinese and European corporations, like Mercedes, BMW, and Huawei, disrupting supply chains. Another difficulty for businesses was the COVID-19 pandemic and the WHO's consequent recommendation to lockdown all global economies to reduce the spread of the virus.

After the pandemic was announced, psychological warfare began between China and the US. The aim of psychological warfare is to use propaganda against an enemy, supported by military, economic, and political measures to demoralize the society of the enemy (Schmid, 2005). One example of psychological warfare was the use of the phrase "Chinese virus", initiated by then-President Donald Trump on Twitter (Zheng et al., 2020). China denied the accusation, blaming the US Army for spreading the virus in October 2019 in Wuhan during the Military World Games (US Department of Defense, 2019).

In March 2020, Trump suspended travel from Europe for 30 days, excluding Great Britain. The main goal of that decision was to stop the spread of COVID-19 in the US. Trump was blaming Europe for the increasing number of COVID-19 cases in the US. The ban had enormous economic implications, because it involved the Schengen economic zone and travel (Wilkie, 2020). The same restriction had been imposed on China before. The second crucial situation was the announcement of a global pandemic by the WHO, which recommended lockdowns in all countries to stop the spread of the virus (Cucinotta & Vanelli, 2020). The third was temporary shortages of key supplies. According to the World Trade Organization, export bans covered over 90% of private goods (Casey & Cimino-Isaacs, 2021).

Referring to the first part of the chapter, geopolitical relations between the US and China have disrupted the global order established by the Americans only within a decade, which impacted international economy and business. As a result, the many European companies relocated their production from China. One of the preferred places for new production location has been Central and Eastern Europe (Consultancy, 2022).

The second part of the chapter will explain reshoring practice from China to Europe and the US before a global pandemic was announced in March 2020.

Reshoring practice from China

The opening of the Chinese market in the 1970s and 1980s allowed the companies to use offshoring practices to profit from low labor costs, or later a business-friendly regulatory environment that included access to raw materials. Offshoring was very popular and profitable, but also contributed to business failures of many companies that underestimated the costs associated with transferring services or production to China (Wiesmann et al., 2016).

Reshoring is considered as a strategic decision to change the location of industrial manufacturing from low-cost to often high-cost environments. Reshoring is a new and emerging practice, even though a few cases have sporadically occurred since the 1980s (Wiesmann et al., 2016). Other researchers, like Cosimato and Vona (2021, p. 8) define reshoring as relocation of value and tasks from offshore location to geographically closer locations. In addition, some authors embed reshoring practice in internationalization theory due to the advantages of minimizing of costs, volatility demand, and smaller or segmented markets. Cosimato and Vona (2021) point out that reshoring decisions are often inspired by specific factors like increasing inequality among countries.

As mentioned in the first part of the chapter, global and economic changes mainly caused by tensions in the US–China relationship have reignited the debate on relocating manufacturing and service units back to the home country (reshoring) or at least to nearby countries (nearshoring) (Brandon-Jones et al., 2017). Relocation trend from China to other destinations, among others to Europe, mainly concern technological companies, including such recognizable companies as HP, Nintendo, Dell, Microsoft, Amazon, or Apple.

Despite the fact that there is no unambiguous consensus among researchers on how to delineate reshoring practices, this chapters contributes to the debate by adding geopolitical perspective to the debate. Reshoring is a practice where technological resources and services are frequently transferred to countries with lower geopolitical potential for disruptions due to the limited capacity of these countries to take over know-how, possibility of increased political influence, and reduced supply chain.

Reshoring includes five types of selecting practice, presented in Table 7.1.

Four groups of reshoring determinants may be identified in the literature: industry-related, firm-related, country-related, and project-related factors (Luo, 2001). Reshoring is closely embedded in few theoretical frameworks that interrelate, namely transaction cost theory, resource-based view, institutional theory, eclectic paradigm, and the Uppsala internationalization model (Schellenberg et al., 2017).

Here, the link between reshoring operations and geopolitical context will be drawn. As mentioned before, the main reason for reshoring undertaken by American companies was increasing diplomatic tensions between the US and China. Foreign capital was originally located in China because of relatively cheap labor, but

Table 7.1 Five types of reshoring practice

No.	*Practice*	*Concepts*
1	In-house reshoring	Relocate whole manufacturing activities or services from offshore wholly owned facilities to deliver them in-house in the home country
2	Reshoring for outsourcing	Relocate manufacturing activities from wholly owned facilities back to domestic suppliers
3	Reshoring for insourcing	Relocate manufacturing activities back to wholly owned facilities in a home country
4	Outsourced reshoring	Relocate manufacturing activities performed by offshore suppliers back to home-based suppliers
5	Nearshoring	Relocate manufacturing activities to neighboring or closely located countries

Source: own elaboration based on Wan et al. (2019)

with time the situation changed due to the rise of wages and global politics. It was a political situation that drove the companies to move their operations back to their respective home countries, in particular to CEE and the US. The reshoring decisions increased in number between 2020 and 2021 (Dikler, 2021). In fact, the phenomenon of reshoring could have been seen much earlier, after 2012 Hilary Clinton's speech about the Pacific Pivot. Moreover, former President Barack Obama in his 2015 State of the Union speech pointed out that reshoring may have been a contributing force to US job growth (Oldenski, 2015).

The process of reshoring US manufacturing activities has several underlying reasons – crucial from both national and international perspectives. The first reason was that the manufacturing sector has declined significantly. According to World Bank data, the manufacturing share (value added as a percentage of the GDP) declined from 16% in 1997 to 11% in 2019. The second reason was the impact of the Financial Crisis in 2008. Furthermore, unemployment rates and income inequality as well as social instability were unproportionable (Pan and Zhu, 2019). The reshoring strategy aimed at getting the US economy back on the right track, which was a necessity after 2008. However, US involvement in the Middle East war and in the Ukrainian crisis in 2014 only deepened the crisis of its global hegemony and caused additional internal problems.

After the Trump administration took office in 2017, the reshoring of manufacturing activities accelerated significantly. Trump proposed many changes regarding tax policy and tariff increases. He also decided to establish an Office of Trade and Manufacturing Policy and promote reshoring through various policies, which has led to the creation of the US tax credit program (Pan & Zhu, 2019). Trump's policy making in fact created greater polarization in international politics and international business. Trump, who was raised on the hard and ruthless rules of Wall Street, took this style into global politics, which made little if no impression on countries such as China, Russia, and Iran. Even Germany, which is heavily dependent on US policy in some aspects, objected to Trump's decision.

Another important destination for reshoring manufacturing from China (besides the US) was the European market, and especially Central and Eastern Europe. The European market has become attractive in many aspects, such as lower production and labor costs, skilled workers, cheap resources, availability and suitability of locations, low corporate taxes, and the availability of investment incentives (Młody, 2016). All of these elements reflect exactly what created the lure of the Chinese market in the 1970s and 1980s. Central and Eastern Europe countries have tried to attract investment through the development of legislation, regulations, and procedures, and these efforts have been successful, e.g., between 2009 and 2010 the capital inflow level in Poland and Hungary increased by over 40%. One of the most important investments in the region was capital from the automotive sector. Its turnover amounted to about 150 billion euros, with growth of 170% between 2009 and 2014. Over 40 manufacturers are in CEE, producing more than 3.5 million vehicles annually (Lőrincz, 2018).

The practice of reshoring decisions is becoming popular among many companies. This new phenomenon has not been fully analyzed and defined, but this does not change the fact that a global shift can be seen in capital relocation (Karatzas et al., 2022). China was an attractive place for global businesses and investments in the 1970s and 1980s because of low labor costs. Geopolitical tensions and rising wage costs in China have contributed to the relocation of manufacturers in two important aspects: the first is to return to the home country due to tax reliefs and benefits. The second aspect is new locations that offer attractive investment conditions like Germany, the Czech Republic, Poland, and Hungary. The final part of the chapter will investigate reshoring practices at the time of the COVID-19 pandemic. The section will aim to see if significant changes (accelerations or stagnation) in the process can be observed.

Reshoring practice in face of COVID-19

The strained relationship between the US and China started to change the landscape of global business, including supply chain networks, tariffs, non-tariff restraints, and others, long before the pandemic started. The struggle for the global businesses was triggered by a lurking economic slowdown. In fact, the global pandemic of COVID-19, announced by the WHO, was a tremendous problem for companies and forced them to rethink their global value chains (GVC).

The COVID-19 pandemic has undoubtedly caused many economic problems that directly affected the functioning of the economies of all countries (Karatzas et al., 2022). Particular restrictions imposed on China resulted in disrupted supply chains. The reshoring that evolved in the pre-pandemic period significantly accelerated after the announcement of the pandemic. The era of globalization, offshoring, and the enrichment of countries such as the US ended in 2008 during the Financial Crisis, which hit not only the US but also most European and Middle Eastern countries. The World Uncertainty Index showed that risk and uncertainty rose 200% after 2008. Based on the same index, the crisis caused by COVID-19 is expected to increase over 300% and GVCs are expected to fall by more than 35% (Propovic & Milijic, 2020).

Generally, two reasons driving the phenomenon of unprecedented outflow of capital from Asia are recognized: the trade war between the US and China and the coronavirus pandemic (Zhang et al., 2020). Supporting this notion is the fact that various countries expecting the return of business to the home country are offering various tax benefits. Trump's administration was a leading supporter of reshoring, so much so that the US Senate has proposed funds for companies that will move their facilities back to the US (Chen et al., 2022). Recently, research studies have shown that many companies were keen on reshoring their resources due to the global pandemic, which resulted in disrupted logistics and business operations (Karatzas et al., 2022). A survey conducted by the Site Selectors Guild indicates that over 80% of sampled companies are interested in reshoring, and there are many indications that "reduced" supply chains are likely to become a new trend (Chen et al., 2022). In addition, a McKinsey survey confirmed that over 90% of companies plan to increase the level of resilience in their supply chains using reshoring mechanisms (Pla-Barber et al., 2021).

Another important note on the matter is a survey prepared by the United Nations Conference on Trade and Development. It shows that the pandemic crisis has increased the challenges associated with globalization, specifically growing economic nationalism. The report also indicates that international cooperation has grown over the past decades, and it is expected that in the post-pandemic, economic stagnation will be widely observable in the next few years. By 2030, however, most companies will have reorganized their operations, which will include reshoring in order to stabilize value chains with higher levels of geographic concentration that will bring additional value thanks to the availability of high tech-driven, GVC-intensive industries (Gupta et al., 2021).

The COVID-19 pandemic has accelerated the trend of reshoring around the world. It is not surprising that the phenomenon itself is weakening China's economy. Reshoring as a trend has been very beneficial for the US. Companies are interested in relocating capital to their home locations or choosing more attractive countries such as Hungary, Poland, and Germany to invest. However, the key determinants shaping the reshoring outcome (like the trade war between China and US and the COVID-19 pandemic) affect the entire GVCs. There is growing uncertainty in the world about the conditions of many companies, as shown in the World Uncertainty Index. Many companies are deciding to move their capital, tempted by a number of tax reliefs and subsidies for reshoring decisions by countries such as the US. In the future, the trend of capital relocation will escalate, mainly due to geopolitical tensions and a potential open kinetic conflict between the US and China in the future.

Summary

In many ways, 2001 was a milestone year for the US and the world. Two factors influenced the current geopolitical situation: 9/11 and China joining the World Trade Organization in December 2001. The US became involved in the Middle East war, where it has been conducting operations since 2003. This fact opened China's first geopolitical window of dynamic national prosperity and economic independence. China has made good use of the offshoring opportunity by attracting major manufacturing and technology companies. Apple, for example, employed more than 700,000 workers in Chinese factories producing cell phone components (Rodríguez & Nieto, 2017).

A deep geopolitical transformation took place after 2008 when US policy makers noticed a few serious problems. First, America has engaged in a that has accelerated polarization of the society. Secondly, the US hegemony, with its international prestige, began to decrease due to new geopolitical players like China and Russia. This means that the previously single-power world became polycentric in a short period of time. This caused deep concerns in the US establishment, and in 2011 the US announced a new strategy for their policy. The announcement was made in the infamous "Pacific Pivot" speech delivered by Hilary Clinton. One of the ways to rebuild the former prestige of the US was a reshoring strategy and leaning of the supply chains. China has read the political situation well, which is why there was a shift in government administration in 2013, when Xi Jinping became the chairman of the Communist Party.

China's strategy has also changed in relation to capital outflow from their country. In order to prevent economic decline, China began to use an offshoring method and to place its capital in Africa. Chinese banks, such as the People's Bank of China, the China Development Bank, and the Export–Import Bank of China, have invested heavily in the development of sub-Saharan Africa (SSA). In 2014, there were more than 2200 private Chinese companies operating in SSA (Pigato & Tang, 2015). In 2017, Donald Trump was announced as the new president of the United States. His policies toward China led to accelerated reshoring of US companies to America or to countries that created friendly political climate and business conditions, such as Germany, Poland, and Hungary. The announcement of the global COVID-19 pandemic in 2020 only intensified the reshoring. Many respondents declared that they were ready to fully reshore their capital from China in fear of sanctions imposed on Chinese goods, spread of the virus, and incentives such as tax reliefs. It is now assumed that the reshoring phenomenon will accelerate to allow for stabilizing the GVCs.

References

Brandon-Jones, E., Dutordoir, M., Quariguasi Frota Neto, J. & Squire, B. (2017). The impact of reshoring decisions on shareholder wealth. *Journal of Operations Management, 49–51*(1), 31–36.

Casey, A. & Cimino-Isaacs, C.D. (2021). Export restrictions in response to the COVID-19 pandemic. *Congressional Research Service*. Retrieved from: https://crsreports.congress.gov/product/pdf/IF/IF11551.

Chen, H., Hsu, C., Shih, Y. & Caskey, D. (2022). The reshoring decision under uncertainty in the post-COVID-19 era. *Journal of Business and Industrial Marketing, 37*(10), 2064–2074. https://doi.org/10.1108/JBIM-01-2021-0066.

Compton, M. (2011). Expanded military ties in Australia. *The Obama White House*. Retrieved from: https://obamawhitehouse.archives.gov/blog/2011/11/16/expanded-military-ties-australia.

Consultancy. (2022). European companies increasingly moving to reshore Asia production. *Consultancy.eu*. Retrieved from: http://www.consultancy.eu/news/7430/european-companies-increasingly-moving-to-reshore-asia-production

Cosimato, S. & Vona, R, (2021). Digital innovation for the sustainability of reshoring strategies: A literature review. *Sustainability*, *13*(14), 7601.

Cucinotta, D. & Vanelli, M. (2020). WHO declares COVID-19 a pandemic. *Acta Bio-Medica: Atenei Parmensis*, *91*(1), 157–160.

Dikler, J. (2021). Reshoring: An overview, recent trends, and predictions for the future. *World Economy Brief*, 21–35.

Furniss, E.S. (1952). The contribution of Nicholas John Spykman to the study of international politics. *World Politics*, *4*(3), 382–401.

Gorman, L. (2022). How the US-China trade war affected the rest of the world. *NBER*. Retrieved from: http://www.nber.org/digest-202204/how-us-china-trade-war-affected-rest-world

Gupta, S., Wang, Y. & Czinkota, M. (2021). Reshoring and sustainable development goals. *British Journal of Management*, 1–4.

Hoek, R. & Dobrzykowski, D. (2021). Towards more balanced sourcing strategies – Are supply chain risks caused by the COVID-19 pandemic driving reshoring considerations? *An International Journal*, *26*(6), 689–701.

Jinping, X. (2013). *Address to the First Session of the 12th National People's Congress*. Retrieved from: http://www.neac.gov.cn/seac/c103372/202201/1156515.shtml (15.07.2022).

Karatzas, A., Ancarani, A., Fratocchi, L., Di Stefano, C. & Godsell, J. (2022). When does the manufacturing reshoring strategy create value? *Journal of Purchasing and Supply Management*, *28*(3).

Lőrincz, N. (2018). Being an investment target in CEE. Country attractiveness and near-shoring. *Vezetéstudomány – Budapest Management Review*, *49*(5), 47–54.

Luo, Y. (2001). Determinants of entry in an emerging economy: A multilevel approach. *Journal of Management Studies*, *38*(3), 443–472.

Manyin, M.E., Daggett, S., Dolven, B., Lawrence, S.V., Martin, M.F., O'Rourke, R. & Vaughn, B. (2012). Pivot to the pacific? The Obama administration's "rebalancing" toward Asia. *CRS Report for Congress*. Retrieved from: https://sgp.fas.org/crs/natsec/R42448.pdf.

Młody, M. (2016). Reshoring trend and CEE: An assessment of possible scenarios on the example of Poland. *Faculty of Management Koper*, *1*(1), 29–50.

Obama White House. (2011). *The Trans-Pacific Partnership What You Need to Know about President Obama's Trade Agreement*. Retrieved from: https://obamawhitehouse.archives.gov/issues/economy/trade.

Oldenski, L. (2015). Reshoring by US firms: What do the data say? *Peterson Institute for International Economics*, 15–14.

Pan, H. & Zhu, D. (2019). The "Manufacturing reshoring" strategy in the United States and its implication to China. *Eurasian Journal of Economics and Finance*, 7(3), 1–14.

Pigato, M. & Tang, W. (2015). *China and Africa: Expanding Economic Ties in an Evolving Global Context*. Washington: World Bank.

Pla-Barber, J., Villar, C. & Narula, R. (2021). Governance of global value chains after the Covid-19 pandemic: A new wave of regionalization? *BRQ Business Research Quarterly*, *24*(3), 204–213.

Propovic, A. & Milijic, A. (2020). *Impact of Reshoring in Industry 4.0 on Economic Development in the Wake of Covid-19 Crisis*. Retrieved from: https://www.researchgate.net/publication/353822254_IMPACT_OF_RESHORING_IN_INDUSTRY_40_ON_ECONOMIC_DEVELOPMENT_IN_THE_WAKE_OF_COVID-19_CRISIS

Rodríguez, A. & Nieto, M. (2017). Taking advantage of R&D offshoring beyond innovation. *Rutgers Business Review, 2*(2), 251–257.
Schellenberg, M., Harker, M.J. & Jafari, A. (2017). International market entry mode – A systematic literature review. *Journal of Strategic Marketing*, 1–27.
Schmid, A. (2005). Terrorism as psychological warfare. *Democracy and Security, 1*(2), 137–146.
US Department of Defense. (2019). *7th International Military Sports Council Military World Games.* Retrieved from: http://www.defense.gov/Spotlights/CISM-Military-World-Games/.
US Department of State. (2011). *America's Pacific Century.* Retrieved from: https://2009-2017.state.gov/secretary/20092013clinton/rm/2011/11/176999.htm.
USTR. (2018). *USTR Finalizes Tariffs on $200 Billion of Chinese Imports in Response to China's Unfair Trade Practices.* Retrieved from: https://ustr.gov/about-us/policy-offices/press-office/press-releases/2018/september/ustr-finalizes-tariffs-200.
Wan, L., Orzes, G., Sartor, M., Di Mauro, C. & Nassimbeni, G. (2019). Entry modes in reshoring strategies: An empirical analysis. *Journal of Purchasing and Supply Management, 25*(3), 10.
Wang, Z. (2017). The economic rise of China: Rule-taker, rule-maker, or rule-breaker? *Asian Survey, 57*(4), 595–617.
Wiesmann, B., Snoei, J.R., Hilletofth, R. & Eriksson, D. (2016). Drivers and barriers to reshoring: A literature review on offshoring in reverse. *European Business Review, 29*(1), 15–42.
Wilkie. (2020). Trump suspends travel from Europe for 30 days as part of response to "foreign" coronavirus. *CNBC.* Retrieved from: http://www.cnbc.com/2020/03/11/coronavirus-trump-suspends-all-travel-from-europe.html.
Womack, B. (2017). International crises and China's rise: Comparing the 2008 global financial crisis and the 2017 global political crisis. *The Chinese Journal of International Politics, 10*(4), 383–401.
Zhang, F., Wu, X., Tang, C.S., Feng, T. & Dai, Y. (2020). Evolution of operations management research: From managing flows to building capabilities. *Production and Operations Management, 29*(10), 2219–2229.
Zheng, Y., Goh, E. & Wen, J. (2020). The effects of misleading media reports about COVID-19 on Chinese tourists' mental health: A perspective article. *Anatolia, 31*(2), 337–340.

8 Companies and their exposure to the COVID-19 pandemic

Aleksandra Kania

Introduction

COVID-19 is commonly said to have taken a great toll on business. Lockdowns and health-focused restrictions have forced companies to adapt to certain changes and governments to look for tools to mitigate the multi-faceted and negative effects of the crisis. The disruption caused by the pandemic exposed a lot of uncharted territory for people, systems, and organizations all over the world. If we compare the pandemic crisis to other previous shocks, we will notice that never before have companies had to act so fast in such uncertain conditions (Gkeredakis et al., 2021; Nasih et al., 2022). The Polish economy has not experienced such a violent shock in response to the COVID-19 pandemic since the systemic transformation in 1989. The first lockdown, when most restrictions were introduced between March 14 and 31, 2020, included, among others: suspension of border traffic and closure of educational institutions, restaurants, hotels, and shopping centers. After May 24, the restrictions were gradually loosened, only to come back again on October 24, 2020. This was a new situation for owners and managers, as well as for politicians. The crisis spread immediately and completely across the real economy, evaporating supply and demand simultaneously (He et al., 2022). Demand was constrained by recommendations to stay at home, cuts in wages and employment, and restrictions abroad. Supply, in turn, was reduced by the necessity of temporarily suspending the activities of some companies, limited availability of supplies from abroad, and increased absence of employees. Sudden stops in economic activity, supply chain disruptions, financial and credit market issues – these were all problems that most businesses had to face.

It is generally agreed that vulnerability of any system (and at any scale) is a function of the exposure and sensitivity of that system to hazardous conditions and the resilience, ability, or capacity of the system to cope, adapt, or recover from the effects of those conditions. Generally, a system more exposed and more sensitive to a certain hazard will be more vulnerable, ceteris paribus, and a system that has more resilience will tend to be less vulnerable, ceteris paribus (Smit & Wandel, 2006; Mroczek-Dąbrowska & Matysek-Jędrych, 2021). Exposure, sensitivity, and resilience together can be seen as three separate yet interconnected elements that are part of a vulnerability model (presented in Figure 8.1). Based on that model, we can assume that **industry exposure increases post-action company sensitivity**.

DOI: 10.4324/9781003345428-8

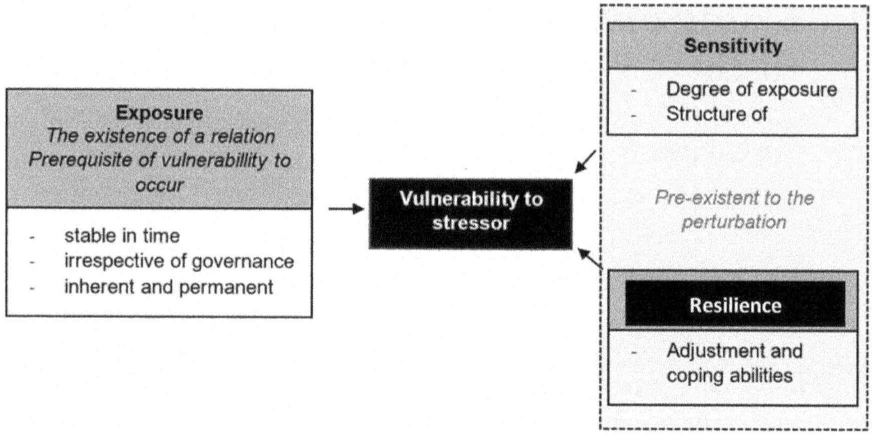

Figure 8.1 Exposure as a part of a vulnerability model

Source: own elaboration based on Mroczek-Dąbrowska and Matysek-Jędrych (2021)

It is also possible to be exposed to a shock but not be vulnerable. However, to be vulnerable to a crisis, it is necessary to be exposed.

We have lived in an era of risk and uncertainty for quite some time now. Globalization, new technologies, and the ever-changing business environment transformed the process of maintaining competitive advantage. The recent COVID-19 pandemic made it even more clear to CEOs all over the world that being able to react to varying conditions without delay has become a new strategy for companies wanting to win the competitive battle on the market. Quickly reading and acting on signals of change can help a company thrive in an uncertain environment. Now, more than ever, it has become crucial to be able to refine or reinvent business models in a dynamic and sustainable way to stay ahead (Reeves & Deimler, 2011).

When we take a look at the current pandemic, it is noticeable that some of the industries suffered a heavier toll than others, since sanitary conditions, social distancing, and state regulations on business operations restricted their functioning to a greater degree (Al-Awadhi et al., 2020; Buchheim et al., 2022; Hassan et al., 2020; Shen et al., 2020). Therefore, industry exposure to COVID-19, including the period in which companies were closed for business, differs, and not all industries were equally exposed to the pandemic impact. Some industries, like tourism and catering in China, have become economic "epicenters" of the pandemic's impact (Shen et al., 2020). The chapter aims to answer the question of which industries in Poland were more sensitive to external shock of the COVID-19 pandemic than others, and why

Research method

In order to answer the above-mentioned question, we conducted surveys among 500 companies in industries affected by the pandemic restrictions.[1] The data for the study was gathered between October 2021 and February 2022 with use of computer-assisted telephone interviews. In order to be included in the study, companies needed to comply with the following criteria: companies needed to be registered in Poland, employ at least ten persons, and prove financial stability through at least three years prior to the pandemic. We interviewed Polish company owners from four different industries, according to NACE Rev 2 level 3, that have been differently affected by the COVID-19 pandemic: wholesale and retail, education, accommodation and catering services, and manufacturing. Please note that our research method is described in further detail in Chapter 9.

Findings

It is generally agreed that economic impacts of COVID-19 were not distributed equally. Some industries were less affected (or even expanded) and others were put on hold. Businesses that rely heavily on face-to-face communication or close physical proximity when manufacturing a product or providing a service were especially vulnerable to social distancing restrictions. The immediate impact of travel bans all over the world and the introduction of further movement restrictions was clearly felt by some industries far more than others – particularly airlines, tourism, entertainment (including e.g. cinemas and gyms) and education.

However, when we take a look at the ability to generate revenue during the whole pandemic, according to our study, the only industry in Poland that has been making money non-stop is education (presented in Figure 8.2.). Throughout all official lockdowns, most education firms moved their businesses to online e-learning platforms and therefore escaped the complete cutoff from making revenue. Moreover,

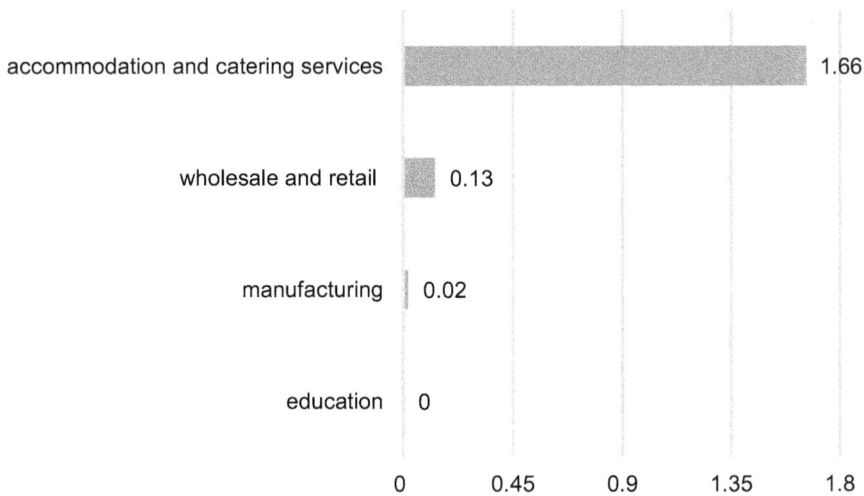

Figure 8.2 Average time (in months) when industries were not able to generate any revenue due to official lockdown

Source: own elaboration

most companies were able to use new communication technologies like Zoom or MS Teams as their survival strategy, which enabled them to continue their activity while staying in touch with employees and pupils/students online. Many private education companies, such as training companies, appreciated the advantages of conducting classes in a remote or hybrid mode long before the pandemic, so during lockdowns they were able to adapt to the situation faster and easier than traditional educational institutions. Some language schools and training agencies quickly saw the niche and tried to fill it. The popularity of dedicated applications used for conversations with native speakers was growing, but professional platforms also appeared, which practically made online classes equal to traditional ones.

In comparison, manufacturing companies were only completely closed off for business for a short average period of 0.02 months, and the companies operating in wholesale and retail for 0.13 months. The latter group of firms partially moved their sales to online channels in order to get away from total shutdown during lockdowns. The most efficient ones with a well-run online business model have even flourished during the pandemic. Lockdowns and all the trade restrictions unexpectedly increased the number of purchases over the internet, which in turn meant that a lot of orders with home delivery were carried out with long delays, because stores were not prepared for such a sudden increase in orders. The prolonged lockdown, which for many people meant remote work and long-term stay at home, resulted in an increased interest in online purchases of products and services that helped fighting boredom or constituted an alternative to traditional forms of entertainment, i.e. electronics, DIY accessories, or interior and garden decoration products.

Accommodation and catering services, which according to our research were not able to generate any revenue for 1.66 months on average, tried to survive the consecutive lockdowns by shifting from one area of activity to another. For example, during official closures of the hotel industry, the researched companies tried to make revenue by offering catering services and take-out. Therefore, the periods of not making any revenue presented by the interviewees in our study are much shorter than the official lockdowns in Poland. It shows how studied companies, even though exposed to a number of difficulties, tried to implement adaptive strategies and survive. Further details in that regard can be found in Chapter 9.

Unfortunately, however agile and brilliant companies were in finding new ways to survive, all of the industries went through a decline in turnover in 2020, in comparison to 2019. The explanation of this situation is twofold. First of all, "non-essential" activity was shut down for some time in 2020. Secondly, a broad range of retailers was also affected as direct job and income losses spilled over to other sectors as businesses reduced spending to stay afloat and as customers who were made redundant decided to cut back.

As can be seen in Figure 8.3, accommodation and catering services recorded the highest decline in turnover – 28%, mostly due to the longest and strongest lockdowns[2] and limited ability to make up for lost sales through catering and other channels.

Education also recorded a substantial decline in turnover – in the height of 23%, which can be explained by many customers dropping out of courses and workshops

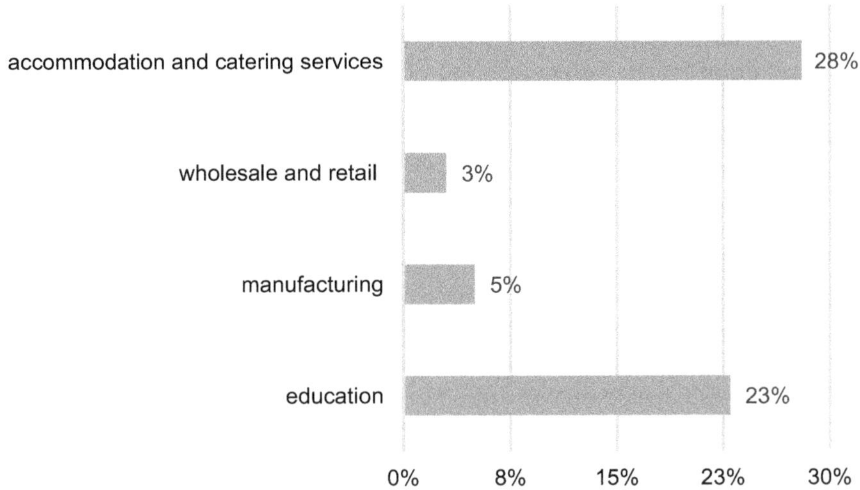

Figure 8.3 Decline in turnover (%) in 2020 of the industry, according to NACE Rev 2 level 3

Source: own elaboration

once they learned they had been moved to an online mode.[3] For example, in eyes of many students, the biggest added value of MBA studies and other highly specialized classes is meeting face to face with fellow colleagues and lecturers and expanding contacts through networking. Without the personal factor, the value of these course depreciates and a certain group of students will naturally withdraw.

Two industries that recorded a relatively small decline in their turnovers, in comparison, were manufacturing (5%) and wholesale and retail (3%). The closure of shopping malls affected the condition of retail sales, in particular in those segments where it was impossible or difficult to replace direct sales with online transactions. However, the whole industry managed to maintain a more or less similar level of turnover, mostly due to the ability to quickly move to online sales channels and because of the fact that food (which is a vital part of this industry) had and would have good prospects as a staple commodity – the food trade generally did fairly well during the pandemic (which has strongly developed the market for home food deliveries). It is also worth noticing that e-commerce was particularly successful in those sectors that had already done their homework, such as electronics and household appliances. There are few strong players that have existed on the internet for a long time, and the pandemic has been an additional stimulus for them to further improve their online presence, since the need to work and learn remotely triggered an impulse among many customers to buy new electronic equipment online.

The situation of manufacturing companies presents itself slightly differently – they are usually part of larger value chains, and to be able to offer their goods, they need first to obtain the required production materials. In the first waves of the pandemic, companies that are part of global supply chains suffered significant delays, and the production process in many cases was also affected, which was one of the reasons for their decreased turnover. Furthermore, export is a key factor determining the success of manufacturers operating in Poland. So, the fact that major disruptions in the supply chain were accompanied by decline in demand and difficulties related to various types of restrictions introduced by individual countries was very disconcerting. This industry has been severely affected by the closure of borders, which corresponds to the opinion that the COVID-19 pandemic was the most major challenge for globalization as it has been so far. What is more, in the industry on the whole, orders fell significantly, in terms of both consumer goods and intermediate goods. Many of the ordered goods were not picked up. There were also critical problems with logistics and the possibility of delivering ordered and manufactured goods. In some cases, the execution of orders was prevented by shortages in the supply of raw materials and semi-finished products, and in some cases problems with completing the crew (due to quarantine[4]). Companies that produce high-end products that require cutting-edge inputs (mainly those that must be sourced from abroad) were in particular heavily exposed to the pandemic shock. Such turmoil arrived in late 2020 in the automotive industry, when low levels of supply from semiconductor producers were met with growing demand from customers located in Poland. The ensuing shortage of chips resulted in automotive manufacturers shutting down entire production lines and sending employees on either paid or unpaid leave. The closure of large companies, in turn, affected sub-suppliers, which are most often small and medium-sized enterprises. At time of writing this chapter, in June 2022, demand still exceeds supply in that sector. It should be noted, however, that most manufacturing companies did not suffer from massive layovers – a characteristic solution often used in the manufacturing industry was resignation from services of temporary employment agencies or cancelation of night shifts, which allowed redundancies of own employees to be limited. This can be explained by the fact that access to qualified staff in that industry has been difficult in recent years, and hence companies were reluctant to get rid of employees, at the same time hoping that the pandemic was a temporary phenomenon.[5]

Even though a lot of firms struggled, in the end very few companies operating in wholesale and retail (0.48%) went bankrupt in 2020 (as we can see in Figure 8.4). Better results can only be seen in education (0.38%), which can be explained by the fact that many companies in that industry are state-owned and managed to survive the pandemic partially thanks to government funding. The entities organizing sports and recreational activities, which could not transfer their services to remote mode, were in the worst situation, but most of these companies tried to offer different services during official lockdowns and therefore minimize the negative impact.

A slightly worse situation can be noticed in manufacturing, where 0.98% of companies ceased operations in 2020 and in accommodation and catering services, with a result of 1.23% bankruptcies. This industry also recorded a decline in employment in 2020, in comparison to 2019 – at a height of 11.73%. These results can be explained by two facts: a relatively small percentage of companies went bankrupt, but far more had to implement redundancy plans in order to stay solvent. The pandemic

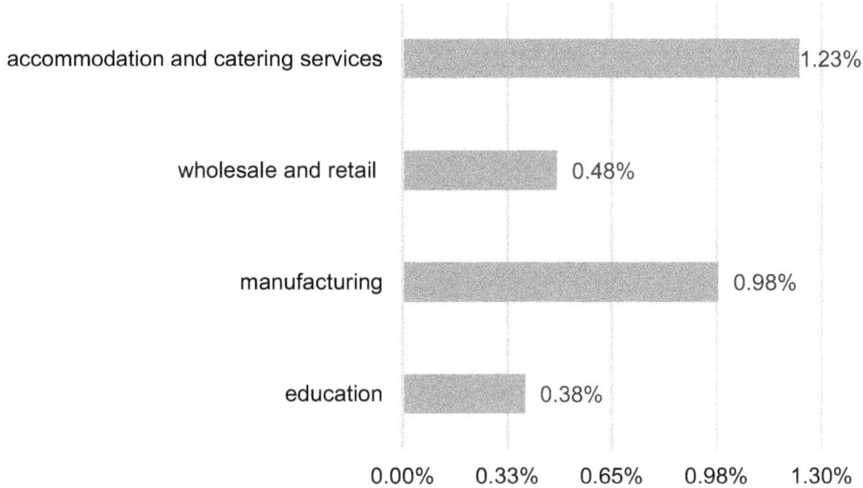

Figure 8.4 Number of companies that ceased operations in 2020 to total number of companies registered in an industry

Source: own elaboration

and related closures have simply forced personnel changes. Closed facilities did not always have the means to maintain full staff, which then reflected negatively on their performance and level of customer service in periods of increased tourist traffic.

Another factor assessed in our study was the debt ratio (understood as amount of leverage used by a company in terms of total debt to total assets), which in accommodation and catering services industry also rose considerably in 2020, in comparison to 2019 – by nearly 20%, which is noticeable in Figure 8.5. Most companies managed to stay in business but paid the price of having to let part of their employees go and increasing their debt ratio. Far better results were recorded in this regard in manufacturing and wholesale and retail with an increase of debt ratio around 5% and in education with a practically unchanged level of total debts to total assets.

Accommodation and catering services was also the industry that recorded the highest decline in their quick ratio, which measures company's capacity to pay its current liabilities without needing to sell its inventory or obtain additional financing – 33.39%. Education suffered by only 4.53% and manufacturing and wholesale and retail by around 10% (as seen in Figure 8.6). Respondents from the hospitality industry also pointed out that it was difficult to negotiate fixed prices with suppliers that could apply for a long time, which was often guaranteed in the contracts before the pandemic. The results of the accommodation and catering services industry can be also explained by the fact that in their situation size does in fact matter. Due to the model of functioning, small and medium-sized companies (which constitute most of the accommodation and catering services industry in Poland) are more vulnerable to rapid changes in their liquidity (Bartik et al., 2020; Ichev & Marinč, 2018; Harel, 2021).

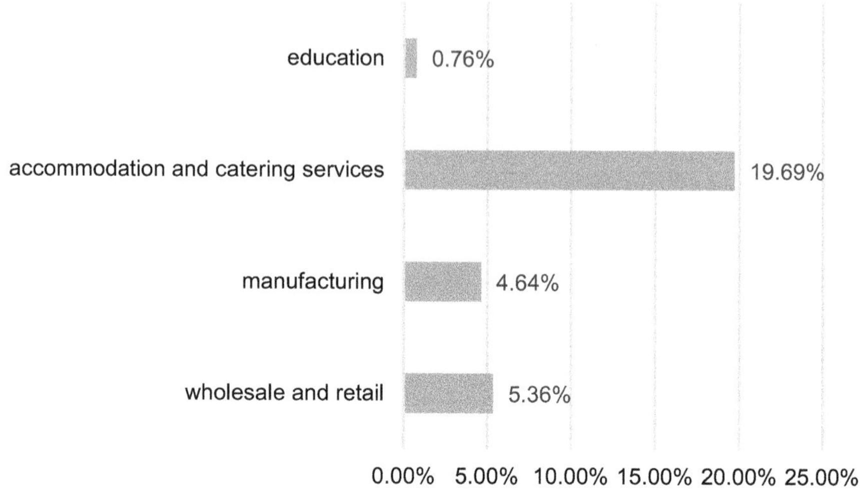

Figure 8.5 Increase in debt ratio in 2020 in comparison to 2019

Source: own elaboration

They need to cover fixed expenses (rent, utilities, employee pay, etc.), which constitute the major part of their monthly cost structure. Generally, micro and small companies do not own cash reserves, which disables them from functioning for longer than the immediate future. Without the ability to quickly acquire capital, they resort to employee dismissal, and shortly after, they are frequently forced to file for bankruptcy (c.f. Obłój, 2020a, 2020b). Large companies often reach for two solutions that extend their expiry date – they compromise with their employees on pay cuts, unpaid vacation, and any other cost-saving tools and – if they constitute part of capital groups – they seek additional cashflows. Additionally, the companies in supply chains – forced to choose between their clients due to limited inventories – tend to turn first to their major recipients due to the effect of scale. This once again gives an upper-hand to the large companies. Another argument for impact differentiation is the fact that most of the prepared anti-crisis tools were aimed at smaller companies, which were expected to suffer a heavy toll in the pandemic. During the pandemic, even such trivial issues as application of sanitary standards was challenging for a lot of small and medium-sized companies, due to low employment and sharp increase in prices of basic protective measures (as much as several hundred percent), and many of them resigned from incurring such additional expenses.

The data obtained from the conducted survey shows us that liquidity threats were a huge problem even in the industries that were not on the front lines of the crisis (e.g. manufacturing and wholesale and retail). In the recent pandemic, even companies that maintained production were at risk of losing financial liquidity, which may, down the road, result in bankruptcy. Therefore, it was very important to maintain access to revolving financing for companies that fulfilled orders on an ongoing basis.

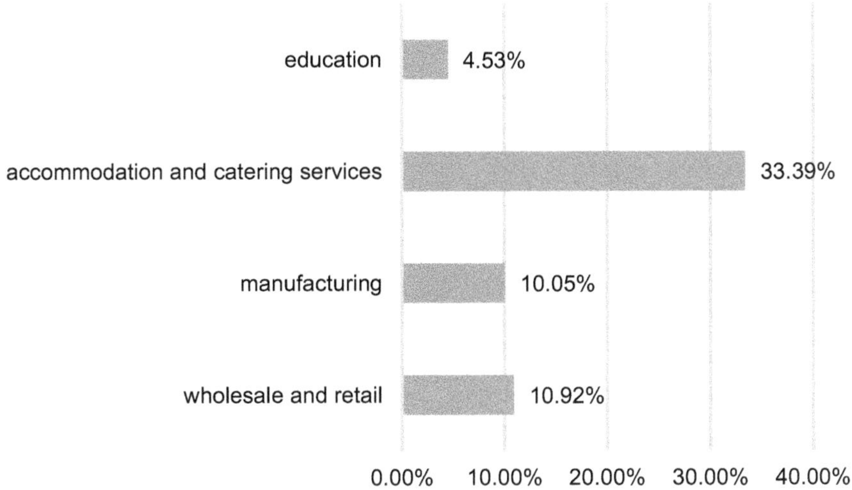

Figure 8.6 Decline in quick ratio (liquidity) in 2020 in comparison to 2019

Source: own elaboration

The last index that we assessed in our study was the receivables turnover ratio, which measures the efficiency with which a company is able to collect on its receivables or the credit it extends to customers. It turns out the ratio was also mostly unfavorable for accommodation and catering services – in 2020, in comparison to 2019, it declined by 16.45%. The other industries recorded smaller drops – manufacturing and retail around 5%, while education's ratio stayed nearly the same (presented in Figure 8.7).

It should be noted, however, that the real crisis caused by the pandemic may show itself once the money from all government anti-crisis tools runs out. These cash transfers, which companies have received and are still getting, can be considered a substantial influx of capital, but they mainly served to ensure that companies survived when the economy stood still, and many industries were generating no profit at all. This means, however, that when the financial support from the government ends, the companies will have to manage by themselves, covering still high operating costs (rents, staff costs, etc.) from their own, probably much smaller income. Many of them will not be able to cope with it, and the effect will be pressure on the reduction of employment and wage cuts. Therefore, in the near future, liquidity problems and payment gridlocks may pose a huge (much greater than usual) challenge for the studied industries and for the entire Polish economy.

In order to compare the exposure of companies between different waves of the pandemic, part of our study was also dedicated to companies' preparedness for potential containment measures in the so-called fourth wave of the pandemic (which started in October 2021). Respondents from all four researched industries assessed their readiness as on average better than a year before, with education and

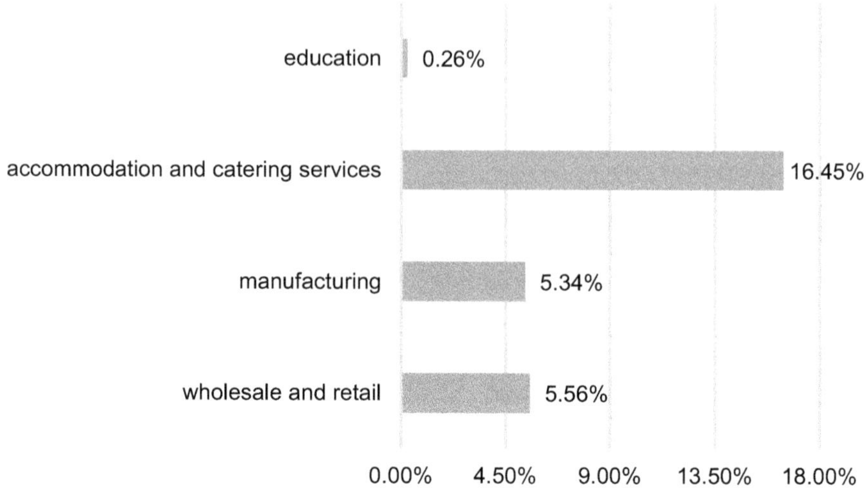

Figure 8.7 Decline in receivables turnover ratio in 2020 in comparison to 2019

Source: own elaboration

manufacturing being slightly better prepared than accommodation and catering services (as seen in Figure 8.8).

For many entrepreneurs, the moments of loosening restrictions in May 2020, and then also in December and February 2021, were of key importance. However, it was only partially possible to make up for the losses – while a large part of goods could be sold with a delay when the shopping malls re-opened, education could not always benefit from increased demand created during lockdowns.

The first year of the pandemic was accompanied by a rotation in demand from services and toward goods, which was a positive factor for a lot of manufacturing companies and the whole wholesale and retail industry. What is more, these sectors didn't suffer from high declines in turnover and employment reductions during first waves of the pandemic, so they felt rightly prepared for the new set of containment measures in October 2021.

On the other hand, accommodation and catering services was the industry that previously recorded highest drops in turnover, had to lay off most employees, and struggled the most to fill in the gap of no revenue in time of official lockdowns. Most companies from that industry tried to survive by expanding their areas of expertise by e.g. offering special stays for professional athletes (which were exempted from lockdowns). However, the months of the lockdown forced a lot of workers to switch to a different industry and resulted in reluctance to take up employment in the unstable hospitality sector again. At the break of the fourth wave of the pandemic, the entire industry was struggling with a shortage of people willing to work, which at the peak of the holiday season was a huge operational challenge. The other problem was the lack of regulations that would

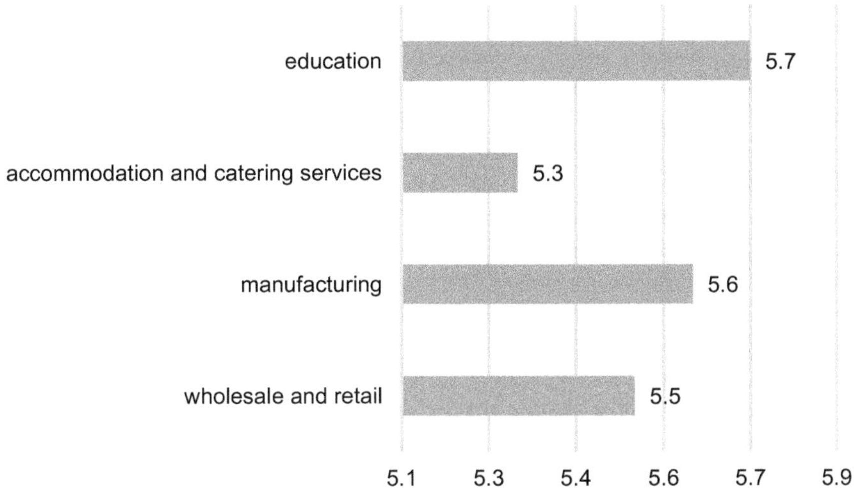

Figure 8.8 How would you rate (on a scale from 1–7) the company's preparation for potential problems resulting from increased restrictions in the so-called fourth wave of the pandemic (from October 2021) compared to 2020?

Source: own elaboration

allow entrepreneurs to verify which employees were vaccinated and which were not. However, even with these limitations, in between COVID-19 waves, accommodation and catering services industry recorded satisfactory results. The holiday period in particular was much more favorable for the domestic hotel industry, due to the loosening of movement restrictions and the fact that a large number of Poles refrained from traveling abroad and decided to spend their holidays in the country. It is also worth highlighting that the Polish accommodation and catering services industry relies to a relatively small degree on incoming tourism (about 20% visitors are foreigners), and thanks to domestic tourism it may recover faster after the crisis.

Conclusions

The crisis related to the COVID-19 pandemic has brought unexpected problems on an unprecedented scale to many sectors of the economy. A lot of firms struggled to predict the evolution of the pandemic and how they could prepare for the next "wave". The collapse of demand, and in extreme cases even the inability to produce and/or sell, deprived companies from these industries of sources of income necessary to cover, for example, fixed operating costs. All this was often combined with large supply problems related to disruptions in global supply chains, operational downtime caused by the pandemic, and/or temporary staff shortages.

The survey results help to understand the scale of the difficulties that Polish companies from various industries were facing during the pandemic and provide information for discussion on areas that might need immediate state support. Conducted research shows that some sectors have not been strongly affected by the pandemic, in particular those producing and selling everyday goods (e.g. food) as well as education, while some have even benefited, e.g. online sales and production of hygiene products.

One of the most severely exposed industries to the COVID-19 pandemic in Poland was accommodation and catering services. The turnover of hotels, restaurants, and other services, where direct contact with the customer prevails, decreased. It was a serious hit to the entire Polish economy, as the broadly understood industry produces as much as 12% GDP. The number of people employed in the hospitality industry is several hundred thousand. If we take into account companies related to hotels – suppliers of products and services and subcontractors, the number of employees dependent on the functioning of this industry reaches up to one million people. While the industry has been constantly affected since the pandemic began, as a result of lockdowns, it may rebound once COVID-19 restrictions are lifted.

One of the reasons for such high sensitivity in the accommodation and catering services was improper communication between the state and entrepreneurs during the crisis. It should have been based on three principles – transparency, solidarity, and adequacy – to reduce uncertainty, not increase it through ever changing and unclear regulations.

The combination of uncertain revenue prospects, high debt levels, lower liquidity, and current or potential capital losses led to a situation in which many companies in Poland were and are under financial stress due to the pandemic. Larger firms could tap into capital markets to weather the COVID-19 storm. Smaller companies have received support through government anti-crisis tools, but they might find themselves particularly exposed once this temporary support is withdrawn and the debt accrued during the crisis falls due. If the pandemic ends up having a more permanent impact on these borrowers, they may struggle to repay this debt, which may lead to higher levels of default in the future.

Interestingly, the pandemic may be conducive to accelerating the consolidation of industries in Poland. Its effects affect the smaller entities, which are weaker economically, with smaller financial reserves and worse access to financing, and are exposed to bankruptcy and/or takeovers by larger entities on a bigger scale. From the point of view of the national economy, this may be a favorable phenomenon in the longer term, as international experience shows that the driving force behind innovation and maintaining dynamic economic growth are large domestic companies, not SMEs.

Acknowledgments

This contribution draws on the final results of the "Determinants of company's adaptability to crisis situation – the case of Covid19" project. The project was co-financed by the Polish National Agency for Academic Exchange within the Urgency Grants program.

Notes

1 Further issues investigated thanks to the mentioned survey are presented in Chapter 9.

2 The outflow of guests from hotels and the first cancellations of reservations took place in the first half of March 2020, when the first cases of coronavirus infections began to be recorded in Poland. The government has shut hotels since April 2020, more than two weeks after the lockdown struck. At that time, they could only operate by accepting guests who were on essential business trips or representatives of a medical profession. The hotels reopened right after the May 3rd long weekend. The re-closing for non-business visitors took place on November 7, 2020.

3 It is worth noticing that the educational industry in Poland encompasses not only schools and universities but also language schools, entities offering practicing various sports and recreational activities, driving lessons, schools preparing for specific professions, and activities supporting education (e.g. additional after-school-hours math classes). In addition, there are also unclassified out-of-school forms of education – otherwise a very broad category.

4 These issues, however, were mostly quickly solved as the infections were usually limited to small groups of workers. The rules of sanitary rigor, introduced after the outbreak of the pandemic, were fruitful. Temperature measurement, disinfectant fluids, masks, lunch shifts – these measures have been used by virtually all factories in Poland and worked quite successfully in most cases.

5 It is worth remembering that at the beginning of the first lockdown, no one knew how long the freeze would last and what the repercussions would be, and new question marks appeared every day. On the whole, most of the pandemic companies were unable to predict how hard would the next "wave" hit them, which made it even more difficult for them to prepare their survival strategies.

References

Al-Awadhi, A.M., Alsaifi, K., Al-Awadhi, A. & Alhammadi, S. (2020). Death and contagious infectious diseases: Impact of the COVID-19 virus on stock market returns. *Journal of Behavioral and Experimental Finance, 27*, 2–5.

Bartik, A.W., Bertrand, M., Cullen, Z., Glaeser, E.L., Luca, M. & Stanton, C. (2020). The impact of COVID-19 on small business outcomes and expectations. *Proceedings of the National Academy of Sciences, 117*(30), 17656–17666.

Buchheim, L., Krolage, C. & Link, S. (2022). Sudden stop: When did firms anticipate the potential consequences of COVID-19? *German Economic Review, 23*(1), 79–119.

Gkeredakis, M., Lifshitz-Assaf, H. & Barrett, M. (2021). Crisis as opportunity, disruption and exposure: Exploring emergent responses to crisis through digital technology. *Information and Organization, 31*(1).

Golubeva, O. (2021). Firms' performance during the COVID-19 outbreak: International evidence from 13 countries. *Corporate Governance, 21*(6), 1011–1027.

Harel, R. (2021). The impact of COVID-19 on small businesses' performance and innovation. *Global Business Review, I*(22).

Hassan, T.A., Hollander, S., Lent, L. & Tahoun, A. (2020). Firm-level exposure to epidemic diseases Covid-19, SARS, and H1N1. *Working Paper, National Bureau of Economic Research*, 26971.

He, Z., Suardi, S., Wang, K. & Zhao, Y. (2022). Firms' COVID-19 pandemic exposure and corporate cash policy: Evidence from China. *Economic Modelling, 116*.

Ichev, R. & Marinč, M. (2018). Stock prices and geographic proximity of information: Evidence from the Ebola outbreak. *International Review of Financial Analysis, 56*, 153–166.

Mroczek-Dąbrowska, K. & Matysek-Jędrych, A. (2021). "To fear or not to fear?" The nature of the EU-27 countries' vulnerability to Brexit. *European Planning Studies, 29*(2), 277–290.

Nasih, M., Wardani, D.A.K., Harymawan, I., Putra, F.K.G. & Sarea, A. (2022). COVID-19 exposure: A risk-averse firms' response. *Journal of Financial Reporting and Accounting*. Ahead-of-Print. Retrieved from: https://doi.org/10.1108/JFRA-12-2021-0430

Obłój, K. (2020a). Płynąc w sztormie (Swimming in a storm). *Rzeczpospolita*, 16 April. Retrieved from: https://www.rp.pl/opinie-ekonomiczne/art769431-prof-krzysztof-obloj-plynac-w-sztormie

Obłój, K. (2020b). Wirus zmusi ład gospodarczy do mutacji (The virus will force the economic order to mutate). *Rzeczpospolita*, 11 May. Retrieved from: https://www.rp.pl/opinie-ekonomiczne/art727101-krzysztof-obloj-wirus-zmusi-lad-gospodarczy-do-mutacji#error=login_required&state=71370b5d-bef3-4828-b2af-f96b7f02a3a2

Reeves, M. & Deimler, M. (2011). Adaptability: The new competitive advantage. *Harvard Business Review*. Retrieved from: https://hbr.org/2011/07/adaptability-the-new-competitive-advantage

Shen, H., Fu, M., Pan, H., Yu, Z. & Chen, Y. (2020). The impact of the COVID-19 pandemic on firm performance. *Emerging Markets Finance and Trade, 56*(10), 2213–2230.

Smit, B. & Wandel, J. (2006). Adaptation, adaptive capacity and vulnerability. *Global Environmental Change, 16*, 282–292.

9 Building companies' adaptive capabilities in the 21st century

Evidence from Poland

Katarzyna Mroczek-Dąbrowska, Aleksandra Kania, and Anna Matysek-Jędrych

Introduction

We live in an era of risk and uncertainty. Globalization, new technologies and the ever-changing business environment transformed the process of maintaining competitive advantage. The COVID-19 pandemic made it even more clear to CEOs all over the world that adaptability has become a new strategy for companies wanting to win the competitive battle on the market. Quickly reading and acting on signals of change can help a company thrive in an uncertain environment. It has become crucial to be able to refine or reinvent business models in a dynamic and sustainable way to stay ahead (Anning-Dorson & Nyamekye, 2020; Brunelli et al., 2022; Reeves & Deimler, 2011). Such ability to constantly and continuously evolve to match or exceed the requirements of the operating environment before those requirements become critical can be defined as adaptive capability[1] (Hamel & Välikangas, 2003). Now, more than ever, the company's survival may be built on this ability to recognize and act on changing market expectations. Adaptive capability is firmly connected to an organization's strategic plan to respond to changing business needs by identifying and nurturing its key resources, competences, and other organizational processes (Ali et al., 2017). Paliokaite (2012) and Tejeiro Koller (2016) suggest that adaptive capability helps to maintain a competitive position, particularly in continuously changing environments.

The chapter's aim is, firstly, to discuss how companies can approach the building of the resilience capacity and, secondly, to discuss what types of adaptive strategies companies in Poland made use of during the early stage of pandemic. Hence, the chapter's structure reflects these aims – first presenting a brief review of resilience-related concepts, following by a discussion on methods and the sample used in the empirical methods, and finally discussing the k-means clustering results, adaptive strategies, and public support used by companies.

Resilience, adaptive capabilities, and disturbance

As Polman & Winston (2021) wisely said, when a storm hits, buildings may collapse, but most palm trees remain standing. Organizations need to build their resilience capacity to withstand the storms they are likely to face: natural disasters, pandemic,

DOI: 10.4324/9781003345428-9

industry disruptions, geopolitical threats, supply chain disruptions. Although crises can differ in nature, impacting organizations through different channels and with different force, companies strive to uphold at least the threshold resilience in order to maintain their operations.

The concept of resilience originates with Holling (1973) as a capacity of a system to withstand any perturbations and return to its original state of equilibrium (c.f. Gunderson, 2000; Folke, 2006; Scheffer, 2009). With time, the understanding of the notion has developed into allowing alternative stable states to substitute for the original state, thus admitting that resilience should be associated with adjusting rather than persisting.[2] We distinguish between specified resilience, where particular parts of a system are immune (or capable of adjusting) to a certain set of shocks and perturbations (Carpenter et al., 2001), and general resilience, where the whole system is prepared to endure all kind of shocks, including novel ones (Folke et al., 2010). Nurturing specified resilience may in fact hinder building the general resilience capacity as organizations often find themselves in a state of denial, imaging that novel perturbations can be overcome with use of the same capabilities. The specific resilience strives to maintain the existing *status quo* by returning to a predetermined state, removing deviations, and keeping company within established boundaries (Weick & Sutcliffe, 2007). General resilience, on the other hand, stimulates a company's behavior toward self-reinforcement and modifying the rules of the game.

To achieve resilience, an organization – or, wider, a system – needs adaptive capabilities. Adaptability reflects the organization's capacity to draw on gained experience and knowledge to adjust to external and internal disruptions and continue developing in a stable state (Folke et al., 2010; Liu et al., 2021; O'Connell et al., 2015). In contrast, the term transformability has been coined to reflect the capacity to construct a new system when external circumstances deem the existing structure untenable (Walker et al., 2004). Resilience, adaptive capabilities, and transformability are all embedded in so-called adaptive cycles, which alternate between the growth phase, where resources are aggregated and nurtured, and the reorganization phase, where the inevitable outcome leads to resource reshuffling and system renewal (Holling et al., 2002). Adaptive cycles are an apt analogy (or, rather, complementarity) for the term *sustainability*, which means a system's ability to maintain its functionality over an infinite time horizon (Fath, 2015).

Resilience and adaptive capabilities are tested by disturbances. Small-scale "shock therapy" is encouraged as it helps build a company's adaptive capacity and promote alternative pathways to create innovation. Self-infused small-scale disturbances provide firms with internal feedback and enable the system to learn from multi-level interactions (Fath et al., 2015), and hence building the company's general resilience by pinpointing the weak links. Eliminating all loopholes is never possible; however, testing allows companies to react agilely to the unknown, as in the case with the COVID-19 pandemic outbreak. In the following part of the chapter, we present a typology of adjustment strategies companies adopted in the first stage of the pandemic. The strategies presented are directly linked to the adaptive capabilities that companies were able to incorporate into their operations.

Method and sample

The data for the study was gathered between October 2021 and February 2022 with use of computer-assisted telephone interviews on a sample of 500 Polish companies. The questionnaire referred to the following aspects of company's behavior during the lockdowns: factors influencing the firm's adaptive capabilities, sensitivity toward the pandemic, and usage of the anti-crisis tools offered by the government. In order to be included in the study, companies needed:

- to be registered in Poland,
- to employ at least ten persons,
- to prove financial stability through at least three years prior to the pandemic,
- to belong to industries highly affected by the pandemic.

Moreover, the sample included companies that were state- or private-owned (or both), were of different size (based on turnover and average employee numbers), were local market–oriented or foreign market–oriented, and belonged to production or non-production industries (Table 9.1).

Based on the data gathered, we conducted k-means clustering where we sought to partition the sample into groups that identify patterns in a company's adaptive capabilities in the face of the COVID-19 pandemic. The analysis included six factors, three referring to a company's agility in adjusting operations once the pandemic started (time elapsed to adjust sales channels, working arrangements, and supply chains) and three characterizing the company itself (market experience, size measured by turnover, and average employee numbers). As Table 9.2 indicates, all of the listed factors were well fitted to determine the final grouping.

The F-values prove that the factors included in the analysis significantly differentiate the adaptive capabilities of companies displayed during the initial phases of pandemic restrictions. This fact meant that the achieved partitioning met the goal of

Table 9.1 Sample characteristics

Feature	*Number of companies in sample*
Between 10 and 49 employees	***125***
wholly owned by the state	5
fully private	120
Between 50 and 249 employees	***125***
wholly owned by the state	28
fully private	97
More than 250 employees	***250***
wholly owned by the state	61
mixed – private and state owned	4
fully private	185
Total	***500***

Source: own elaboration

Table 9.2 Variance analysis – results

Factor	*Between cluster*	*df*	*Within clusters*	*df*	*F-value*	*p-sig*
Agility in adjusting sales channels	98.24	2	354.71	497	68.83	0.00
Agility in adjusting working operations	30.48	2	300.73	497	25.19	0.00
Agility in adjusting supply chains	295.28	2	527.55	497	139.09	0.00
Market experience	44076.82	2	25017.69	497	437.81	0.00
Employee	498.00	2	705.928	497	175.46	0.00
Turnover	9053904.19	2	54785271.60	497	4107.08	0.00

Source: own elaboration

Table 9.3 Cluster mean values

	Cluster 1	*Cluster 2*	*Cluster 3*
Agility in adjusting sales channels	0.99	1.38	2.20
Agility in adjusting working operations	0.53	0.93	1.17
Agility in adjusting supply chains	1.63	0.51	2.50
Market experience	16.67	37.24	32.31
Turnover	40 434 506	29 910 625	283 177 939
Employee	205.79	237.31	555.54

Source: own elaboration

minimizing the within-cluster variance and maximizing the between-cluster variance. Using Ward's method, we established that the appropriate number of clusters would be three, and the results of the analysis were achieved within three iterations (Table 9.3).

Using the mean values (Table 9.3), we were able to delineate three types of adjustment patterns that companies adopted in the first stage of the pandemic lockdown:

- cluster 1: *young demand-driven flexibles*: companies where adjustments were quick and mostly triggered by the demand-side of the operations,
- cluster 2: *established supply-driven flexibles*: companies where adjustments were quick and mostly triggered by the supply-side of the operations,
- cluster 3: *mature adopters*: companies where adjustments were significantly slower in all areas of operations.

The *young demand-driven flexibles* are the most diversified companies as there is no dominant industry to which they belong nor any specific size (in terms of employee numbers). They are, however, relatively young, with the youngest companies established in 2018, and the turnover they generate is significantly smaller than in the other two clusters. The *established supply-driven flexibles* are the most sizable group, with companies operating mostly in education and accommodation and food service activities. These are the most experienced market players of significant size –in terms of both employee numbers and turnover generated. The group includes almost all state-owned companies, which contradicts the common claim that such companies are the slowest on the adoption curve. The final cluster, *mature adopters*, includes companies that belong to manufacturing as well as retail and wholesale industries. They were the slowest to introduce changes in their business models in all three areas of operations: sales, working arrangements, and supply chains.

We have also studied whether companies saw a need to actively change their market behavior by: attracting new customers, adjusting the existing product/service offer, introducing new products/services to offer, entering a new industry, entering new geographical markets, or finding new suppliers. Since the variables did not display normal distribution, we have used the non-parametric Kruskal-Wallis test to verify whether there were significant differences in how companies belonging to the identified clusters used those strategies (Table 9.5).

Table 9.5 indicates that significant differences can be observed in four out of six considered variables (where the p-value is lower than 0.05). In the case of decision to attract new customers, the biggest difference can be observed between young demand-driven flexibles and mature adopters. Mature adopters rarely seen the need to expand the client base, but if they did, they assessed the effectiveness of their actions as high, whereas young demand-driven flexibles made such a choice much more often but as often were disappointed with the effect. In adjusting the existing market offer, differences were observable among all the clusters. Again, mature adopters rarely reached for such an option, and if they did, they performed with an above average success rate. Young demand-driven flexibles used it frequently, though not

Table 9.4 Characteristics of companies in the identified clusters

Feature	*Young demand-driven flexibles*	*Established supply-driven flexibles*	*Mature adopters*
Number of companies in the sample	191	208	101
Dominant size (turnover)	<45 mln euro	> 45 mln euro	<45 mln euro
Dominant size (employee number)	no pattern	>250 employees	>250 employees
Dominant industries	no pattern	education, accommodation	manufacturing, wholesale and retail
Company age	majority between 11 and 22	majority between 31 and 46	majority between 23 and 41
Dominant ownership structure	private	state- and private-owned	private
Dominant equity	Polish capital	Polish capital	Polish capital

Source: own elaboration

Table 9.5 Kruskal-Wallis test results

Actions undertaken	*H-value*	*p-value*
attracting new customers	8.83	0.01
adjusting product/service offer (price, sales schedule, payments arrangement etc.) to the current market requirements	45.44	0.00
introducing new products/services to offer	2.47	0.30
entering a new industry	5.62	0.06
entering new geographical markets	27.02	0.00
finding new suppliers	32.70	0.00

Source: own elaboration

with satisfactory results, while established supply-driven flexibles made use of it as frequently but with a high effectiveness rate. Generally, companies in all three clusters were not eager either to expand their portfolio by introducing new products/services or to enter completely new business activities. Firms in all groups were also generally reluctant to undertake new ventures in new geographical markets. However, if such decisions were made again, mature adopters performed best with high, established supply-driven flexibles with average and young demand-driven flexibles with below average effectiveness rates. Finally, the decision to expand the supplier base also differed significantly. Again, most companies saw no need to pursue this option; however, those mature adopters did perform significantly worse than established supply-driven flexibles.

Public support in pandemic times

Like most countries, the Polish government prepared and enforced anti-crisis tools to support companies and citizens during the consecutive lockdown phases. The support covered five main areas: employee support, company support, financial system support, investment, and healthcare. Companies were offered a substantial package of support tools that included, among others: exemption from social security contribution payment; furlough; microloans; co-financing of employees' wages; the Smart Growth Operations Program guarantee with a subsidy for entrepreneurs; shortening the bad debt relief period on the seller's side; Smart Growth Operations Program liquidity loans to cover current liabilities; reduced interest rates on loans; or loans for technological innovations. The accessibility of tools was, however, conditioned by certain financial and size indicators, as not all tools were designed for and targeted at each company. In total, the government has spent ca. 65 billion EUR to minimize the coronavirus impact, out of which more than 15 billion EUR was spent on financial support for companies.

The government offered the so-called Anti-Crisis Shield (with numerous updates appearing in time), which constitutes a set of policies that aimed to (PFR, 2022):

- improve the financial liquidity of companies;
- compensate companies for the damage they sustained as a result of the pandemic;

- protect jobs, especially in micro-firms and SMEs;
- enhance the performance of industries most affected by the pandemic.

The support within this program was granted to 347,000 entities, constituting ca. 13.3% of the entities registered in Poland (information derived from the REGON database for 2020). As mentioned in the method section, our questionnaire used in the CATI study included a part that referred to the enforced COVID-19–related risk mitigation policies as well. That part of the study aimed to examine the extent of support usage among the companies registered in the sampled industries and discuss the complexity and clarity of the policies offered. Figure 9.1 shows the frequency of the use of the support offered by the government.

Application for anti-crisis support did not differ significantly within the identified clusters. Overall, 19% of the sampled companies did not apply for any support, 22% of the companies did it once, and the majority of companies (59%) were granted more than one type of support. Among the companies that sought no governmental aid, most belonged to the education industry (70 companies) and only a small part to the retail and wholesale (12 companies) and manufacturing industries (10 companies).

The list of support tools presented in Table 9.6 does not exhaust the forms of support offered by the government in time of pandemic. It has however been created (and modified according to the feedback obtained during a test-round) to

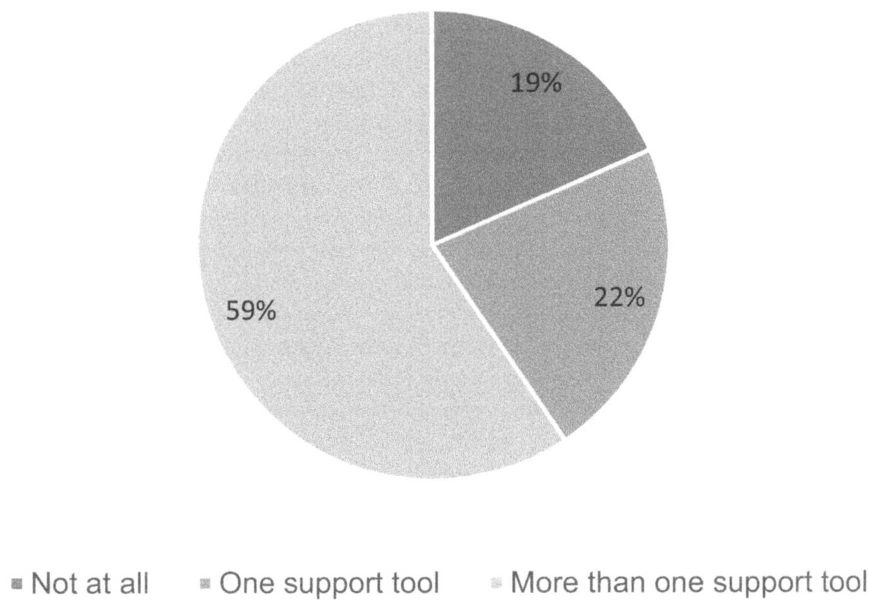

Figure 9.1 Frequency of the use of support tool (N=500)

Source: own elaboration

Table 9.6 Frequency of usage of selected anti-crisis support tools

Support tool	*Submitted application*	*Young demand-driven flexibles*	*Established supply-driven flexibles*	*Mature adopters*
exemption from social security contribution payment	No	24%	35%	35%
	Yes	76%	65%	65%
furlough	No	54%	62%	93%
	Yes	46%	38%	7%
non-returnable loans	No	73%	66%	72%
	Yes	27%	34%	28%
co-financing of employees' wages	No	30%	47%	45%
	Yes	70%	53%	55%
Smart Growth Operations Program guarantee with a subsidy for entrepreneurs	No	86%	87%	80%
	Yes	14%	13%	20%
shortening the bad debt relief period on the seller's side	No	83%	93%	80%
	Yes	17%	7%	20%
Smart Growth Operations Program liquidity loan to cover current liabilities	No	88%	88%	83%
	Yes	12%	13%	17%
reduced interest rates on loans	No	79%	82%	83%
	Yes	21%	18%	17%
loans for technological innovations	No	94%	96%	93%
	Yes	6%	4%	7%

Source: own elaboration

reflect the most commonly used tools that companies of different size and industries reached for. As Table 9.6 specifies, the first four forms of support – namely: exemption from social security contribution payment, furlough, non-returnable loans, and co-financing of employees' wages – were acknowledged as those most frequently applied for. Furthermore, it has been observed that furlough was very little used by *mature adopters*, mostly due to their industry specificity. Furlough could only be used in reference to specific industries (e.g. not applicable for manufacturing) and therefore had been expected not to be applicable for that group of companies. Other tools were generally accessible; however, certain conditions differentiated their attractiveness among individual companies. For instance, the value of the non-returnable loans depended on a drop in the sales revenue for SMEs and on a drop in the sales revenue combined with the number of employees for micro companies. At the same time, only 75% of the loan was non-returnable while the remaining 25% was subject to specific conditions like business continuity, need for upholding previous number of employees, industry affiliation, level of sales revenue drop, etc.

We also inquired as to why companies decided to forego any public support offered to them even while, from the formal perspective, they complied with the regulations. The most commonly mentioned reasons entailed:

- the complexity of the regulations and "strings" attached to support that in case of non-compliance would result in the necessity to repay the financial aid or even in additional penalties;

- the belief that the impact of the support would not bring tangible change to the situation while restricting the application of any structural modifications to the company's operations;
- mismatch between the monetary value of support and restrain cap imposed by the funding agency;
- lack of knowledge and predictability on the ever-changing policies concerning the public support;
- lack of suitable human resources to tackle extensive red tape associated with submitting the application for support and – in case the support was granted – settle the end date formalities;
- in case of large companies (which accounted for ca. 69% of the no application rate), the belief that the support was designed and targeted mostly at the micro companies and SMEs;
- in case of foreign corporate groups, the belief that joint corporate actions would bring more favorable outcomes than entanglement in public support.

Conclusions

Building a general capacity of a company to respond to crisis situations has always been a vital ability. Nowadays, companies tend to be exposed to external threats with increasing intensity. In the CEE region, after years of relative prosperity where the major disturbances were industry-related, companies are now forced to face global challenges affecting whole economies. Therefore, in our study we focused on seeing what strategies companies adopted during the crisis induced by the COVID-19 and the restrictions that followed.

We have identified three types of behavior companies displayed in face of the disruption. Although the first two clusters were significantly faster and more agile in implementing changes to their operations, the companies that belonged to the third group – mature adopters – were the ones that performed best during the restriction period. Therefore, the results indicate that the common COVID-19-related words by Baldwin and Weder di Mauro (2020), "Act fast and do whatever it takes", do not enhance company performance or resilience.

Acknowledgments

This contribution draws on the final results of the "Determinants of company's adaptability to crisis situation – the case of Covid19" project. The project was co-financed by the Polish National Agency for Academic Exchange within the Urgency Grants program.

Notes

1 Adaptive capability and adaptive capacity are often used interchangeably in the literature of the subject.

2 Resilience, adaptive capabilities and adaptive capacity are not unambiguous terms. A very throughout discussion on the meaning and proper usage of the terms is conducted by

Madani and Parast (2021). The present chapter does not aim at revisiting the terminologies but focuses on companies' adaptive capabilities in the recent COVID-19 outbreak, at the same time encouraging the readers to deepen their understanding of resilience-related issues in the suggested sources.

References

Ali, Z., Sun, H. & Ali, M. (2017). The impact of managerial and adaptive capabilities to stimulate organizational innovation in SMEs: A complementary PLS – SEM approach. *Sustainability, 9*, 2157.

Anning-Dorson, T. & Nyamekye, M.B. (2020). Be flexible: Turning innovativeness into competitive advantage in hospitality firms. *International Journal of Contemporary Hospitality Management, 32*(2), 605–624.

Brunelli, S., Gjergji, R., Lazzarotti, V., Sciascia, S. & Visconti, F. (2023). Effective business model adaptations in family SMEs in response to the COVID-19 crisis. *Journal of Family Business Management, 13*(1), 101–117. Retrieved from: https://www.emerald.com/insight/content/doi/10.1108/JFBM-02-2022-0020/full/html

Carpenter, S.R., Walker, B.H., Anderies, J.M. & Abel, N. (2001). From metaphor to measurement: Resilience of what to what? *Ecosystems, 4*, 765–781.

Fath, B.D. (2015). Quantifying economic and ecological sustainability. *Ocean and Coastal Management, 108*, 13–19.

Fath, B.D., Dean, C.A. & Katzmair, H. (2015). Navigating the adaptive cycle: An approach to managing the resilience of social systems. *Ecology and Society, 20*(2). Retrieved from: http://www.jstor.org/stable/26270208.

Folke, C. (2006). Resilience: The emergence of a perspective for social – Ecological systems analyses. *Global Environmental Change, 16*, 253–267.

Folke, C., Carpenter, S.R., Walker, B., Scheffer, M., Chapin, T. & Rockström, J. (2010). Resilience thinking: Integrating resilience, adaptability and transformability. *Ecology and Society, 15*(4). Retrieved from: http://www.jstor.org/stable/26268226.

Gunderson, L.H. (2000). Ecological resilience: In theory and application. *Annual Review of Ecology and Systematics, 31*, 425–439.

Hamel, G. & Välikangas, L. (2003). The quest for resilience. *Harvard Business Review, 81*, 52–63. Retrieved from: https://hbr.org/2003/09/the-quest-for-resilience.

Holling, C.S. (1973). Resilience and stability of ecological systems. *Annual Review of Ecology and Systematics, 4*, 1–23.

Holling, C.S., Gunderson, L. & Ludwig, D. (2002). In quest of a theory of adaptive change. In L.H. Gunderson, & C.S. Holling (Eds.), *Panarchy: Understanding Transformations in Human and Natural Systems* (pp. 3–24). Washington: Island Press.

Liu, J., Yang, W. & Liu, W. (2021). Adaptive capacity configurations for the digital transformation: A fuzzy-set analysis of Chinese manufacturing firms. *Journal of Organizational Change Management, 34*(6), 1222–1241.

Madani, F. & Parast, M.M. (2021). An integrated approach to organizational resilience: A quality perspective. *International Journal of Quality and Reliability Management, 40*(1), 192–225.

O'Connell, D., Walker, B., Abel, N. & Grigg, N. (2015). The resilience, adaptation and transformation assessment framework: From theory to application. *CSIRO* (Canberra, Australia). Retrieved from: http://www.stapgef.org/sites/default/files/documents/CSIRO-STAP-Resilience-Adaptation-Transformation-Assessment-Framework-Report.pdf

Paliokaite, A. (2012). The relationship between organisational foresight and product innovation in small and medium enterprises. In *Proceedings of the 8th International Ph.D. School on*

National Systems of Innovation and Economic Development, Globelics Academy, Rio de Janeiro, Brazil, 20–31 August. Retrieved from: http://www.redesist.ie.ufrj.br/ga2012/paper/AgnePaliokaite.pdf

Polman P. & Winston, A. (2021). 6 types of resilience companies need today. *Harvard Business Review Digital Articles*. Retrieved from: https://hbr.org/2021/11/6-types-of-resilience-companies-need-today

Polski Fundusz Rozwoju. (2022). *Tarcza Finansowa PFR dla Firm i Pracowników*. Retrieved from: https://pfrsa.pl/tarcza-finansowa-pfr.html/

Reeves, M. & Deimler, M. (2011). Adaptability: The new competitive advantage. *Harvard Business Review*. Retrieved from: https://hbr.org/2011/07/adaptability-the-new-competitive-advantage

Scheffer, M. (2009). *Critical Transitions in Nature and Society*. Princeton: Princeton University Press.

Tejeiro Koller, M.R. (2016). Exploring adaptability in organizations: Where adaptive advantage comes from and what it is based upon. *Journal of Organizational Change Management, 29*(6), 837–854.

Walker, B., Holling, C.S., Carpenter, S.R. & Kinzig, A. (2004). Resilience, adaptability and transformability in social – Ecological systems. *Ecology and Society*, *9*(2). Retrieved from: http://www.ecologyandsociety.org/vol9/iss2/art5/.

Weick, K.E. & Sutcliffe, K.M. (2007), *Managing the Unexpected: Resilient Performance in an Age of Uncertainty* (2nd ed.). San Francisco, CA: Jossey-Bass.

10 Building and enacting organisational resilience

Firms' responses to the COVID-19 crisis

Anže Burger, Iris Koleša, and Andreja Jaklič*

Introduction

'Bad companies are destroyed by crises. Good companies survive them. Great companies are improved by them', once said Andrew Grove, the former president and CEO of Intel (in Yu, 1998). This notion of businesses' varying degrees of resilience under the circumstances of inherent entropy, sustained disruption, and radical uncertainty has come back to light in the 21st century. According to the United Nations 2019 global assessment report on disaster risk reduction, '[s]urprise is the new normal' (pp. iv). In line with this, Makridakis (1996) argues that '[c]ompanies will stand a much higher chance of success in the future if they follow a strategy of expecting change' (pp. 1). This is because high-risk events that challenge humankind, such as extreme weather events, water and food crises, natural disasters, cybercrime, financial crises, economic recessions, terrorist attacks, and global health crises, have increased from approximately 350 in 1980 to almost 1,000 in 2014 (World Economic Forum, 2015). They have diversified, intensified, become more frequent, and are often also more destructive. They may present a direct threat to human lives as well as indirectly impact people's wellbeing by bringing about significant economic losses. The United Nations (2015), for example, reports a notable rise in the latter: from 50 to 250 and even 300 billion USD annually between the 1980s and 2010s. Further increases in negative economic impacts of crises and the related multidimensional uncertainties are anticipated for the future, as (combined with an increased scale and scope of such events) the greater connectedness of people, organisations, and countries through business practices such as lean manufacturing and extended supply chain networks causes the seemingly local and isolated events to snowball and have systemic regional or even global consequences (Van der Vegt et al., 2015).

In this chapter, we focus on organisational resilience, defined as an organisation's ability to continue to operate in the face of pervasive risk and uncertainty (Hamel & Välikangas, 2003),[1] at either the same or improved capacity (Butler, 2018), through different strategies involving flexibility, adaptability, reactiveness, and proactiveness (Supardi & Hadi, 2020), especially in relation to business processes and relationships. We address this in light of the recent COVID-19 pandemic.[2] The latter has prompted

*Corresponding author

DOI: 10.4324/9781003345428-10

fundamental changes in the underlying assumptions about what it means to do business; and which entities can survive and potentially thrive in the absence of relative stability (Anker, 2021). In other words, it has reiterated the importance of organisational resilience and flexibility, adaptability, reactiveness, and proactiveness in business for successful (immediate as well as long-term) risk management during systemic crises that often involve environmental, industry, firm-specific, and individual-level uncertainties simultaneously (Bordia et al., 2004; Buono & Bowditch, 1989; Jackson et al., 1987) and thus require a strategic approach to risk management at all levels of governance. Even during the early stages of the COVID-19 outbreak, the cascade effects of the pandemic on business have been evident. The business environment changed drastically: some businesses were forced to stop production and other operations to support the efforts aimed at preserving public health and safety, while others operated in the realm of new rules and limitations. Central banks cut interest rates and deployed other contingency measures in expectation of recession; access to lending or investment has become much more challenging and revenues and cash-flows dropped while input costs increased (see e.g. Cheng et al., 2021). Regional and global value chains were disrupted (Javorcik, 2020; Mirodout, 2020; UNCTAD, 2020).

Not all organisations have been capable and able to respond to the new conditions successfully and maintain a status quo in light of the crisis – let alone develop and grow further. In fact, business history demonstrates that organisational resilience is a relatively rare competence. Lack of resilience has been well documented: from the Schumpeterian creative destruction (Schumpeter, 1934) to the well-known permanent changes in the Fortune 500 or Standard and Poor's rankings, also described by Christensen (1997), Foster and Kaplan (2001), and Hamel and Välikangas (2003). This is because companies have been primarily focused on creating and executing stable plans, maximising short-term returns, and increasing shareholder value, but have rarely measured resilience beyond very specific material risks (Reeves & Whitaker, 2020).[3] An additional factor contributing to organisational lack of resilience is the business education and managerial practice being focused on managing performance and less on the questions of the antecedents and management of outcomes related to organisational resilience. Lack of organisational resilience (or its realisation) also results in the absence of swift action at multiple levels needed to address crises (i.e. low-probability, high-impact events that occur in the firms' external environments and pose a systemic threat to individual businesses and the overall economy; Pearson & Clair, 1998). This is often difficult, as the causes, effects, and means of resolution of a crisis are usually ambiguous (Pearson & Clair, 1998; Van der Vegt et al., 2015), but also because addressing them requires adequate resources and capabilities (see also Kitching et al., 2009; Pecujlija et al., 2017).

The organisations' capability and ability to (reactively or proactively) respond to different types of external (or internal) shocks[4] and emerge from crises as winners is likely to vary based on their age, size, ownership and organisational structure, industry and sector, integration in regional and global value chains, domestic and international business orientation, employee base, and other factors (including the institutional environment at subnational, national, and supranational levels that determine both access to and the need for specific resources). Different organisations are also likely to employ different strategies aimed at establishing, maintaining, or enacting their resilience and generate different outcomes with respect to organisational performance in the short and long run. However, extant research rarely addresses the antecedents of organisational resilience (other than from the human resources management perspective; see e.g. Akgün & Keskin, 2014; Lengnick-Hall et al., 2011); the different dimensions of resilience as suggested by Supardi and Hadi (2020); the types of firm-level strategies aimed at building, maintaining, and enacting resilience (especially from the process-focused perspective and at the time of crises for crisis management); and the impact of the selected strategy on firm performance. Conz and Magnani (2020) call for a more thorough analysis and systematisation of the different types of outcomes of different organisational resilience building and enactment paths, and explication of whether the more resilient firms are able to outperform the less resilient firms.

In this chapter, we aim to (1) propose a typology of firms based on crisis management strategies aimed at establishing, maintaining, and enacting organisational resilience that they employ *during* crises, (2) identify the antecedents of these strategies, and (3) explain the association between the firms' strategic orientation and their business performance (more specifically, future growth plans in light of crises). We base our exploratory study on data from two surveys conducted on two separate samples after the first wave of the COVID-19 pandemic in Slovenia: 227 respondents participated in the first study, whereas 213 respondents participated in the second study. Cluster analyses are first conducted on a joint dataset to identify the number of groups and differences among the types of organisations based on the strategies they employ to manage risks introduced by the pandemic. To control for relevant firm characteristics and to identify the possible antecedents of the broad strategic types, we then link the survey data with detailed firm-level data on Slovenian firms (i.e. balance sheets and financial statements for 2019) provided by the Agency of the Republic of Slovenia for Public Legal Records and Related Services (AJPES). Finally, we analyse the association between firms' strategic orientations and firm performance based on regression analyses.

Our study contributes to the literature on crisis management by demonstrating the importance of a multidimensional strategic approach to managing systemic crises that requires flexibility and adaptability, but can be reactive or proactive. We also show that interorganisational collaboration and process-focused changes can be crucial for establishing, maintaining, and enacting organisational resilience under great uncertainties. We develop an empirically grounded typology of firms based on their strategies aimed at risk management, as well as identify the determinants and potential outcomes of these strategies. We identify defensive, wait-and-see, omnibus, and innovation-oriented crisis response strategies and discover that the choice of a specific strategy depends on characteristics and internationalisation of firms. We moreover show that the firms' risk management–related strategic orientations have implications for firm performance and that wait-and-see, innovation-oriented, and omnibus strategies all enable the enactment of resilience, but only omnibus strategies are likely to result in immediate growth of revenues.

The chapter is structured as follows. We first provide an overview of extant research on organisational resilience as a multifaceted proxy for the risk management capacity of a firm. We then explain the methods used to analyse the phenomenon in this study. The methods section is followed by a presentation of research results from the two surveys described above. We conclude the chapter with a discussion of the main findings, their managerial and methodological implications, the limitations of the study and recommendations for future research, and a summary of key takeaway messages.

Literature review

Defining resilience

The term resilience originates from the Latin word *resilio*. It translates into going, leaping or springing back, recoiling or rebounding. It was initially used in physics to express materials' quality of resisting pressure, easily bending, and regaining original shape (Salanova, 2020). Through the use of the concept across different disciplines, its conceptualisation has become fragmented (Conz & Magnani, 2020; Hillman & Guenther, 2021; Mamouni Limnios et al., 2014; Sutcliffe & Vogus, 2003). There are several definitions of organisational resilience: as a capacity (e.g. Koronis & Ponis, 2018), capability (e.g. Annarelli & Nonino, 2016; Ma et al., 2018), process, outcome, management system, behaviour, strategy, or a static organisational characteristic (Bell, 2019; Hillmann & Guenther, 2021). Based on a review of organisational resilience definitions across disciplines, Chan (2011) identifies five broad approaches to studying the phenomenon:

- **the behavioural approach**, which suggests that a resilient organisation has the collective behaviour and robust response capability to recognise environmental changes swiftly and to apply adaptive responses early;
- **the sense-making approach**, which describes the resilient organisation as capable of timely sense-making of disruptions and threats;
- **the self-renewal process approach**, which focuses on the organisation's capability to establish early warning signals about events that could damage or even prevent the organisation's self-renewal process;
- **the risk management approach**, which stresses the organisational capacity to cope with uncertain, destructive, and collective events; and
- **the systems approach**, which suggests that organisational resilience can be achieved by identifying potential factors of a viable organisation to cope with adverse events.

As indicated in the introduction, we follow the risk management approach to studying organisational resilience building, maintenance, and enactment during crises.

Alternatively, Linnenluecke (2017) identifies five research streams with different definitions, theoretical approaches, and conceptualisations of resilience just in business and management literatures. These focus on organisational responses to external threats, organisational reliability, employee strengths, the adaptability of business models, or resilient supply chains. They nonetheless have one communality: a focus on processual and informal characteristics of organisations, such as competencies, learning, and culture (see also Andersson et al., 2019).

Butler (2018) summarises the common characteristics of different definitions of resilience and describes resilience as 'having the will, skill and ability to adapt in a positive manner to a changing environment' (pp. 104). He emphasises (1) the ability (i.e. the will, skill, and power) as opposed to capability (i.e. just the power); (2) the ability to adapt in response to a stimulus; and (3) positive outcomes despite negative stresses as crucial features of organisational resilience.

Bresch et al. (2014), on the other hand, propose a set of resilience approaches based on three dimensions these approaches are focused on:

- **structural resilience**, which focuses on the systemic nature of the organisation in order to improve business continuity management;
- **integrative resilience**, which stresses the complex interconnections of the organisation with its environment; and
- **transformative resilience**, which takes a longitudinal perspective in order to ensure and enhance a company's transformability.

Shashi et al. (2020) note that organisational resilience literature is predominantly based on the positivist notion of resilience as the entities' ability to 'bounce back' to an initial state of equilibrium (see also Halkos et al., 2018; Holling, 1996). However, they also highlight that some authors have started emphasising a non-positivist perspective to resilience, which centres on the idea of ecological resilience, or the ability to 'bounce forth' (i.e. to persist and adapt) (Shashi et al., 2020). In business, the meaning of resilience is thus not limited to resisting and maintaining the status quo. It also refers to the ability to overcome adversity, continue to function well in adverse situations, and rebuild from and in spite of difficulties – i.e. it implies action aimed at perseverance or adaptation and the possibility of some form of progress (Butler, 2018; Salanova, 2020). More specifically, it is defined as an organisation's 'ability to effectively absorb, develop situation-specific responses to, and ultimately engage in transformative activities to capitalise on disruptive surprises that potentially threaten organisation survival' (Lengnick-Hall et al., 2011, pp. 244). It is a multilevel,[5] multifactor, multidimensional, and procedural (i.e. dynamic) construct that consists of (1) cognitive, (2) behavioural, and (3) contextual resilience aspects[6] at individual and collective (i.e. group or team, organisational, subnational, national, and supranational) levels and often involves learning and unlearning of specific sense-making and behavioural patterns, as well as activation of psychological and social capital and broad resource networks (see e.g. Lengnick-Hall et al., 2011; Xiao & Cao, 2017). Van der Vegt et al. (2015), for instance, explicitly stress the importance of structural transformation and adaptation of the means for functioning in the face of long-term stresses, change, and uncertainty.

While there are several definitions of organisational resilience, which differ in the aspects of resilience they are addressing (e.g. firm-level resources needed for resilience, tools used for battling crises, and other disruptive events or processes adapted to foster resilience), we assume an outcome view to organisational resilience that requires process adaptations. This is consistent with Ma et al. (2018), who highlight the importance of organisational resources, routines, and processes in building organisational resilience, as well as the acknowledgement that the capabilities needed for resilience are not necessarily the same before, during, and after shocks (Conz & Magnani, 2020). We suggest that such an approach is also particularly valuable for practitioners, who – in light of the multitude of definitions and approaches – are presented with the challenge of choosing the appropriate one and developing and realising organisational resilience in a given situation (Chan, 2011).

To address the confusion in terminology and the related approaches to studying resilience that influence the outcomes of resilience, we use the framework proposed by Supardi and Hadi (2020) as the basis of our study. Supardi and Hadi (2020) propose **a process-focused model of business resilience** that integrates the different aspects of resilience (i.e. resilience as a proactive, absorptive/adaptive, reactive, and dynamic attribute). They suggest that business resilience dynamics start with the proactive phase of anticipation that occurs before the turbulence. This continues with the responsive and adaptive phase during turbulence, followed by a reactive phase after the turbulence. They thereby explain that proactive resilience is an antecedent of responsiveness and adaptive ability of an organisation, whereas responsiveness and adaptive ability have consequences for the company's reactive ability. The authors add that the direction of the process reverses from the reactive phase to the proactive phase, which means that building and enacting resilience is an iterative process determined by the changes in internal and external organisational environments. Both reactive and proactive ability are thereby crucial for an organisation's resilience to enable stable or improved performance in the short and long run. The potential benefits of organisational resilience and the different paths leading to them are presented in more detail hereinafter.

The benefits of resilience for businesses and approaches to their realisation

Organisational resilience may help firms in many ways and increases in importance especially in dynamic and unpredictable business environments. Butler (2018) emphasises the following benefits of organisational resilience:

- **competitiveness:** a highly resilient organisation is able to anticipate, identify, and adapt to change and uncertainty before the case for change becomes urgent, as well as quicker and more efficiently than its competitors, which can result in advantages over them;
- **coherence:** a highly resilient organisation aligns operational resilience measures with strategic resilience objectives, across partners and supply chains, which suggests its survival during crises is longer term and consistent with its strategy, as well as has spill-over effects on other stakeholders (especially business partners); and
- **efficiency:** reduced uncertainty results in better estimation of the situation as well as resources and capabilities required for perseverance or growth. Working within a coherent and integrated framework has time and cost-saving implications.

The concept of resilience may thus help to explain the performance differentials among firms. Types of organisational resilience by processes being adapted or employed may thereby elucidate not only the difference among survivals and non-survivals, but also differences in firm growth. Though organisational resilience may be insufficient to fully account for competitive advantage (some authors suggest that a sole focus on resilience as a core competency can create a competitive disadvantage – see e.g. Webb & Schlemmer, 2006), there is a wide consensus on its benefits. However, the scope and the content of resilience advantages may vary – both across firms and in time – and the antecedents determining the different outcomes of organisational resilience remain largely unexplored.

Another advantage of resilience is that a resilient organisation can more than recover. The resilient organisation has the ability to learn (or unlearn) and adapt in real time, to recognise crises as an opportunity, and to emerge from the crisis stronger and better than before (Butler, 2018). In other words: it can build responsiveness as well as adaptive, reactive, and proactive abilities for different contexts and at different points in time through experience and resource acquisition (see also Supardi & Hadi, 2020). Reeves and Whitaker (2020) propose that a company employing resilient principles meets multiple opportunities for advantage that play out sequentially and may cumulatively give a company a significant edge in value over competitors.

Reeves and Whitaker (2020) map the potential advantages of resilience for performance during the process of adaptation. They identify four main benefits of resilience. First, an **anticipation benefit** refers to the organisation's ability to recognise threats faster. Though this may not be immediately manifested in performance, it can be detected via other signals, such as when a company articulates its resilience plans (something most companies were slow to do during the outbreak of COVID-19). Speed and the nature of response can also drive advantages in subsequent phases. Second, an **impact benefit** refers to the organisation's ability to better resist or withstand the initial shock caused by a crisis or a high-risk event. This can be achieved through better preparation or a more agile response. Availability of resources and capabilities (e.g. knowledge, skills, or social capital) also influences the extent of the impact. Third, the **recovery speed benefit** represents the organisation's ability to rebound from the shock quicker by identifying the adjustments needed to return to the prior operating level and implementing them swiftly and effectively (i.e. it refers to the realisation of anticipatory adjustments). Finally, an eventual **outcomes benefit** represents increased fitness for the new post-shock environment. Cumulatively, the four benefits (focused on the different stages of resilience) create gaps between resilient and non-resilient organisations that produce a significant difference in value.[7]

Organisations can reap these benefits by employing different strategies. Reeves and Whitaker (2020), for example, propose (1) structuring organisations by embracing six principles of long-lasting systems (i.e. redundancy, diversity, modularity, adaptability, prudence, and embeddedness), (2) introducing migration strategies, such as shifting the organisation's business portfolio mix across products, channels, geographies, or business models to maximise opportunities and minimise adversity, (3) engaging in environmental shaping, and/or (4) establishing collaboration with other players and sharing platforms. Koronis and Ponis (2018) argue that organisational resilience is driven by preparedness, responsiveness, adaptability, and learning (some authors add to this unlearning; e.g. Klammer & Gueldenberg, 2019; Starbuck, 2017), which are further supported by cultural and social capital foundations, such as trust and strong perceived organisational identity. Andersson et al. (2019) furthermore identify four principles that contribute to organisational resilience i.e. risk awareness, preference for cooperation, agility, and improvisation. This suggests that while resources and capabilities (including knowledge, skills, information, and relationships) are needed for resilience, planning is not always its foundation. We argue that resilience can be coincidental and circumstantial and that planning it can be difficult due to its contextual nature (see also Anker, 2021). We posit that with an outcome focus and by assuming different scenarios, this is nonetheless somewhat possible and advisable for more strategic crisis management – proactively or reactively.

In reference to the latter, Butler (2018) proposes that organisations can follow **a defensive or an offensive approach** to taking advantage of the opportunities presented by crises and other adverse events – depending on their adaptive and resistance capacities.[8] Andersson et al. (2019) similarly explain that resilience can be enacted through either **anticipation** (i.e. sensing events early and directing activities towards stopping the development of undesirable events before they occur) or **containment** (i.e. directing activities toward unexpected events after they have occurred): i.e. firms can use **a proactive or a reactive approach** to building, nurturing, and enacting resilience for risk and crisis management. Annarelli and Nonino (2016) describe this distinction as that between **static and dynamic resilience**, with the former being grounded in preparedness and preventive measures to minimise probability of threats and to reduce any impact that may occur, and the latter on the ability of managing disruptions and unexpected events to shorten unfavourable aftermaths and maximise the organisation's speed of recovery to the original or to a new more desirable state. Conz and Magnani (2020), on the other hand, distinguish between an **adaptive and absorptive path** to facing disturbance. They suggest that redundancy, robustness, and agility are the essential capabilities that characterise the absorptive path, whereas resourcefulness, adaptability, and flexibility are the essential capabilities that characterise the adaptive path. In reference to this, Mamouni Limnios et al. (2014) explain that organisations exhibit a combination of both adaptive capacity (which enables a system to react to disturbance by changing its structure, processes, and functions in order to increase its ability to persist) and resistance to change (which results in a system maintaining its current structure and processes by absorbing shocks rather than adapting to them). They distinguish between rigid, adaptable, transient, and vulnerable systems and define their characteristics as determinants of the magnitude of resilience and a more or less successful defensive or offensive crisis response. They observe that highly resilient systems assume a primarily defensive character and resist change when the system operates at an undesirable system state, whereas they assume a primarily offensive character and adapt when they operate at a desirable system state.

Finally, based on a literature review, Ramezani and Camarinha-Matos (2020) identify the following **resilience aiming strategies**: (1) buffering, where businesses establish safeguards that protect them from disturbances, (2) insurance, where businesses transfer (mostly financial) risks onto the insurer, (3) the Barbell strategy, where businesses invest most of their assets conservatively, wishing to stay robust to negative disruptions, and take risks with the rest, in order to remain open to positive disruptions, (4) hormesis, where businesses achieve growth by adapting to a reasonable amount of a harmful stressor, and (5) collaboration, where businesses reduce uncertainty and increase the system's capability to respond to unforeseen circumstances through enhancing access to relevant resources and capabilities, as well as reduce risks by focusing on optionality and diversification for more success opportunities. The authors classify disruption-coping strategies according to six meta-levels: (1) discovering, which includes strategies aimed at detecting critical sources of disruptions and estimating how the system is expected to change with disruption, (2) avoiding, which involves strategies aimed at preventing threatening situations, (3) doing nothing, which refers to strategies that accept the risk of disruption, (4) reducing, which involves strategies aimed at mitigating vulnerability and negative consequences, (5) managing, which includes strategies aimed at managing system complexity, and (6) learning and adapting, which refers to strategies targeted towards creative problem solving. They relate these strategies to three phases of disaster management: readiness, response, and recovery.

While Ramezani and Camarinha-Matos (2020) do indicate that organisational resilience is a process and that strategies vary based on the stage of crisis response, none of the above described approaches explicitly focus on the resilience-related changes in *organisational processes* – or the process of resilience building and realisation. Though the presented approaches do not directly relate the benefits of resilience to specific dimensions or strategies of resilience, they suggest that different strategies aimed at building and capitalising on resilience result in different outcomes. In our empirical study, we thus address the different strategies to organisational resilience building and enactment from the process-based perspective (i.e. we look at the processes taking place within firms aimed at implementing and capitalising on resilience rather than the stages of resilience building) and also study the antecedents and outcomes of the firm-level selected strategies. The methodology and results are presented hereinafter.

Data and methodology

Data

Empirical research was performed on data from two distinct structured questionnaires developed by the Centre of International Relations (CIR, Faculty of Social Sciences at the University of Ljubljana) research team in collaboration with the Chamber of Commerce and Industry of Slovenia (GZS) and the Public Agency for Entrepreneurship, Internationalisation, Foreign Investments, and Technology – SPIRIT Slovenia.

Both questionnaires had been tested on a small number of individuals before they were sent to firms. The first survey conducted in partnership with GZS was carried out online between 27 May and 18 June 2020 (i.e. immediately after the first wave of the COVID-19 pandemic) and sent to a sample of approximately 1,500 firms (members of GZS). The response rate was 15% and can be regarded as acceptable (Harzing, 2000). The questionnaire comprised 49 questions of both closed and open types and focused solely on the (expected) impact[9] of the COVID-19 pandemic on businesses and their responses to the shock. The second questionnaire prepared for SPIRIT Slovenia was launched on 3 September 2020, whereby data collection lasted until 2 October 2020. The questionnaire was sent to a representative sample of 993 foreign-owned entities in Slovenia. The survey was performed online as well as in print and yielded a 21.5% response rate. It consisted of 29 questions of both closed and open types, which were primarily centred on foreign investors' evaluation of the business environment in Slovenia for business internationalisation. However, it also included a set of questions on the impact of the Covid-19 pandemic on businesses with foreign equity. Both surveys included questions on (1) the impact of the COVID-19 pandemic on business performance and internationalisation, (2) business responses to COVID-19 (including investments in digitalisation and automation, employee development, process, product and service innovations all refer to different types of innovations),[10] (3) and the use of individual state measures targeted at reducing the impact of the pandemic on the economy.

Overall, there were six questions related to the firms' strategic orientation that appeared in both surveys (220 firms responded to all of them) and could thus be analysed jointly. The first strategy is focused on employment adjustment and as such describes an important aspect of operational cost orientation during the crisis. The next three strategies belong to international business orientation. Firms can recalibrate their export market geographic scope, focus their attention towards export product portfolio, or re-evaluate their network of foreign suppliers. The fifth is the innovation orientation where firms consider introducing a new product/service, new processes, digital solutions, and automation. Lastly, we consider human capital orientation through which firms can upgrade the skills of their employees by providing training. In addition to strategic orientations, we use a subjective performance measure. Respondents were asked to assess the impact of COVID-19 on total revenue in 2020. The measures of strategic orientation and performance are listed in Table 10.1, together with frequencies and shares of firms reporting a decrease, no change, or an increase for each measure.

Both surveys gathered data on the firms' responses to the COVID-19 pandemic in a single country to control for the effect of country-level measures and focus on the responses to the crisis by firms operating in Slovenia (i.e. both domestic and foreign-owned firms are included in the surveys). Both surveys also included identification of respondents based on the company registration number, which allowed further analyses of organisational resilience antecedents and actual outcomes at firm level based on the data from the AJPES database that includes detailed annual balance sheets and income statements for all firms in Slovenia.

Table 10.1 Measures of strategic orientation and performance

	Response		
Survey question	*Decrease*	*No change*	*Increase*
Strategic orientation			
What will be the impact of COVID-19 on your firm performance in 2020 in terms of employment?	101 (36.2%)	130 (46.6%)	48 (17.2%)
State your firm's response to COVID-19 in terms of the number of export markets:	55 (18.1%)	230 (75.7%)	19 (6.3%)
State your firm's response to COVID-19 in terms of the number of export products:	56 (18.7%)	196 (65.3%)	48 (16.0%)
State your firm's response to COVID-19 in terms of the number of foreign suppliers:	55 (16.7%)	256 (77.6%)	19 (5.8%)
State your firm's response to COVID-19 in terms of introducing new technological solutions (digitalisation, automation):	45 (13.7%)	158 (48.0%)	126 (38.3%)
State your firm's response to COVID-19 in terms of employee training/development:	58 (17.0%)	214 (62.8%)	69 (20.2%)
Performance			
What will be the impact of COVID-19 on your firm performance in terms of total revenue for 2020?	247 (69.2%)	59 (16.5%)	51 (14.3%)

Source: own elaboration

Methodology

Our goal in the empirical analysis is to identify distinct classes of business strategies in confronting the economic downturn, to discover their antecedents, and to examine the association between strategic orientations and firm performance. To detect homogeneous and distinctive strategic groups, we employ cluster analysis. It is a commonly used statistical method to obtain a taxonomy of business strategies (e.g. Hagen et al., 2012; Kabanoff & Brown, 2008; Peneder, 2010; Slater & Olson, 2001; Zahra & Covin, 1993). Cluster analysis can be used as an exploratory method to identify distinct groups within a dataset, but as such is sometimes criticised for being atheoretical (Ketchen & Shook, 1996). When used in such an exploratory way, it is more appropriate to treat it as generating theory inductively (Crum et al., 2020). However, cluster analysis can also be used deductively, as a confirmatory method to corroborate a taxonomy based on an extant theoretical rationale (Fisher & Ransom, 1995). In our study, clustering was implemented in two stages.

First, we performed agglomerative hierarchical clustering using several different linkage algorithms and examined the Caliński–Harabasz pseudo-F stopping-rule values and the Duda–Hart stopping rule for each of them in order to determine the optimal number of groups. In addition, we examined the dendrograms and clustergrams proposed by Schonlau (2002). The latter depict how cluster members are assigned to clusters as the number of clusters increases. They are useful in exploratory analysis for non-hierarchical clustering algorithms such as k-means and for hierarchical cluster algorithms when the number of observations is large enough to make dendrograms impractical. In the first stage, cluster analysis stopping rules indicated two groups in two linkage algorithms (single and centroid), three groups in three linkage algorithms (average, complete, and Ward), four groups for weighted-average linkage, and five groups for median linkage algorithm. Clustergrams produced from single linkage k-means partitioning clustering method for 14 different binary similarity measures indicated mostly three and four clusters. Based on the information on the optimal number of groups, the k-means clustering procedure was performed in the second step of the analysis to derive the best configuration of the predefined groups, placing similar firms together and forming a cluster. We decided to form three and four groups based on 12 binary clustering variables, two for each of the six strategic orientations listed in Table 10.1 (one for increase and the other for decrease in strategic channel, with no-change serving as the omitted baseline).

In the last part of the empirical analysis, we ran an OLS regression, with the dependent variables being the growth rate of revenue from 2019 (the year prior to the pandemic) to 2021, as well as the short-term 2019–2020 revenue growth rate.[11] A positive coefficient for an explanatory variable implies that the variable is positively correlated with a firm's reported performance measure. To control for relevant firm characteristics and to identify the possible antecedents of broad strategic types, we linked the survey data with detailed firm-level data on the total population of non-financial Slovenian firms' balance sheets and income statements for the years 2019–2021 provided by AJPES.

Results

Three approaches were taken in the first step of cluster analysis, with the goal to determine the optimal number of groups to be formed in the second step. Initially, we examined dendrograms based on several different linkage algorithms and several different matching coefficients for binary variables. We first report two dendrograms, where we show weighted-average linkage (Figure 10.1) and Ward's linkage (Figure 10.2) clustering techniques with Anderberg (dis)similarity measure. Both figures indicate that the optimum number of groups is between two and five.

Next, we calculated and examined the Caliński–Harabasz pseudo-F stopping-rule values and the Duda–Hart stopping index for several different linkage algorithms. The results point to a 2–5 optimal number of clusters, with three groups suggested most frequently. Finally, we observe clustergrams for single linkage k-means partitioning clustering method for 14 different binary similarity measures, two of which are shown below (Figure 10.3 and Figure 10.4). These indicate three or four clusters to be the optimal number of partitions of the firms. Hence, in the following part of the analysis we show results for three and four groups of firms clustered according to six different strategic measures undertaken by firms during the crisis. The significance ($F = 44.26$, $p<0.0001$ for four clusters; $F = 31.23$, $p < 0.0001$ for three clusters) of the cluster differences was tested by employing a MANOVA method. Both three and four clusters were confirmed to characterise distinctive strategic types.

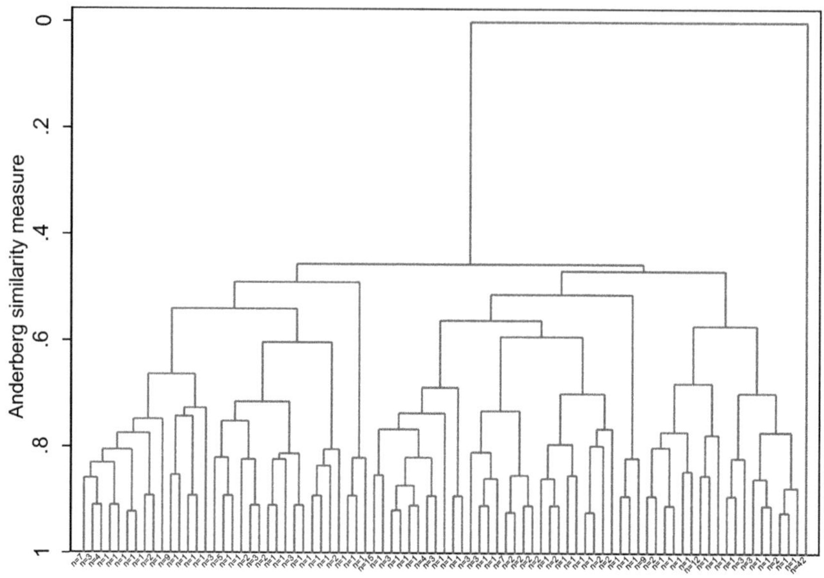

Figure 10.1 Dendrogram of weighted-average linkage hierarchical cluster analysis with Anderberg similarity measure for binary data

Source: own elaboration

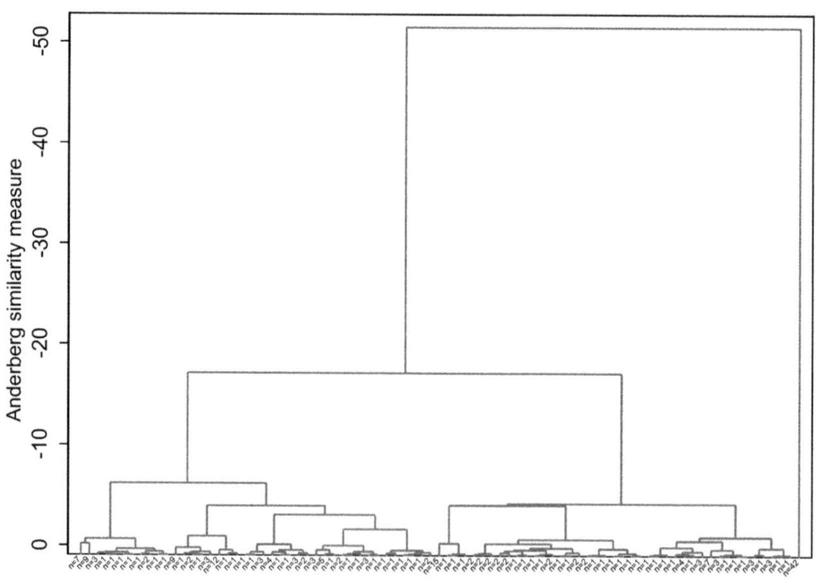

Figure 10.2 Dendrogram of Ward's linkage hierarchical cluster analysis with Anderberg similarity measure for binary data

Source: own elaboration

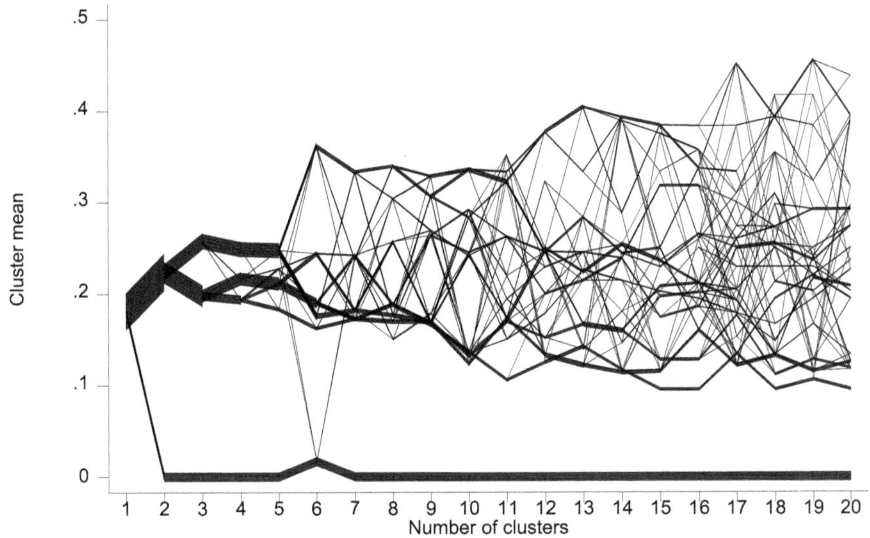

Figure 10.3 Clustergram for the K-means clustering with the Anderberg similarity measure

Source: own elaboration

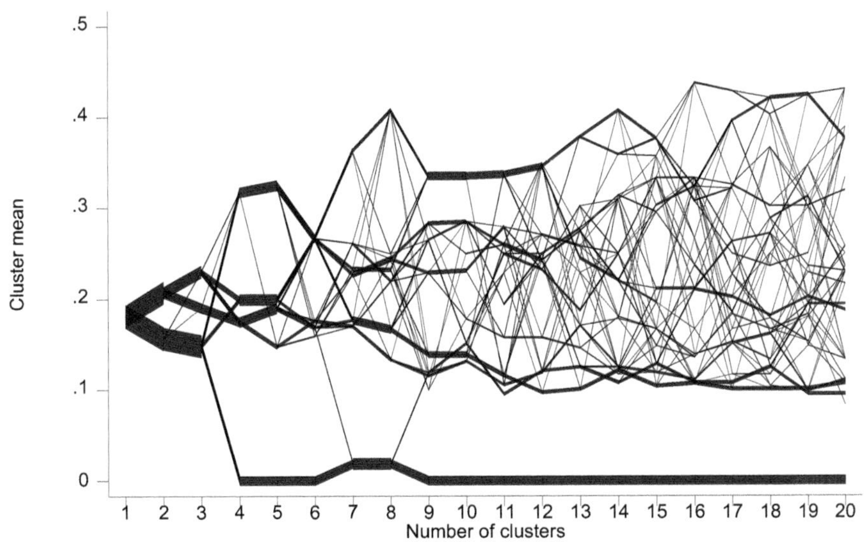

Figure 10.4 Clustergram for the K-means clustering with the Jaccard similarity measure

Source: own elaboration

Having ascertained that the three and four groups are statistically homogeneous within clusters and heterogeneous across clusters, we now describe the strategic profiles and the corresponding labels we attached to them. Figure 10.5 shows the average score of the six strategic orientation dimensions (employment adjustment, changes in export market presence, export product scope modification, reconfiguration of foreign supplier network, amendments to automation/digitalisation process, and adjustments in employee training and development) for each of the clusters. The uppermost seventh dimension in the radar graphs shows the average scores of subjective performance indicator about the expected future growth of a firm's revenue. Both clustering variants clearly define a group of firms with retreating activities on all six strategy dimensions (labelled 'defensive' and depicted in black) and a group of firms reporting no changes in any of the strategic components (named 'wait-and-see' and coloured in dark grey). The third cluster of firms is distinctive in its proactive application of several strategies simultaneously, which we label the 'omnibus' strategic type and designate with light grey. Finally, in the four-group clustering, an 'innovation-oriented' strategic type emerges (medium grey). These firms push intensively towards increased introduction of new technologies, introduce new products on export markets, and invest in employee skill upgrading.

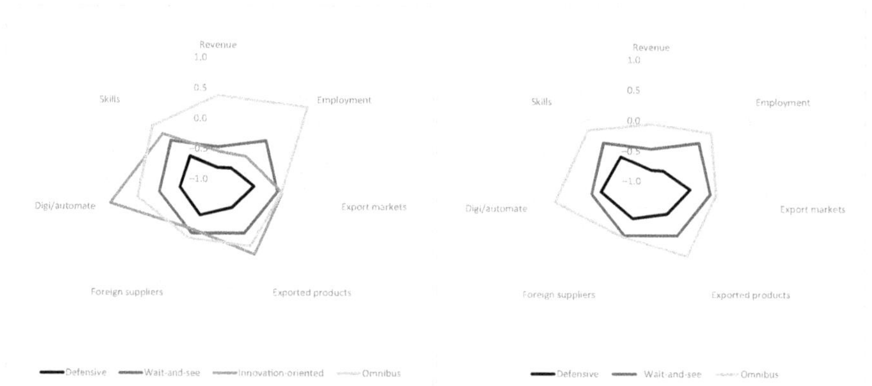

Figure 10.5 Strategic profiles and performance scores of firms during the COVID-19 crisis after the four-group (left) and three-group (right) K-means clustering

Source: own elaboration

Table 10.2 summarises the mean demographic and performance characteristics of the four clusters in 2019, just prior to the outbreak of the COVID-19 pandemic. Based on this information, we are able to propose key antecedents of each strategic profile. We perform a two-group t-test for the equality of means between each pair of clusters and denote statistically significant differences between the groups with superscripts a–f. Cluster 1 firms use a defensive strategy and are old and large in terms of the number of employees, but among the smallest in the sample in terms of revenue. Consequently, this group exhibits the lowest labour productivity measure and had negative return on assets (ROA) in 2019. Its export profile is characterised by the highest export intensity and high dependency on the European Union (EU) market (the lowest share of exports to non-EU countries). As expected, this strategic profile reports the bleakest expectations of future revenue. Indeed, the realised revenue growth eventually turned out significantly lower compared to other groups.

Cluster 2 firms perform a passive strategy on all six dimensions. This wait-and-see strategy is characteristic of the youngest and smallest firms in our sample. However, these are the firms with the greatest stamina in terms of productivity and profitability and are the most globally oriented enterprises. The third strategic type are innovation-oriented firms that are the oldest and the largest firms, but also the firms that are already the most productive. They are the least internationalised as measured by export intensity, but nevertheless earn as much as 47% of their revenue abroad. Lastly, the omnibus strategy is used by the most profitable firms. These firms report by far the most optimistic prospects about their future revenue. Again, their mid-crisis projections turned out to be correct in ordinal terms as the official revenue growth rates in 2019–2020 and 2019–2021 are significantly higher for these firms compared to other strategic groups.

Table 10.2 Key performance and strategy characteristics of the four clusters

	Cluster 1	*Cluster 2*	*Cluster 3*	*Cluster 4*
	Defensive	*Wait-and-see*	*Innovation-oriented*	*Omnibus*
N	73	42	62	43
Demographic and performance characteristics (2019)				
Age	18.5[a]	15.5[a,d]	18.6[d]	17.3
Employment	191.5[a,c]	49.5[a]	251.6	97.5[c]
Total revenue	23.29[a]	10.68[a,d]	72.85[d]	68.39
Value added/emp	37,289[a,b,c]	59,515[a,e]	62,574[b]	49,445[c,e]
ROA	−1.3%[a,b,c]	8.6%[a]	7.4%[b]	8.2%[c]
ROE	12.8%[c]	10.5%[e]	10.6%	27.3%[c,e]
Export intensity	60.4%[b]	52.9%	46.6%[b]	55.5%
Non-EU export share	9.2%[a]	18.0%[a]	12.4%	10.5%
Strategic orientation questionnaire scores (2020)				
Employment	−0.73[a,b,c]	0.00[a,d,e]	−0.42[b,d,f]	0.88[c,e,f]
Export markets	−0.40[a,b,c]	0.00[a]	0.08[b]	0.07[c]
Export products	−0.47[a,b,c]	0.00[a,d,e]	0.39[b,d]	0.23[c,e]
Foreign suppliers	−0.33[a,b,c]	0.00[a]	−0.06[b,f]	0.09[c,f]
Digi/automate	−0.36[a,b,c]	0.00[a,d,e]	0.84[b,d,f]	0.37[c,e,f]
Skills	−0.41[a,b,c]	0.00[a,d,e]	0.18[b,d,f]	0.40[c,e,f]
Performance questionnaire scores (2020)				
Revenue	−0.82[a,b,c]	−0.48[a,e]	−0.55[b,f]	0.37[c,e,f]
Realised revenue growth (%)				
2019–2020	−68.7[a,b,c]	−7.3[a,e]	−8.0 [b,f]	+4.5 [c,e,f]
2019–2021	−16.3[b,c]	−0.1[e]	+6.5[b,f]	+20.3[c,e,f]

Notes: [a], [b], [c], [d], [e], [f] denote statistically significant differences in mean values between clusters 1 and 2, 1 and 3, 1 and 4, 2 and 3, 2 and 4, 3 and 4, respectively (at 5% significance level).

Source: own elaboration

Table 10.3 Key performance and strategy characteristics of the three clusters

	Cluster 1	*Cluster 2*	*Cluster 3*
	Defensive	*Wait-and-see*	*Omnibus*
N	87	42	91
Demographic and performance characteristics (2019)			
Age	18.5[a]	15.5[a]	17.9
Employment	185.3[a]	49.5[a]	193.1
Total revenue	22.63[a,b]	10.68[a,c]	79.04[b,c]
Value added/emp	39,714[a,b]	59,515[a]	57,971[b]
ROA	0.5%[a]	8.6%[a]	7.5%
ROE	13.5%	10.5%	17.5%
Export intensity	57.2%	52.9%	51.6%
Non-EU export share	9.6%	18.0%	11.7%
Strategic orientation questionnaire scores (2020)			
Employment	−0.75[a,b]	0.00[a,c]	0.26[b,c]
Export markets	−0.34[a,b]	0.00[a,c]	0.10[b,c]
Export products	−0.39[a,b]	0.00[a,c]	0.37[b,c]
Foreign suppliers	−0.31[a,b]	0.00[a]	0.03[b]
Digi/automate	−0.16[a,b]	0.00[a,c]	0.62[b,c]
Skills	−0.37[a,b]	0.00[a,c]	0.33[b,c]
Performance questionnaire scores (2020)			
Revenue	−0.83[a,b]	−0.48[a,c]	−0.07[b,c]
Realised revenue growth (%)			
2019–2020	−59.7[a,b]	−7.3[a,c]	−1.0[b,c]
2019–2021	−13.2[b]	−0.1[b,c]	+13.4[b,c]

Notes: [a], [b], [c] denote statistically significant differences in mean values between clusters 1 and 2, 1 and 3, 2 and 3, respectively (at 5% significance level).

Source: own elaboration

Table 10.3 presents key demographic and performance indicators for the clusters of firms after three-group k-means cluster analysis. As before, a defensive strategy is characteristic of old and large firms in terms of employment, but among the smallest in terms of revenue. The defensive strategy using firms are again the least productive and hardly have a positive ROA. A wait-and-see strategy is chosen by the youngest and smallest firms with the highest value added per employee and ROA. As before, they are the most globally oriented enterprises, yet the premium is not statistically significant. Finally, an omnibus strategy is chosen by the largest and the most profitable firms in terms of return on equity (ROE). These firms again report the most buoyant revenue forecasts and ultimately achieve the highest revenue growth during the crisis relative to other two classes of firms.

In the final part of the empirical analysis, we explore the association between firm resilience strategy and revenue growth during the two pandemic years. Our hypothesis is that firms with a clear proactive strategic orientation during the crisis exhibit better prospects in terms of future revenue growth. The dependent variable is the reported revenue growth rate during the 2019–2020 period and during the 2019–2021 period. OLS regression was employed and for each dependent variable (2019–2020 and 2019–2021 growth rate) specifications were run on the sample with three and four strategic groups separately. Several control variables were included in specifications: firm age in years in 2019, log of the number of employees, log of total revenue, log of labour productivity (value added per employee), export intensity (share of total exports in total revenue), non-EU export share (share of exports to non-EU countries in total revenue), and profitability measures ROA and ROE. All control variables correspond to year 2019 in order to avoid simultaneity bias. In addition, a set of strategic orientation dummies was included, corresponding to clusters 2, 3, and 4 (clusters 2 and 3 in specifications with only three groups formed). Cluster 1 (defensive strategy) was set as the baseline category.

The regression results are reported in Table 10.4. Firms with a higher share of non-EU exports in total revenue achieved higher revenue growth in the 2019–2021

Table 10.4 Association between strategic orientation and revenue growth during the COVID-19 crisis

	(1)	*(2)*	*(3)*	*(4)*
Dependent variable	*Revenue growth*	*Revenue growth*	*Revenue growth*	*Revenue growth*
Period	*2019/2021*	*2019/2021*	*2019/2020*	*2019/2020*
Age	0.000234	−0.000145	0.00146	0.000918
	(0.00243)	(0.00245)	(0.00427)	(0.00412)
logEmployment	−0.0593	−0.0542	−0.191	−0.196
	(0.0373)	(0.0383)	(0.154)	(0.162)
logRevenue	0.0422	0.0370	0.0959	0.0997
	(0.0337)	(0.0337)	(0.152)	(0.154)
logValue added/emp	−0.0280	−0.0278	−0.0763	−0.0747
	(0.0219)	(0.0223)	(0.0613)	(0.0616)
Export intensity	0.0754	0.0680	0.240	0.194
	(0.0828)	(0.0842)	(0.328)	(0.329)
Non-EU export share	0.272**	0.278**	0.241	0.284
	(0.129)	(0.130)	(0.218)	(0.232)
ROA	−0.204**	−0.174*	0.187	0.235**
	(0.103)	(0.0931)	(0.134)	(0.113)
ROE	−0.0124	−0.0133	−0.0306	−0.0271
	(0.0470)	(0.0475)	(0.0391)	(0.0385)
Group 2	0.143	0.105	0.502*	0.397*
(Wait-and-see)	(0.105)	(0.0918)	(0.273)	(0.207)
Group 3	0.225**		0.557*	
(Innovation-oriented)	(0.103)		(0.318)	
Group 4	0.367***	0.258***	0.663**	0.511**
(Omnibus)	(0.105)	(0.0855)	(0.306)	(0.246)
Constant	−0.361	−0.257	−0.784	−0.717
	(0.426)	(0.412)	(1.507)	(1.490)
N	211	211	214	214
R-squared	0.106	0.088	0.048	0.041
F	3.817	3.780	3.037	3.477
Prob > F	0.0001	0.0001	0.0009	0.0003

Notes: heteroscedasticity robust standard errors in parentheses; *, **, *** correspond to significance at 10%, 5%, and 1% level, respectively.

Source: own elaboration

period. The coefficients of three clusters (wait-and-see orientation, innovation strategy, and omnibus strategy) in all specifications are jointly highly significant and positively related to revenue growth rate. In the short run (specifications (3) and (4)), only the omnibus strategy exhibits statistically significant growth premium relative to the defensive strategy set as the benchmark. The growth premium ranges between 51% (specification (4)) and 66% (specification (3)). Over the longer 2019–2021 period, both innovation-oriented and omnibus strategies outperform the defensive strategy. The revenue growth premiums for the omnibus strategy is between 26% (specification (2)) and 37% (specification (1)). Innovation-oriented firms, on the other hand, outperform the defensive strategy by 23% (1). Results therefore show that using omnibus and innovation-oriented strategies raised the probability of higher or less depressed revenue over the course of the crisis period (2019–2021), whereas only the omnibus strategy also correlated positively with short-term revenue growth during the first and the most severe phase of the COVID-19 crisis. The results therefore support the hypothesis that proactive multifaceted business strategies have a positive impact on business performance during the economic downturn.

Discussion

Exploring the strategies of risk management through building, maintaining, and enacting (different dimensions and types of) resilience to the COVID-19 crisis reveals both variation and multidimensionality in businesses' strategic responses and resilience to high-risk and extreme events. With our research, we demonstrate that a process-based perspective to studying resilience enables exploring the linkages between antecedents, strategies, and outcomes of organisational resilience. In the cluster analysis, we identify four groups of businesses based on the different strategies they use to tackle the pandemic. These are: (1) defensive, (2) wait-and-see, (3) omnibus, and (4) innovation-oriented firms. We show that the firms' resources acquired pre-crisis are crucial for the realisation of organisational resilience capabilities, as firm size, firm age, labour productivity, profitability, export intensity, and the global orientation all impact the choice of strategies used by firms when responding to the COVID-19 pandemic. Our findings are inconsistent with past evidence of larger and more mature firms being less responsive to turbulence and unlikely to maintain continuous growth over time than the smaller, more flexible, and entrepreneurial firms due to the diseconomies of scale related to their bureaucratisation (Conz & Magnani, 2020; Makridakis, 1996; Shashi et al., 2020). They support the claims by authors such as Butler (2018) and Supardi and Hadi (2020) that resilience can be built through (experiential) learning and resource acquisition. Our study indicates that size, rigidity, and maturity do not necessarily hinder a firm's resilience, but (in the context of the COVID-19 pandemic) rather result in its greater likelihood to not just cope with but also capitalise on a crisis. We argue that it is likely related to the type of crisis that makes a specific type of resources and capabilities more important than the structural limitations. These resources and capabilities include well-established change management routines, processes, and business functions such as effective supplier management,[12] accurate inventory control system, and effective performance measurement system combined with and managed by skilled individuals and/or groups within the firm (see also Conz & Magnani, 2020; Shashi et al., 2020). They also encompass business-to-business and governmental networks (see e.g. Azadegan & Dooley, 2021). Involvement in business-to-business collectives and collaboration with governments may be particularly relevant for resilience during and after the COVID-19 pandemic due to high levels of interventionism that mark the related crisis management. We thus encourage future research on this.

We also show that different types of resilience strategies result in different outcomes in terms of firm performance. The results of our regression analyses demonstrate that three clusters of resilience strategies are related to stable operation or even growth. While the wait-and-see and innovation-oriented strategies raise the probability of stable revenue growth in the long run, the omnibus strategy also correlates positively with the immediate growth of firm revenue during crises (in other words: while it may be resource consuming, multidimensional proactiveness pays off the most as it facilitates growth in both the short and long run). Furthermore, firms' global presence improves their ability to anticipate, identify, estimate, and adapt to change and uncertainty before the case for change becomes urgent, which results in higher efficiency (due to cost savings, speed, and scope of adaptation). These findings support prior claims about the multidimensionality of the construct (see e.g. Bhamra et al., 2011; Schriber et al., 2019; Van der Vegt et al., 2015), but also highlight an additional aspect of this multidimensionality: i.e. its process-based underpinnings. They namely suggest that firms can build their resilience through focusing on strengthening and adapting the processes by relevant business functions. Firms that are systematically building the resilience in one or multiple selected business functions or areas (for example, ICT, corporate security, and supply change management) may be better able to capitalise on organisational resilience (in the long term) and do so faster. Speed of recovery and positive outcomes (resulting in the increase in revenues) are related to a multidimensional strategic response, though. The elements of strategic responses that are particularly important for high levels of organisational resilience in our sample are related to process change: digitalisation and automation, employee development, and process, product, and service innovation. Firms that pursue an innovation-oriented and omnibus strategy have increased digitalisation and automation, their investments in employee development, as well as the number of employees. An omnibus strategy is the only identified strategy also related to both immediate growth of revenues during the crisis and long-term growth after the crisis.[13]

Accumulation of resources and capabilities seems to be an important source of resilience during crises. The antecedents of an omnibus strategy include experience, abundance of resources (profit, employees), and (internal) relations, which help firms to adapt and respond to stresses and changes in the environment. Innovation-oriented strategies are often linked to firms that are agile, highly adaptive, and able to change very quickly.[14] Our results suggest that stable external relations beyond the region of residence are a particularly important resource for innovation-oriented firms to overcome crises. In other words, internationalisation is a vital component of organisational resilience. This is because a global presence reflected in the majority of export revenues generated outside EU provides access to ideas, technology, and other resources crucial for product and service innovation or market development (see also Akgün & Keskin, 2014; Blyth & Mallett, 2020). Stabilisation of revenues in the short run after crises, typical for a 'wait-and-see' strategic approach, may also be seen as a process. Young, small, but mostly highly productive and globally oriented enterprises that pursue this strategy have limited resources and thus cautious responses to exogenous disruptions. Finally, a defensive strategic response to external shocks, according to our findings, is related to a lack of resources or flexibility. This results in high levels of business vulnerability to high-risk events and contraction of business. Old, large, and less productive firms more likely lack the ability to resist shocks. Vulnerable firms that have experienced contraction of business operations during the pandemic dominate in our sample. All in all, the findings from our exploratory study show that the abundance of resources (as well as capabilities) and the way they are utilised for process-based adaptation and innovation in crises play a central role in the enactment of organisational resilience.

The study has both managerial and methodological implications. One of the key managerial implications is that the benefits of organisational resilience vary by type of strategy to handle disruptions and that each approach used also requires specific resources and capabilities. Long-term positive outcomes of crisis responses are related to multidimensional strategies of resilience, such as the omnibus strategy. The empirically developed typology of strategic responses to COVID-19 from this chapter may thus help enterprises to acknowledge the need for a process-based approach to organisational resilience and to identify the resources and capabilities they need to build (or maintain) for the latter. As pointed out by Salanova (2020), resilience can be learnt, so the links between antecedents, responses, and outcomes identified in our typology can provide practical guidelines on how to approach organisational resilience development and enactment for managers. Awareness about the process-based nature of resilience is of particular relevance in this respect. Developing, nurturing, and utilising the appropriate 'resources and capabilities for resilience' before, during, or after an external shock can help organisations manage the outcomes of the crisis and capitalise on the opportunities brought about by a disruptive event. With respect to methodological implications, we show that a process-based approach can better explain the development and use of organisational resilience. A multitude of processes need to be considered, as each facet of disruption can cascade into a series of associated disruptions that cause a widespread and seemingly endless wave of risks for an organisation and the economy (see also Blyth & Mallett, 2020; Jones, 2020; United Nations, 2019).

While the study presents an important contribution to examining organisational resilience, it has several limitations that lend opportunities for future research. It pertains to a particular type of crisis and context, as it is based on survey responses by firms operating in a small European economy during the COVID-19 pandemic. Surveys on different crises as well as on samples from large and developed economies may generate additional insights. Since our sample includes foreign-owned firms and internationalised domestic enterprises, the second limitation is less profound. However, studying the phenomenon longitudinally (following different stages of a crisis or different crises) and from a multilevel perspective, including individual, team, interorganisational, subnational, national, and supranational resilience measures, tools and strategies, and their outcomes was beyond the scope of the study. This is its main limitation, since multiple levels of analysis are likely to influence one another and do so differently depending on the context. We thus encourage future studies to incorporate a multilevel process-based view as well as to employ a comparative and mixed methods approach that would better explain the mechanisms driving the connections between antecedents, strategies, and outcomes of organisational resilience to different crises.

Conclusion

The COVID-19 pandemic has reiterated the importance of organisational resilience and a proactive approach to risk management during systemic crises at individual, organisational, subnational, national, and supranational levels. Our exploratory study provides a process-based typology of organisational strategies aimed at (re)building and enacting resilience in such contexts. It links both the antecedents and the outcomes of the different types of organisational strategies to developing and capitalising on resilience. Overall, our study shows that building business resilience requires changes in multiple processes within and outside the firm. The most resilient firms take a dynamic, innovative, and proactive approach in managing risks internally (especially in the areas of employee development, digitalisation, and automation), externally (in collaboration with suppliers and buyers, as well as in terms of market development), and combined (through product and service innovation). The study has both theoretical and practical implications for planning, designing, monitoring, and managing organisational resilience and offers several suggestions for future research of organisational resilience from process-based, comparative, and multilevel perspectives. With COVID-19, companies face shocks, but also have a unique opportunity and necessity to revisit their business models to build greater systemic resilience.

Notes

1 Risk refers to measurable probability of future events, whereas uncertainty occurs when the likelihood of future events is indefinite or incalculable (Knight, 1921). In crises, both are usually present.

2 Like Hillmann and Guenther (2021), we acknowledge that different types of crises require different responses and that any conceptualisation of organisational resilience needs to take into consideration the nature, magnitude, and desirability of change (see also Mamouni Limnios et al., 2014). In relation to the COVID-19 pandemic, this includes (1) its character of an exogenous natural system that is beyond (complete) human control, affecting another (social) system beyond complete human control (e.g. due to the unpredictable psychological factors) (Anker, 2021), (2) an impact on health and social welfare – nationally and globally, and (3) high levels of state interventionism, whereby change to business operations may not be desired but is required.

3 Creating and executing stable plans only works well when causal relationships are clear, predictable, and unchanging, but less with the unknown, changeable, unpredictable, and improbable, yet highly impactful events – like the Covid-19 pandemic (see also Reeves & Whitaker, 2020).

4 Perrow (1984) and Annarelli and Nonino (2016) note that organisational resilience can also refer to actions aimed at internal organisational reliability. However, this is beyond the scope of our study.
5 According to Schriber et al. (2019) and Ma et al. (2018), individual, group, and organisational levels of resilience are intertwined (see also Bhamra et al., 2011). Van der Vegt et al. (2015) thereby warn against automatically assuming reciprocity across levels when it comes to resilience: while resilience at one level may lead to resilience at other levels, developing capacity for resilience at lower levels does not always increase the overall resilience of the system and *vice versa*. Although we acknowledge these potential interplays in the interpretation of results, a multilevel empirical study is beyond the scope of this chapter and thus presents an opportunity for further analyses and research.
6 Ma et al. (2018) suggest that the development of organisational resilience lies in the continuous flux between these three dimensions.
7 As observed in China during the early Covid-19 shock, most sectors and companies deteriorated swiftly and simultaneously. However, during recovery, there was a noticeable divergence in company performance (Reeves & Whitaker, 2020).
8 When neither approach is used, the organisation is described as vulnerable (Butler, 2018).
9 The results based on analyses of expected revenue growth as projected by the firms were compared to those based on actual revenue growth data provided by AJPES (see the Results section of the chapter).
10 This corresponds to the multidimensional uncertainties caused by the pandemic that need to be addressed by companies.
11 To check how the actual revenue growth rate corresponds to the subjective projections of the future revenue growth, we also ran a specification using firms' revenue forecasts from the two surveys. A discrete variable from both questionnaires was used, constructed from the question 'What will be the impact of Covid-19 on your firm performance in terms of total revenue for 2020?' In these robustness regressions, we applied logistic regression and an ordered logit model, where the dependent variable was a binary indicator for expected increase of firm revenue in 2020 and an ordinal discrete version of this variable with three distinct values (decrease, no change, and increase), respectively. The results are in line with the actual revenue growth, which corroborates ex-post the validity of subjective performance forecasts provided by firms through the survey. They are available upon request.
12 Most firms in our study report maintaining rather than changing their supplier networks. They do not report additional supply chain splitting, suggested as a risk management strategy by Anker (2021) and Shashi et al. (2020), but they also do not report supply network optimisation, which might mean that they had had sufficiently diversified networks prior to the pandemic or that the impact of the pandemic had not yet hit this area of operations in the early stages of the crisis. Future research is encouraged to look into this more in depth.
13 Ramezani and Camarinha-Matos (2020) describe this as antifragility.
14 According to Akgün and Keskin (2014), the resilience capacity influences firm performance through product innovativeness.

References

Akgün, A.E. & Keskin, H. (2014). Organisational resilience capacity and firm product innovativeness and performance. *International Journal of Production Research*, *52*(23), 6918–6937.

Andersson, T., Cäkerb, M., Tengblada, S. & Wickelgrena, M. (2019). Building traits for organizational resilience through balancing organizational structures. *Scandinavian Journal of Management*, *35*, 36–45.

Anker, T.B. (2021). At the boundary: Post-COVID agenda for business and management research in Europe and beyond. *European Management Journal*, *39*(2), 171–178.

Annarelli, A. & Nonino, F. (2016). Strategic and operational management of organizational resilience: Current state of research and future directions. *Omega*, *62*, 1–18.
Azadegan, A. & Dooley, K. (2021). A typology of supply network resilience strategies: Complex collaborations in a complex world. *Journal of Supply Chain Management*, *57*(1), 17–26.
Bell, S. (2019). Organisational resilience: A matter of organisational life and death. *Continuity and Resilience Review*, *1*(1), 5–16.
Bhamra, R., Dani, S. & Burnard, K. (2011). Resilience: The concept, a literature review and future directions. *International Journal of Production Research*, *49*(18), 5375–5393.
Blyth, M. & Mallett, S. (2020). Epidemics and pandemics: Effects on societal and organisational resilience. *Journal of Business Continuity and Emergency Planning*, *14*(1), 17–36. PMID: 32847651.
Bordia, P., Hobman, E., Jones, E., Gallois, C. & Callan, V.J. (2004). Uncertainty during organizational change: Types, consequences, and management strategies. *Journal of Business and Psychology*, *18*(4), 507–532.
Bresch, D.N., Berghuijs, J., Egloff, R. & Kupers, R. (2014). A resilience lens for enterprise risk management. In R. Kupers (Ed.), *Turbulence: A Corporate Perspective on Collaborating for Resilience* (pp. 49–65). Amsterdam: Amsterdam University Press.
Buono, J. & Bowditch, J. (1989). *The Human Side of Mergers and Acquisitions*. San Francisco: Jossey-Bass Publishers.
Butler, C. (2018). Five steps to organisational resilience: Being adaptive and flexible during both normal operations and times of disruption. *Journal of Business Continuity and Emergency Planning*, *12*(2), 103–112.
Chan, J.W.K. (2011). Enhancing organisational resilience: Application of viable system model and MCDA in a small Hong Kong company. *International Journal of Production Research*, *49*(18), 5545–5563.
Cheng, J., Powell, T., Skidmore, D. & Wessel, D. (2021). What's the Fed doing in response to the COVID-19 crisis? What more could it do? *Brookings*, January. Retrieved from: http://www.brookings.edu/research/fed-response-to-covid19/.
Christensen, C.M. (1997). *The Innovator's Dilemma: When New Technologies Cause Great Firms to Fail*. Boston: Harvard Business School Press.
Conz, E. & Magnani, G. (2020). A dynamic perspective on the resilience of firms: A systematic literature review and a framework for future research. *European Management Journal*, *38*, 400–412.
Crum, M., Nelson, T., de Borst, J. & Byrnes, P. (2020). The use of cluster analysis in entrepreneurship research: Review of past research and future directions. *Journal of Small Business Management*, 1–40.
Fisher, L. & Ransom, D.C. (1995). An empirically derived typology of families: I. Relationships with adult health. *Family Process*, *34*(2), 161–182.
Foster, R.N. & Kaplan, S. (2001). *Creative Destruction: Why Companies That are Built to Last Underperform the Market, and How to Successfully Transform Them*. New York, London, Toronto, Sydney and Auckland: Currency/Doubleday.
Hagen, B., Zucchella, A., Cerchiello, P. & De Giovanni, N. (2012). International strategy and performance – Clustering strategic types of SMEs. *International Business Review*, *21*(3), 369–382.
Halkos, G., Skouloudis, A., Malesios, C. & Evangelinos, K. (2018). Bouncing back from extreme weather events: Some preliminary findings on resilience barriers facing small and medium-sized enterprises. *Business Strategy and the Environment*, *27*(4), 547–559.
Hamel, G. & Välikangas, L. (2003). The quest for resilience. *Harvard Business Review*, 52–62. Retrieved from: https://hbr.org/2003/09/the-quest-for-resilience.

Harzing, A.W. (2000). Cross-national mail surveys: Why do response rates differ between countries? *Industrial Marketing Management, 29*(3), 243–254.

Hillmann, J. & Guenther, E. (2021). Organizational resilience: A valuable construct for management research? *International Journal of Management Reviews, 23*, 7–44.

Holling, C.S. (1996). Engineering resilience versus ecological resilience. In P. Schulze (Ed.), *Engineering within Ecological Constraints* (pp. 31–44). Washington: National Academy Press.

Jackson, S., Schuler, R. & Vredenburgh, D. (1987). Managing stress in turbulent times. In A. Riley & S. Zaccaro (Eds.), *Occupational Stress and Organizational Effectiveness* (pp. 141–166). New York: Praeger.

Javorcik, B. (2020). Global supply chains will not be the same in the post-COVID-19 world. In R.E. Baldwin & S.J. Evenett (Eds.), *COVID-19 and Trade Policy: Why Turning Inward Won't Work* (pp. 111–116). London: CEPR Press.

Jones, M. (2020). COVID-19's ripple effect: Mapping out the societal and economic consequences. *Notion.so*, March. Retrieved from http://www.notion.so/COVID-19-s-Ripple-Effect-Mapping-Out-The-Societal-Economic-Consequencesee320975f0d64cb-c8a6c9df92b14348b.

Kabanoff, B. & Brown, S. (2008). Knowledge structures of prospectors, analyzers, and defenders: Content, structure, stability, and performance. *Strategic Management Journal, 29*(2), 149–171.

Ketchen, D.J. & Shook, C.L. (1996). The application of cluster analysis in strategic management research: An analysis and critique. *Strategic Management Journal, 17*, 441–458.

Kitching, J., Smallbone, D. & Xheneti, M. (2009, November). Have small businesses beaten the recession? *32nd Institute for Small Business and Entrepreneurship (ISBE) Conference*, Liverpool. ISBN 9781900862165. Retrieved from: https://eprints.kingston.ac.uk/id/eprint/6917/1/Kitching-J-6917.pdf.

Klammer, A. & Gueldenberg, S. (2019). Unlearning and forgetting in organizations: A systematic review of literature. *Journal of Knowledge Management, 23*(5), 860–888.

Knight, F.H. (1921). *Risk, Uncertainty, and Profit.* Boston and Cambridge: Hart, Schaffner, Marx and Houghton Mifflin.

Koronis, E. & Ponis, S. (2018). Better than before: the resilient organization in crisis mode. *Journal of Business Strategy, 39*(1), 32–42.

Lengnick-Hall, C.A., Beck, T.E. & Lengnick-Hall, M.L. (2011). Developing a capacity for organizational resilience through strategic human resource management. *Human Resource Management Review, 21*(3), 243–255.

Linnenluecke, M. (2017). Resilience in business and management research: A review of influential publications and research agenda. *International Journal of Management Reviews, 19*, 4–30.

Ma, Z., Xiao, L. & Yin, J. (2018). Toward a dynamic model of organizational resilience. *Nankai Business Review International, 9*(3), 246–263.

Makridakis, S. (1996). Factors affecting success in business: Management theories/tools versus predicting changes. *European Management Journal, 14*(1), 1–20.

Mamouni Limnios, E.A., Mazzarol, T., Ghadouani, A. & Schilizzi, S.G.M. (2014). The resilience architecture framework: Four organizational archetypes. *European Management Journal, 32*, 104–116.

Mirodout, S. (2020). Resilience versus robustness in global value chains: Some policy implications. In R.E. Baldwin & S.J. Evenett (Eds.), *COVID-19 and Trade Policy: Why Turning Inward Won't Work* (pp. 117–130). London: CEPR Press.

Pearson, C.M. & Clair, J.A. (1998). Reframing crisis management. *Academy of Management Review, 23*, 59–76.

Pecujlija, M., Jaksic, K., Drobnjak, S., Cosic, I., Kesetovic, Z. & Seslija, D. (2017). Serbian companies reactivity and flexibility and their crisis management efficiency and effectiveness. *Journal of East European Management Studies, 22*(2), 257–270.

Peneder, M. (2010). Technological regimes and the variety of innovation behaviour: Creating integrated taxonomies of firms and sectors. *Research Policy, 39*(3), 323–334.

Perrow, C. (1984). *Normal Accidents: Living with High-Risk Technologies*. New York: Basic Books.

Ramezani, J. & Camarinha-Matos, L.M. (2020). Approaches for resilience and antifragility in collaborative business ecosystems. *Technological Forecasting and Social Change, 151*, 1–26.

Reeves, M. & Whitaker, K. (2020). A guide to building a more resilient business. *Harvard Business Review*, June. Retrieved from: https://hbr.org/2020/07/a-guide-to-building-a-more-resilient-business.

Salanova, M. (2020). How to survive COVID-19? Notes from organisational resilience. *International Journal of Social Psychology/Revista De Psicología Social, 35*(3), 670–676.

Schonlau, M. (2002). The clustergram: A graph for visualizing hierarchical and non-hierarchical cluster analyses. *The Stata Journal, 2002*(3), 316–327. Retrieved from https://citeseerx.ist.psu.edu/viewdoc/download?doi=10.1.1.459.5318andrep=rep1andtype=pdf.

Schriber, S., Bauer, F. & King, D.R. (2019). Organisational resilience in acquisition: Integration – Organisational antecedents and contingency effects of flexibility and redundancy. *Applied Psychology: An International Review, 68*(4), 759–796.

Schumpeter, J.A. (1934). *The Theory of Economic Development: An Inquiry into Profits, Capital, Credit, Interest, and the Business Cycle*. Cambridge: Harvard University Press.

Shashi, Centobelli, P., Cerchione, R. & Ertz, M. (2020). Managing supply chain resilience to pursue business and environmental strategies. *Business Strategy and the Environment, 29*(3), 1215–1246.

Slater, S.F. & Olson, E.M. (2001). Marketing's contribution to the implementation of business strategy: An empirical analysis. *Strategic Management Journal, 22*(11), 1055–1067.

Starbuck, W.H. (2017). Organizational learning and unlearning. *The Learning Organization, 24*(1), 30–38.

Supardi, S. & Hadi, S. (2020). New perspective on the resilience of SMEs proactive, adaptive, reactive from a business turbulence: A systematic review. *Journal of Xi'an University of Architecture and Technology, XII*(V), 1265–1275.

Sutcliffe, K. & Vogus, T. (2003). Organizing for resilience. In K. Cameron (Ed.), *Positive Organizational Scholarship: Foundations of a New Discipline* (pp. 94–110). San Francisco: Berrett-Koehler Publishers Inc.

UNCTAD. (2020). *World Investment Report*. Geneva: United Nations.

United Nations. (2015). *Global Assessment Report on Disaster Risk Reduction 2015: Making Development Sustainable: The Future of Disaster Risk Management*. Retrieved from: http://www.preventionweb.net/english/hyogo/gar/2015/en/gar-pdf/GAR2015_EN.pdf.

United Nations. (2019). *Global Assessment Report on Disaster Risk Reduction 2019*. Retrieved from: https://gar.undrr.org/sites/default/files/reports/2019-05/full_gar_report.pdf.

Van der Vegt, G.S., Essens, P., Wahlström, M. & George, G. (2015). From the editors: Managing risk and resilience. *The Academy of Management Journal, 58*(4), 971–980.

Webb, B. & Schlemmer, F. (2006). Resilience as a source of competitive advantage for small information technology companies. In B. Donnellan, T. Larsen, L. Levine, & J. DeGross (Eds.), *The Transfer and Diffusion of Information Technology for Organisational Resilience* (pp. 181–197). New York: IFIP and Springer.

World Economic Forum. (2015). *Global Risks 2015* (10th ed.). World Economic Forum. Retrieved from: http://reports.weforum.org/global-risks-2015/

Xiao, L. & Cao, H. (2017). Organizational resilience: The theoretical model and research implication. *ITM Web of Conferences, 12*, 1–4.

Yu, A. (1998). *Creating the Digital Future: The Secrets of Consistent Innovation at Intel* (1st ed.). New York: Free Press.

Zahra, S.A. & Covin, J.G. (1993). Business strategy, technology policy, and firm performance. *Strategic Management Journal, 14*(6), 451–478.

11 The relevance of business-tailored government support for foreign affiliates during crises

The case of the COVID-19 pandemic

*Andreja Jaklič and Iris Koleša**

Introduction

To mitigate the immediate, medium-, and long-term effects of the COVID-19 pandemic (declared in 2020) on business and the economy as well as accelerate recovery, numerous countries and governments introduced a range of COVID-19 emergency measures aimed at firms. Despite the significant time and resource constraints that they were facing at the height of the COVID-19 crisis, many understood the need to tailor these measures and draw lessons from policy responses to the pandemic throughout its different stages in this respect. In some cases, support measures were even developed in collaboration with firms, as the unpredictability and complexity of the COVID-19–triggered crisis necessitated prompt, differentiated, and targeted measures grounded in user needs and inputs.

One of the questions that arises when designing anti-crisis policies or government support measures for firms (and was reiterated during the COVID-19 pandemic as well) is whether to distinguish between domestic and foreign-owned firms. Studies namely show performance differences between multinationals and their domestic counterparts in areas such as productivity, technology, profitability, wages, skills, and growth (Bellak, 2004). In general, national industrial policies and emergency government assistance often favour domestic firms, which on average demonstrate lower performance indicators. However, foreign-owned enterprises can constitute an important part of an economy, generate knowledge and technology spill-over effects on domestic businesses, and contribute to stable and durable supply, production, and financial linkages between domestic and foreign enterprises and between economies – also during crises. Foreign affiliates and foreign direct investment (FDI) in general have therefore long been recognised as engines of growth and development. In the global financial crisis of 2008, subsidiaries of multinational enterprises coped better with the crisis than local counterparts with similar characteristics (Alfaro & Chen, 2012). Although FDI is seen as a driver of stimulating economic activity, it is also vulnerable to economic crises and other types of shocks (Hayakawa et al., 2022). Foreign affiliates may curtail their activities, slow or reduce their investment, or even cease operations due to such events. Previous studies recorded negative

*Corresponding author

DOI: 10.4324/9781003345428-11

effects of crises on FDI (see e.g. Dornean et al., 2012; Dornean & Oanea, 2015; Poulsen & Hufbauer, 2011; Stoddard & Noy, 2015). Reduced FDI can result in notable challenges for foreign affiliates' host countries' economies, such as unemployment, supply, and solvency issues, which can be particularly damaging during crises.

The COVID-19 pandemic strongly influenced the dynamics of FDI flows. In 2020, the global FDI flows fell sharply to 885 billion EUR, which was 35% less than in 2019, when FDI flows had already reached significantly lower levels than those a year earlier (i.e. in 2018). In the EU, the COVID-19 pandemic produced even harsher effects compared to the world average, with inward FDI decreasing by 71% to 98 billion EUR in 2020 (in 2019, inward FDI amounted to 335 billion EUR). In 2020, inward FDI accounted for a mere 0.7% of the EU-27 GDP. This was a sharp decrease from the 3.6% it had reached in 2018 (OECD, 2021; European Commission, 2021a).

Due to the effects of decreased FDI flows on national economies, several governments started to re-examine their approaches to FDI and assumed an active role for FDI in their pandemic recovery plans. This shift was particularly important, as prior to the pandemic (following the global recession between 2007 and 2009) the number of investment restrictions had been increasing (UNCTAD, 2020). Effective policy interventions were thus crucial for many countries when trying to mitigate the economic effects of the pandemic also with the support of (and for) FDI.

This chapter summarises the design of, availability for, and the use of COVID-19 emergency government support measures by foreign affiliates in Slovenia. The COVID-19 pandemic has significantly affected this small CEE country, which is largely dependent on foreign markets, integration in the global value chains (GVCs), and FDI. Since the first confirmed COVID-19 case on March 4, 2020, there have been 1,122,870 confirmed infections and over 6,000 deaths with or from COVID-19 (based on data from August 2022). Slovenia experienced a strong second wave of COVID-19 cases in fall 2020 and a less steep third wave during the March–April 2021 period (IMF, 2022).[1] The threat to public health also had spill-over effects on business operations as many businesses were forced to temporarily (and some permanently) seize their operations. Real GDP contracted by 5.5% in 2020 but in the first quarter of 2021, it grew by 1.6% (IMAD, 2021 – IMAD Spring Forecast).

From March 2020 to the end of 2021, the Slovenian authorities took, a series of measures to delay the spread of the coronavirus and mitigate the negative impact of the pandemic on people and businesses with ten so-called anti-corona packages. Businesses were actively engaged in the creation of these measures (through business associations or directly) and also introduced several tailor-made responses at firm-level. In January 2022, Slovenia ranked second (outperformed only by Denmark) among 23 OECD countries on the list of countries with successful recovery measures during the COVID-19 pandemic (Economist, 2022, January 1), making it a relevant case study for anti-crisis policy and government support design.

This chapter provides an overview of the measures and short-term support available to businesses in Slovenia immediately after the pandemic being declared in March 2020. Different types and the overall scope of support are presented. The chapter then discusses the use and relevance of these measures for foreign affiliates in Slovenia and their uptake, as well as outlines the actions taken at firm-level by businesses themselves. Based on a comprehensive survey of foreign affiliates in Slovenia conducted in 2020, we examine how affiliates of multinational enterprises (MNEs) perceive and evaluate different types of government support and how they use and integrate emergency measures into their recovery plans. Finally, we discuss the relevance of government emergency measures to foreign affiliates and the importance of supporting foreign affiliates for national economies. The results of the study presented in this chapter provide rare insights into the propensity and ability of foreign affiliates to benefit from national (and to an extent regional and municipal) support measures and give rise to reflections on how foreign affiliate support can contribute to the recovery of small economies.

The COVID-19 emergency government support measures

With the outbreak of the COVID-19 pandemic, most governments around the world introduced a range of interventions to achieve wider policy objectives related to social security and stabilisation of economic activity. This is because governmental inaction during downturns and crises can lead to failure of otherwise viable firms, which results in job and skill losses that often prolong the recovery time for economies affected by such events (see also OFT, 2009).

The unprecedented economic shock of the COVID-19 pandemic prompted governments to financially support jobs, livelihoods, and distressed businesses on a historic scale. These programmes were crucial in managing the economic impact on individuals and businesses, including the probability of default by fundamentally viable firms, and in stabilising wider credit market conditions (OECD, 2021). At the same time, policymakers around the world were faced with challenges related to the supply of crucial resources, such as food, fuel, and alternative energy sources, raw materials, etc.

Governments thus also intervened to ensure the security of particular supply chains considered essential for the functioning of economies. Ensuring security of health care and food and energy supply in the face of potential world shortages were some of the focal areas in emergency government support programmes.

In several developed countries, the recovery from the pandemi coincided with (or promoted) a green transition, which required a drastic (and systemic) transformation of the economy, including a wide-reaching set of policies supporting such transition (see e.g. de Vet et al., 2021).[2] The growing geopolitical tensions also resulted in countries (and supranational entities, such as the European Union – EU) aiming to achieve open strategic autonomy (see e.g. Miró, 2022), diversifying their suppliers, and therefore limiting excessive dependencies on single trade partners for sectors (or raw materials) considered strategic (e.g. European Commission, 2021b). COVID-19 emergency measures in the EU mostly considered this broader policy framework.

The success of intervention measures depends on not only their consistency with the general economic policy framework but also several other factors (see e.g. Hudson et al., 2019). Our study shows that the speed of response, the number of resources available, and the quality of information (i.e. knowledge of and about the challenges and problems faced by firms) are among the most important factors contributing to the success of government interventions aimed at business during crises.

The heterogeneity of companies and their different needs thereby introduce additional challenges that necessitate coordination and a more complex (also collaborative) decision-making process. Collaboration between companies and governments in developing anti-crisis strategies and their joint development of interventions (i.e. co-creation of measures by companies, so that these are tailored to their differing needs) is thus crucial for effective and efficient addressing of crises such as the COVID-19 pandemic. Effective communication strategies also maximise both the use of support and business participation in recovery plans. Finally, success of government support depends on the willingness (as well as ability and capability) to change and adapt the measures and policies in companies (this can also be enhanced through collaboration and communication, along with resource provision – including know-how and knowledge).

Due to their complexity and multidimensional effects on the economy (including businesses, individuals, subnational, national, and supranational entities), the external shocks of the COVID-19 pandemic have been the object of public policy, business strategy, and concerted social action by public interest groups. The crisis thus also posed a challenge in terms of strengthening government capacity when supporting the private sector while also maintaining legitimacy in doing so (see e.g. Eadi & Rasmussen, 2022; Reeskens & Muis, 2021). The recovery tasks thereby required both investments in financial stability of businesses and employee development (e.g. through promoting digital literacy when work from home was introduced in various organisations or promoting health and safety measures in the workplace specific to the pandemic). The process of designing government support for businesses considered the key issues at country, firm, and to an extent also individual levels that emerged immediately after the COVID-19 pandemic.

Several EU member states announced support measures for companies in order to mitigate economic impact very quickly. The discretionary fiscal measures introduced by EU countries in the first phase of the fight against the pandemic could be divided into three categories:

- An immediate fiscal stimulus in the form of additional government spending (increased spending on health care, maintenance of employment, subsidies to small and medium-sized enterprises, public investment) and partial compensation of revenue losses through tax write-offs. Such measures directly lead to a deterioration in the budget balance.
- Deferrals of tax and contribution payments, which improve the liquidity position of individuals and enterprises but do not eliminate their obligations. Some of these deferrals lasted only a few months and had to be settled in 2020, while those that expired in 2021 or later caused a deterioration in the budget balance in 2020. Some countries decided to help service loans or pay utility bills, which also significantly improved their liquidity position.
- Other liquidity schemes and guarantees, including export guarantees, liquidity assistance, and credit lines through national development banks. Some of these measures improve the liquidity situation of the private sector, but unlike deferrals, which are automatic and usually apply to specific target groups, credit lines require proactive action by the affected firms (Franca et al., 2020).

Slovenia was among EU member states that adopted an emergency fiscal stimulus package very quickly (i.e. within a month after the first declaration of the epidemic). This was worth 3 billion EUR and was designed to help undertakings and the self-employed (see the so-called mega COVID-19 law – ZIUZEOP, 2020; ZIUZEOP-A, 2020;[3] and the list of intervention measures introduced in Slovenia[4]). The specific goals of the abovementioned measures were to preserve jobs and keep businesses in operation. These measures included, in particular, assistance to employers in the form of compensation for "waiting for work"[5] and exemption from social security contributions. The emergency law furthermore tried to improve the liquidity of undertakings with several types of aid (deferral of payment, government guarantees, freezing of payment of advance tax, shortening of payment deadlines for public sector payments, etc.). Measures were also taken to assist scientific research projects (extending project implementation, funding deadlines, and equipment purchase deadlines) and to help the self-employed (see e.g. PISRS, 2021; STA, 2020).

The European Commission approved a 2 billion EUR Slovenian state aid scheme to support the Slovenian economy in the context of the coronavirus outbreak. The Temporary Framework provided the public support in the form of direct grants, wage subsidies, exemption from paying social security contributions, reduction of certain taxes and water fees, bank guarantees, deferred payment of certain credits, and compensatory payments (for more details see Eur-LEX, 2020a). The scheme was approved under the state aid Temporary Framework adopted by the Commission on 19 March 2020, as amended on 3 April 2020 (see Eur-LEX, 2020b). The Temporary Framework enabled member states to combine all support measures, except for loans and guarantees for the same loan or amounts exceeding the thresholds foreseen by the Temporary Framework.[6]

Slovenian government actions to support citizens and businesses during the coronavirus pandemic were both diverse and characterised by continuity. COVID-19 support resulted in a total of ten continued anti-corona packages. Six of the ten packages were released in 2020, the additional four in 2021.[7] Businesses were involved in developing support measures – in particular through business associations and the Chamber of Commerce and Industry. Before each new round of measures, the government also organised consultations with business representatives, where companies had the opportunity to submit proposals for the necessary measures and comment on the government's proposals (e.g. Gov.si, 2022).

The increase in public spending in the period between March and September 2020 amounted to 7.9% in Slovenia, indicating an extremely strong response to the first wave of the epidemic, while the volume of liquidity assistance to enterprises was lower at 6.6% of GDP, with 20% of this assistance going to recapitalisations and loan repayment support, while the rest was used for the guarantee scheme (Franca et al., 2020; IMF, Fiscal Monitor Database, 2020). A cross-country comparison of fiscal measures between March and September 2020 based on the IMF Fiscal Monitor Database (2020) showed that EU member states increased public spending to combat the virus by an average of 5%; with 0.6 percentage points of the increase due to higher spending on health care and 4.4% due to other fiscal measures. Liquidity support to enterprises averaged 8.3% of GDP.

According to the assessment of the Financial Council of the Republic of Slovenia (in 2021), the results of the simulations of the measures implemented by the time of evaluation showed that economic activity in 2020 was 3% higher than predicted in the scenario without these measures. The measures taken, moreover, mitigated the decline in economic activity by about one-third of the decline compared to the baseline scenario, which is comparable to the model assessment of the impact of measures in the EU prepared by the European Commission (Financial Council of the Republic of Slovenia, 2021). IMAD (2021) and the Bank of Slovenia (2020) projected only a slightly larger effect of these measures on economic activity. Simulations demonstrated that the overall effect of the adopted measures on economic activity had been positive and significant, but relatively small from the point of view of multiplier effects.

This was to be expected, as the measures were primarily aimed at preventing a significant economic contraction and an excessive increase in unemployment. Although the adopted measures had positive macroeconomic effects, they were also reflected in a deterioration of public finance aggregates. Simulations showed that the public sector deficit increased by about 4% in the first year exclusively due to the impact of the adopted measures. At the same time, public sector debt increased by about 2% in the year in which the measures were introduced (Financial Council of the Republic of Slovenia, 2021).

The relevance of emergency government support measures for foreign affiliates

In this section, we examine the relevance of emergency government support for foreign affiliates in a case study of Slovenia. Rather than measuring the success of intervention measures introduced in Slovenia (IUS-INFO, 2023; PISRS, 2021; ZIUZEOP, 2020), we explore how foreign affiliates used and perceived emergency measures after the first wave of the pandemic. We also analyse business engagement in developing support measures put in place during the COVID-19 pandemic. The methodological approach includes secondary research, interviews, and a 2020 survey among foreign affiliates in Slovenia (see also Jaklič & Koleša, 2020)[8] to examine how affiliates of multinational enterprises (MNEs) perceive and estimate different types of government support, what additional measures they would need, how they use and integrate existing emergency measures into their recovery plans, and what additional (complementary or supplementary) measures they develop at the firm level.

The survey among foreign affiliates in Slovenia between September and November 2020 was carried out with a sample framework of approximately 1000 firms. Two hundred and thirteen companies with foreign capital answered the questionnaire, which represents a 21.55% response rate and a 17.7% share of the population.

The survey sample represents the population of foreign affiliates in Slovenia well in terms of firm size, industry, market orientation, and the geographical structure of inward investments (for more details see Jaklič & Koleša, 2020; or contact the authors). In line with the inward FDI geographical breakdown for Slovenia (see Bank of Slovenia, 2020), the largest share of investors in foreign affiliates in Slovenia came from the EU countries that are Slovenia's most important trade partners; i.e. Austria (23.7%), Germany (19 %), Italy (8.5%), and Croatia (5.7%). The sample affiliates reported having investors from 25 different countries. With regard to the size structure, small firms dominated the sample (62.3%), followed by medium-sized (22%) and large firms (11.6%). Micro-sized firms represent 4% of sample firms.[9] In terms of industry, service companies dominated the sample: 65.8% of the sample companies operate in the service sector and 34.2% in the production sector. In terms of sales revenue, the sample companies are quite evenly distributed. The majority (55.3%) of the companies in the sample generate most of their revenues in foreign markets (they are mainly exporters), while 44.7% of the companies in the sample operate mainly in the domestic market. Large and medium-sized enterprises are thereby mainly export-oriented, micro enterprises focus mainly on the domestic market, while small enterprises are similarly distributed across domestic and foreign markets. As far as the duration of the foreign investors' presence in Slovenia is concerned, companies with years of experience in the Slovenian business environment dominate the sample. More than 58% of the companies have been operating in Slovenia with foreign investment for more than ten years, in one-fifth, the foreign investor entered the ownership structure in the last five years, and a good fifth of the companies' foreign investors have less than ten and more than five years of experience in the Slovenian business environment. Ten per cent of the sample companies' foreign investors came to Slovenia after 2018 (1% in 2020).

The survey covered the evaluation of business environment in Slovenia and in the region, as well as the impact of COVID-19 on:

- business performance (including the difference between the experienced and planned performance),
- investment, innovation, and internationalisation activities,
- the firm's reactions to the COVID-19 crisis,
- the use of existing governmental (and local) measures, and
- the firm's proposals for developing new and adaptating existing emergency measures.

Survey findings demonstrate that the majority of foreign-owned firms (as much as 52%) operated on a reduced scale during the first wave of the COVID-19 pandemic. Twelve per cent of firms completely suspended their business operations. However, almost one-third of foreign affiliates operated within the planned scope and 4% of sample firms managed to increase the scale of their business operations (see Figure 11.1).

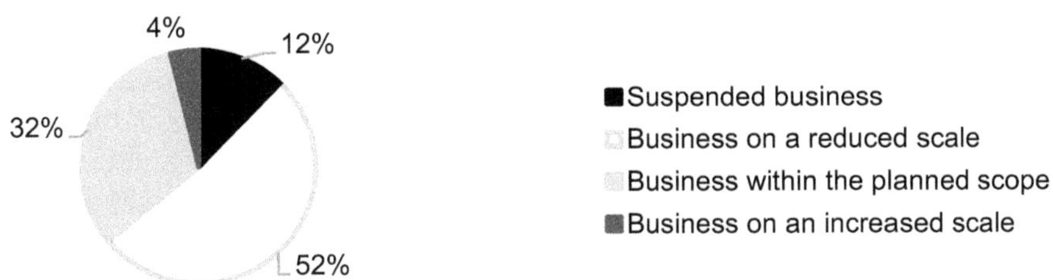

Figure 11.1 Foreign affiliates' business operation during the COVID-19 pandemic in 2020

Source: own elaboration based on Jaklič & Koleša (2020)

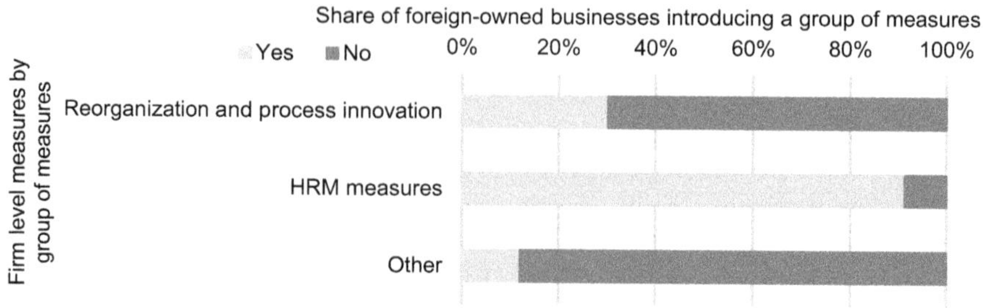

Figure 11.2 Firm-level measures introduced by foreign affiliates during the COVID-19 pandemic by groups of measures in 2020

Source: own elaboration based on Jaklič & Koleša (2020)

Foreign affiliates moreover immediately introduced a number of measures in their units (see Figure 11.2). Most of these measures were related to human resource management (HRM), such as safety measures, remote work, flexible or shortened working hours, reduction (or cancellation) of travel, introduction of virtual meetings and virtual teams, additional training, and psychological support for employees. Companies that introduced reorganisation and process innovation (30% of sample firms) mainly sped up digitalisation and automation and introduced new machinery and equipment, online sales, and/or other organisational innovations.

The impact of the COVID-19 pandemic on business operations was assessed in more detail using data on changes in the number of employees, sales revenue, profit, and business volume (see Figure 11.3). Most companies in the first wave of the COVID-19 pandemic recorded a decline in the volume of profits (61% of companies), revenues (58% of companies), and production or services (51% of companies). A minority (27 %) of the surveyed foreign-owned companies also reduced the number of employees (through redundancies, but also early retirement and other soft measures). In general, companies reported the smallest (negative or positive) impact of the pandemic on the number of foreign suppliers, foreign buyers, and export markets, but also on their process, product and service innovations, investments in automation, digitisation and personnel development, and on the number of employees.

Nevertheless, some foreign affiliates managed the crisis well. More than a tenth of the companies in the sample recorded a positive impact of the pandemic on all aspects of the business studied. Ten per cent of the companies also increased their profits, while 15% of companies increased employment and sales revenue. Half of the companies surveyed also recorded an increase in investments in the safety and health of employees.[10] Foreign firms focused on job continuity and security of their employees. Therefore, they highly appreciated and used HRM focused measures. They thereby aimed to achieve greater flexibility through adapted working arrangements and to develop (knowledge) capacities that would allow them to adjust production methods to the new conditions. Many foreign firms were able to mitigate disruptions caused by widespread lockdown measures by switching to

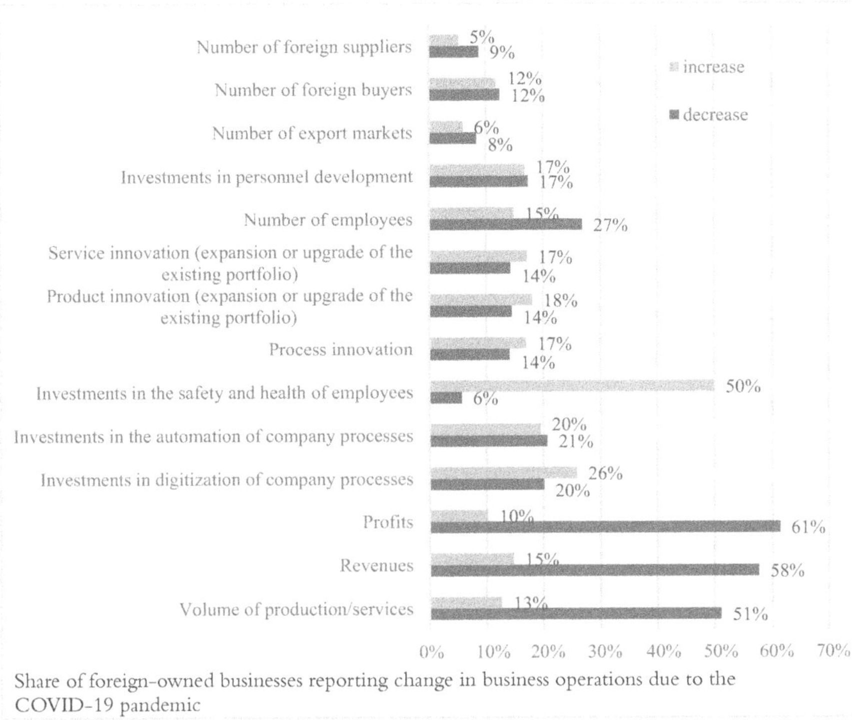

Figure 11.3 Influence of the COVID-19 pandemic on different aspects of business operations in foreign affiliates (% share of companies, 2020)

Source: own elaboration based on Jaklič & Koleša (2020)

remote working arrangements, which tend to be more feasible for skilled workers and administrative jobs.

In the majority of companies (52%), foreign investments also influenced an increase in investments in employee development; only 3% of the sample companies perceived a decrease in investments in personnel development due to the entry of a foreign investor. The largest share of companies that had new investments in employee development was recorded among medium-sized companies; as many as 63% of the surveyed medium-sized companies perceived an increase in this type of investment with the entry of a foreign investor. A similar experience was reported by 48% of the small and 59% of the large companies. Employment growth mostly occurred simultaneously with investment in personnel development. A larger share of companies investing in personnel was present among manufacturing companies (44%) and a smaller share among service companies (28%). When it came to investing in personnel, there were no differences between domestically and export-oriented firms (the share of companies investing in their personnel during the pandemic was the same among both exporters and those operating mainly on the domestic market; it amounted to 51%).

More than a quarter of the surveyed companies also increased investments in digitisation, about a fifth in automation and product innovation, and more than a sixth in service and process innovation and personnel development. In 15% of the surveyed companies, the number of employees and sales revenues also increased. Among the sample companies that increased sales revenue and the number of employees during the first wave of the pandemic, trading companies and companies that deal with business consulting (especially regarding e-business, finance, etc.), as well as some logistics, ICT, and pharmaceutical companies prevailed. There were also manufacturing companies among the companies that increased the number of employees.

The use of emergency government measures, however, was not limited to companies with limited or suspended operations, but was also observed among companies operating at planned or expanded scales. According to the survey, 67% of foreign affiliates resorted to at least one form of anti-corona assistance offered at state level, and most of them resorted to more than one. The use of emergency measures does not seem to be related to performance indicators, and no clear pattern could be identified. On the other hand, the use of emergency measures appears to be related to firm size. Both firms with decreased operating, employment, and business performance and those that met or exceeded the plan resorted to interventionist government measures. Large and medium-sized firms made more intensive use of government emergency measures, suggesting that the use of measures also requires access to information and greater management capacity. Manufacturing firms also used anti-corona packages more intensively than service sector firms (see Figure 11.4).

Multinational companies and their foreign subsidiaries appear to be more active and flexible in obtaining anti-crisis assistance than domestic companies or compared to the average of the entire business sector. According to the survey conducted by the Chamber of Commerce and Industry among a broader sample of companies (including domestic companies), the share of companies that used government support measures amounted to 57% (Chamber of Commerce & Industry, 2020).

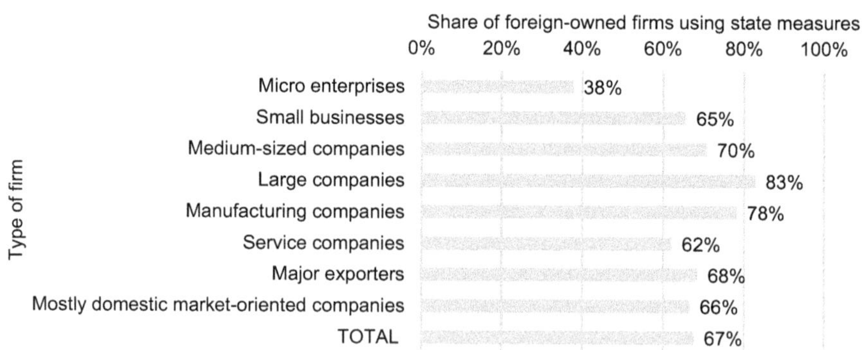

Figure 11.4 Utilisation of state measures aimed at mitigating the effects of COVID-19 on business by foreign affiliates (% share of companies by group, 2020)

Source: own elaboration based on Jaklič and Koleša (2020)

Most likely, the affiliates of multinational companies have recognised that the Temporary Framework (Eur-LEX, 2020a, 2020b) allows a bonus for cross-border cooperation projects between member states (e.g. support for coronavirus-related research and development to address the current health crisis in the form of direct grants, repayable advances, or tax incentives) if their investment is supported by more than one member state and if the investment is completed within two months of the grant (support for the construction and expansion of testing facilities for the development and testing of products). A bonus can be granted for cross-border cooperation projects between member states. Companies can benefit from a bonus when their investment is supported by more than one member state and when the investment is concluded within two months after the granting of the aid.

Among the measures provided at the national level, companies in our sample used mostly those related to human resources (e.g. subsidised "waiting for work" and sick leave, reduction of working hours, working from home, compensation for childcare leave). Measures related to the management of financial flows were also frequently used. These included: exemption/reduction/refund of contributions, tax credits, advance payment of profit tax, VAT deferral, subsidies/write-off of contributions for the pension fund and crisis assistance, work activity subsidy, non-refundable grants, grants in general, and staff incentives, liquidity loans, Slovenian export corporation loans, and a moratorium on loans, taxes, and payments. Companies also benefited from or complied with workplace safety measures (these were measures taken by the National Institute for Health Protection and/or under government regulations).

To a much lesser extent, companies also engaged in subsidies provided at the municipal level. Percentage of companies that benefited from regional and municipal measures by September 2020 was much lower than that for the state measures: only 4% of the sample companies benefited from these measures (compared to the 67% utilising state measures).

Foreign-owned companies' response to the government measures aimed at mitigating the negative effects of the COVID-19 pandemic on the economy was generally very positive: companies benefited massively from the measures and used them to maintain their staffing levels and business volumes. The users of these measures described them as "sufficient" and "correct." According to the respondents, the measures "provided significant relief to labour costs during the critical period." For the most part, they thus saw "no need for additional measures."

Most of the criticism was related to communication or the existence of preventive measures. Some companies called for "clear(er) instructions and clear interpretation of laws, measures . . . without repeated changes and corrections." Others called for "more information for the organization to be able to plan activities and operations . . . and to reduce uncertainty." The most dissatisfied proposed to "eliminate all measures and stop deceiving people." In other words, companies desired consistency and clarity in measures to be able to plan their operations. They also desired consistency and clarity in how the measures were communicated, whereby reasoning for the introduction of the more disruptive measures to their operations (and the later countermeasures) were also desired. The wish to maintain independence in crisis management was highlighted by some firms as well.

The management of many foreign affiliates in Slovenia also actively approached the government and professional associations with proposals. They actively participated in consultations at the Chamber of Commerce and Industry, used all established communication channels, and proposed their own initiatives and necessary measures before each round of anti-corona packages was launched.

In their responses to our survey (Jaklič & Koleša, 2020), companies also made suggestions for dealing with the consequences of the COVID-19 pandemic that referred to different aspects of business: some pertained to improving the business environment, some to government measures, while others focused on financing, personnel, and health and safety measures (see Table 11.1).

Table 11.1 Foreign affiliates' proposals for anti-crisis measures during COVID-19

Area	*Proposals*
Business environment	• clear and stable legislation, • favourable tax regulations, • securing liquidity of end customers (lower taxation of food) and business partners (purchase of receivables for independent entrepreneurs), • digitisation of public administration, • digitisation of health care, • e-business;
Government measures	• not restricting business/boosting the economy/ensuring that the system works, • access to measures for large companies, foreign-owned companies, SMEs, disability companies, and companies in distress, • clear and timely information on measures/clarity and stability of measures (clear division into measures for natural and legal persons), • control of compliance with the measures introduced by the National Institute for Health Protection in companies, • opening of borders (for foreign citizens with a negative test without quarantine, relaxation of measures for countries not classified as "red" – i.e. most exposed to COVID-19, free movement of goods), • measures to support HoReCa (cooperation of hotels, restaurants and cafés)/international tourism (importance of personal contact);
Financing	• grants and subsidies (grants to counteract stopped traffic, funds for optimisation, digitalisation, acquisition of protective gear, modernisation and acquisition of new equipment, wages/labour costs/"waiting for work", fixed costs, job preservation, technological modernisation, and employee development; funds linked to income decline and without restrictions for individual sectors; funds for foreign-owned enterprises, SMEs, disability companies, and large enterprises), • tax deductions/exemptions (pension fund depreciation, tax deduction on purchasing e-vehicles, lower taxation on food and wages – explicitly for younger, highly qualified staff, income), • favourable loans (including for foreign investors, for reverse capital with repayment waivers, insurance of business receivables from customers against credit risks, relaxation of banking restrictions, purchase of receivables from business partners);

Area	*Proposals*
Personnel	• "waiting for work" (financing, accessible to SMEs and disability companies; extension of the measure until the end of the crisis) and sickness benefits, • reduction of working hours (financing, better scheme than the existing one), • payment of wage supplements, • home office (amendment of the health and labour legislation to allow flexible working hours, assistance in organising the home work environment, with lower compliance requirements/simplified legislation, flexible labour law), • flexibility in staff deployment and/or working time arrangements (including staff exchanges between companies), • temporary employment to replace an employee in quarantine (without a tender process), • early retirement, • provision of seasonal workers, • ensuring rapid access to foreign labour markets, • bases for internal communication of measures;
Health and safety measures	• assistance in the purchase of protective equipment, • vaccination, • free swabbing for employees, • testing for infected only, • lifting quarantine for healthy groups, • ensuring/improving the functioning of the health system, • supporting investment in projects that directly improve the environment during the COVID-19 crisis (e.g. electronic UV disinfectants, counting people in the room, measuring temperature, etc.);
Other	• no action required – the situation is under control, • actions were sufficient/adequate/helpful (they provided sufficient relief to labour costs), • as few measures as possible, • limit export of under-processed raw materials; limit the export of logs and wood, • flexibility of the company and its employees, • the importance of preventive examinations and validation of company machines by hospitals.

Source: own elaboration based on Jaklič & Koleša (2020)

Positive experience with crisis management and emergency governmental measures resulted in persisting presence of foreign investments in the country. Although some foreign locations recorded the withdrawal of foreign investment (FDI Intelligence Unit, 2022), the COVID-19 pandemic did not change investment behaviour for the most part and did not affect the presence of foreign investors in Slovenia. Eighty-five per cent of foreign affiliates reported unchanged investment plans, 11% reported a decreased presence of foreign investors in their ownership structure, and 4% recorded an increase in the presence of foreign investors in Slovenia (Figure 11.5).

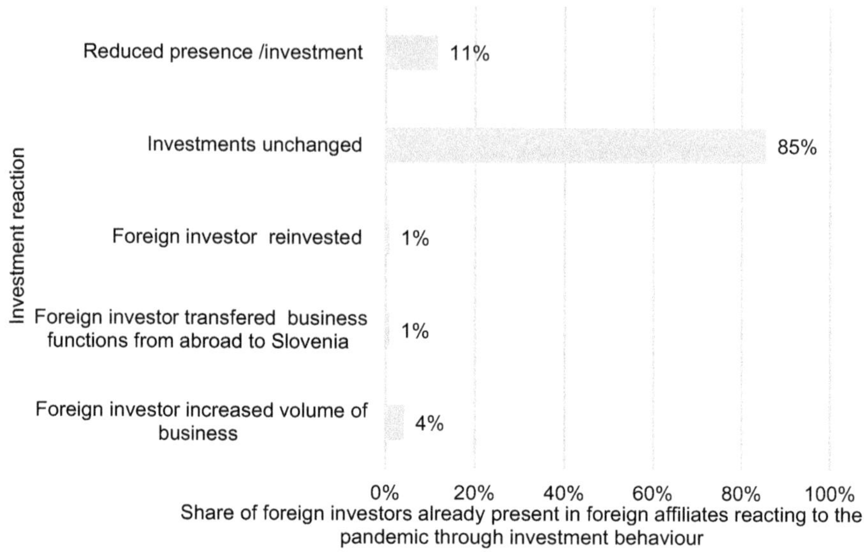

Figure 11.5 Investment reactions of foreign investors already present in foreign affiliates' ownership structure to the COVID-19 pandemic (in % share of firms experiencing a certain type of reaction)

Source: own elaboration based on Jaklič & Koleša (2020)

The reasons for foreign investors' increased presence in Slovenian affiliates reported by respondents to the survey were both environment- and relationship-related. Companies reported government measures and relations with business partners and staff in foreign affiliates as relevant factors for increased presence of foreign investors in their structures. They also reported on novel business opportunities driven by digitalisation and other internal process innovations (see Table 11.2). In contrast, the reasons for reduced presence of foreign investors were more often related to deterioration of health conditions, travel and mobility restrictions, poorer business results, or difficulties in the company headquarters (outside Slovenia).

Discussion

The results give rare insights into the inclination and ability of foreign affiliates to engage in developing as well as benefiting from national (and to an extent regional and municipal) support measures. They also reveal the factors that contribute to the uptake and success of support measures in small economies.

Our findings show that businesses were involved in developing support measures – in particular through business associations and the Chamber of Commerce and Industry. Before each new round of measures, the government also organised consultations with business representatives, where companies had the opportunity

Table 11.2 Reasons for increased/decreased presence of foreign investors, 2020

The reasons for the increased presence of foreign investors as cited by companies:	*The reasons for reduced presence of foreign investors as cited by companies:*
– "The government measures, the stability of the health situation in the country, and the personnel have increased the presence." – "Actually, we do not know the reasons. But some business partners took a new path that brought them more work, and so we had more work." – "More online orders." – "We have become more efficient."	– "Worsening health conditions." (the most common response) – "Poor business results." (very common response) – "Very poor business results. The owner cannot promise help for 2020." – "Declining demand." – "Lower order volume and fewer new projects." – "Deteriorating health situation, government actions restricting travel." – "Poor business results and problems in the headquarters." – "Government measures that restricted mobility, work from home." – "Deterioration of the health situation – closure of the country, limited mobility." – "Health situation at the headquarters (Sweden) as well as nearly disabled traveling through Europe (14 days of quarantine on entering Slovenia, 48-hour validity of a negative COVID-19 test was impossible to provide)." – "The headquarters were closed and in a restructuring phase even before the pandemic outbreak."

Source: own elaboration based on survey responses

to submit proposals for the necessary measures and comment on the government's proposals. Surveys funded by governmental agencies acted as an additional tool to gain business inputs on adjustments of measures. The survey from our study was one such example. Its results confirmed that foreign investors (despite investment stagnation in 2020) constantly monitored global and regional trends as well as intentions and reactions of policymakers and changes in national and international investment policy developments. More than 67% of the surveyed companies with foreign capital benefited from state measures aimed at reducing the negative effects of the COVID-19 pandemic on companies. Survey findings showed that foreign affiliates were on average more proactive in using governmental support than Slovenian firms in general; the survey that was conducted in parallel at the Slovenian Chamber of Commerce and Industry disclosed a lower (56%) share of business users of governmental support measures.

The impact of the COVID-19 pandemic on the operation of foreign affiliates was evident. However, the presence of foreign investors during the first wave was maintained. Manufacturing foreign affiliates did not shift their production to other locations. Although the majority of companies operated at a lower level, only a minority (less than 30%) reduced the number of employees, which implies that companies recognise the importance of maintaining staff (and their skills) for crisis management and recovery. The use of emergency governmental support was not limited to less successful firms, but spread over all businesses: those with reduced operation as well as those with more positive prospects that bridged temporary difficulties. The use of state measures was thus a tool not only to manage the crisis in the short-term, but also to build competitiveness in the medium and long term.

Several businesses also desired additional measures. These included stable and transparent legislation, control over the implementation of measures, clear and consistent communication, ease of international travel and trade, increased digitalisation, financial support (including access to credit), and support for guaranteeing health and safety in the workplace. Most suggestions were focused on securing stability of employment – also through allowing greater flexibility in terms of employment format, reorganisation, and international recruitment.

We also explored the effects of the pandemic on foreign investments in Slovenian companies. The noticeable changes were found in terms of the number of employees and business functions in local entities, but also in investments in personnel development and research and development, automation and digitalisation, and the number of foreign suppliers, buyers, and export markets of these entities. In all the mentioned areas, the positive effects were much more frequent than the negative effects. Foreign-owned firms demonstrated adaptation capabilities and resilience through both the use of their internal resources as well as the use of host country governmental measures. Intensive use of measures oriented to maintaining employment and training personnel gave an important message to the government, as well as to domestic companies that needed to introduce similar measures to maintain their competitiveness. Businesses' participation in public debates, signalling their needs and intentions, and shaping of attitudes and activities within professional associations further strengthened the awareness that firms in general (not just foreign-owned affiliates) appreciate quick and tailor-made measures aimed at recovery. Business environments that enable cooperation and dialogue between the government and businesses are therefore more attractive to foreign investors during (recurring) economic crises. Dialogue, participation, and collaboration thereby give interventionism additional legitimacy to that provided by environmental uncertainty.

Conclusions

Coping with the crisis brought about by the COVID-19 pandemic has presented most governments with an unprecedented challenge. The process aimed at addressing the crisis demonstrated the importance of multistakeholder collaboration that promotes introduction and utilisation of effective measures tailored to specific stakeholder groups. The latter include foreign investors who can have important spillover effects on domestic businesses and the overall economy. They tend to monitor the business environment even more closely during complex, multidimensional and dynamic crises – paying close attention to the content of policies, the ability of governments to coordinate the introduction and implementation of measures, and their flexibility and responsiveness, as well as opportunities for inter-organisational collaboration (including that pertaining to co-creation of measures).

In the case of the COVID-19 crisis in Slovenia, many foreign affiliates within the corporate sector emerged as proactive stakeholders; making suggestions, promoting collaboration and networking within the broader corporate ecosystem, and pushing for clear mechanisms to review milestones and targets that form the basis for disbursing funds to countries. In general, foreign affiliates were well-informed about government policies, aware of the opportunities for government support and its business potential, and able to take advantage of the transparent EU policies and actions. They were also able to integrate contingency measures into their recovery plans. This can be an important driver of economic recovery and stabilisation of supply lines. With increased uncertainty, business success in the coming decade will depend more on how governments shape the business environment and promote business–government relations that enable policy and strategy co-creation.

Notes

1 The first wave of the COVID-19 (i.e. coronavirus) infections in spring 2020 was followed by a gradual reopening of businesses and economies, facilitated by the containment measures and made possible by the decline in the number of COVID-19 cases. Restrictions were relaxed in April 2020 and on May 15, 2020, Slovenia was the first EU country to declare the end of the COVID-19 epidemic in the country. Nonetheless, some anti-COVID-19 restrictions remained in place. In the face of a new wave of infections in the fall, the authorities set the economy in a partial lockdown, which started in October 2020. The government decided to relax some of the containment measures in mid-December 2020, when public transport resumed at reduced capacity and certain other businesses were allowed to resume their operations. Schools for children with special needs reopened in early January 2021, followed by kindergartens, primary and secondary schools (IMF, 2022). For a more detailed overview of the course of the pandemic and key policy responses to it at its different stages see IMF (2022).

2 In the EU, this is exemplified by the breadth of the European Green Deal (EGD) agenda (European Commission, 2019). A more active green industrial policy to serve the goals of the EGD is therefore warranted, also as a part of Europe's new green growth strategy.

3 Act on Amendments and Supplements to the Act on Intervention Measures to Contain the COVID-19 Epidemic and Mitigate Its Consequences for Citizens and the Economy (ZIUZEOP-A, Official Gazette RS, No. 49/20 in 61/20).

4 An overview of covid-related measures introduced in Slovenia is available on PISRS (2021) and IUS-INFO (2023).

5 According to the Slovenian legislation, "waiting for work" refers to extraordinary events during which employers cannot guarantee sufficient work for all their employees in the short run. In such cases, employees are entitled to compensation, which amounts to 80% of their monthly pay (ZDR-1, 2013). During the COVID-19 pandemic this compensation was covered by the government. The measure was aimed at job preservation (ZIUZEOP, 2020).

6 It also enabled member states to combine all support measures granted under the Temporary Framework (Eur-LEX, 2020a, 2020b) with existing possibilities to grant *de minimis* to a company of up to 25,000 EUR over three fiscal years for companies active in the primary agricultural sector, 30,000 EUR over three fiscal years for companies active in the fishery and aquaculture sector, and 200,000 EUR over three fiscal years for companies active in all other sectors. At the same time, member states had to commit to avoiding undue accumulation of support measures for the same companies to limit support to meet their actual needs. Furthermore, the Temporary Framework complemented the many other possibilities already available to member states to mitigate the socio-economic impact of the coronavirus outbreak, in line with EU State aid rules.

7 All ten anti-corona packages are available at IUS-INFO (2023). In this study, we analyse the government support developed after the outbreak of the corona pandemic; i.e. the first six anti-corona packages.
8 The Centre for International Relations at the Faculty of Social Sciences at the University of Ljubljana (Slovenia) regularly conducts surveys of foreign affiliates to determine how foreign affiliates view the business environment in Slovenia. The 2020 survey focused on Covid-19 and related government and enterprise actions.
9 In Slovenia, micro-sized enterprises have up to 10 employees, small businesses are comprised of 11–50 employees, medium-sized firms have between 51 and 250 employees, and large firms have more than 250 employees.
10 While mandatory, this also enabled them to maintain their operations.

References

Alfaro, L. & Chen, M.X. (2012). Surviving the global financial crisis: Foreign ownership and establishment performance. *American Economic Journal: Economic Policy*, *4*(3), 30–55.

Bank of Slovenia. (2020). *Direct Investment 2020*. Ljubljana: Bank of Slovenia.

Bellak, C. (2004). How domestic and foreign firms differ and why does it matter? *Journal of Economic Surveys*, *18*(4), 483–514.

Chamber of Commerce and Industry, 2020. Ljubljana. Internal reports.

de Vet, M.J., Nigohosyan, D., Núñez Ferrer, J., Gross, A.-K., Kuehl, S. & Flickenschild, M. (2021). *Impacts of the COVID-19 Pandemic on EU Industries*. Publication for the committee on Industry, Research and Energy, Policy Department for Economic, Scientific and Quality of Life Policies, European Parliament: Luxembourg. Retrieved from: https://www.europarl.europa.eu/RegData/etudes/STUD/2021/662903/IPOL_STU(2021)662903_EN.pdf.

Dornean, A., Işan, V. & Oanea, D.C. (2012). The impact of the recent global crisis on foreign direct investment. Evidence from central and Eastern European countries. *Procedia Economics and Finance*, *3*, 1012–1017.

Dornean, A. & Oanea, D.C. (2015). Impact of the economic crisis on FDI in central and Eastern Europe. *Review of Economic and Business Studies*, *8*(2), 53–68.

Eadi, G. & Rasmussen, A. (2022). The unequal effects of the Covid-19 pandemic on political interest representation. *Political Behavior*, 1–25. https://doi.org/10.1007/s11109-022-09842-x

Economist (2022, January 1). *Which Economies Have Done Best and Worst During the Pandemic?* Retrieved from: https://www.economist.com/finance-and-economics/which-economies-have-done-best-and-worst-during-the-pandemic/21806917

Eur-LEX. (2020a). Communication from the commission temporary framework for State aid measures to support the economy in the current COVID-19 outbreak 2020/C 91 I/01. *Official Journal of the European Union, CI 91/1*, March. Retrieved from: https://eur-lex.europa.eu/legal-content/EN/TXT/?uri=OJ%3AJOC_2020_091_I_0001

Eur-LEX. (2020b). Communication from the commission amendment to the temporary framework for State aid measures to support the economy in the current COVID-19 outbreak 2020/C 112 I/01. *Official Journal of the European Union, CI 112/1*, April. Retrieved from: https://eur-lex.europa.eu/legal-content/EN/TXT/?uri=uriserv:OJ.CI.2020.112.01.0001.01.ENG&toc=OJ:C:2020:112I:TOC

European Commission (2019). *Communication from the Commission: The European Green Deal*. COM(2019)640, Brussels, 11 December.

European Commission. (2021a). *Report from the Commission to the European Parliament and the Council. First Annual Report on the Screening of Foreign Direct Investments into the Union –*

Brussels, November. Retrieved from: https://trade.ec.europa.eu/doclib/docs/2021/november/tradoc_159935.pdf

European Commission. (2021b). *A Competition Policy Fit for New Challenges*. COM(2021)713, Brussels, 18 November.

FDI Intelligence Unit. (2022). *The fDi Report 2022*. Retrieved from: http://www.fdiintelligence.com/

Financial Council of the Republic of Slovenia (2021). *Dolg sektorja država v Sloveniji: značilnosti, srednjeročna vzdržnost in dolgoročne simulacije* [Debt of the sector country in Slovenia: characteristics, medium term sustainability and long term simulations]. Report from 30 March 2021. Retrieved from: http://www.fs-rs.si/dolg-sektorja-drzava-v-sloveniji-znacilnosti-srednjerocna-vzdrznost-in-dolgorocne-simulacije/.

Franca, V., Domadenik, P. & Redek, T. (2020). *Raziskava o učinkovitosti protikoronskih ukrepov – PKP* [A study of the efficiency of anticorona measures]. Retrieved from: https://www.zds.si/home/getfile?f=d028090a565f1d9804c8af70ddb59933

Gov.si. (2022). *Vladni posvet z gospodarstveniki* [Governmental consultation with business representatives]. Retrieved from: https://www.gov.si/novice/2022-01-06-vladni-posvet-z-gospodarstveniki/

Hayakawa, K., Lee, H.H. & Park, C.Y. (2022). The effect of COVID-19 on foreign direct investment. *ADB Economics Working Paper Series*, 653. Retrieved from: https://www.adb.org/sites/default/files/publication/781381/ewp-653-effect-covid-19-foreign-direct-investment.pdf

Hudson, B., Hunter, D. & Peckham, S. (2019). Policy failure and the policy-implementation gap: Can policy support programs help? *Policy Design and Practice, 2*(1), 1–14. https://doi.org/10.1080/25741292.2018.1540378

IMAD. (2021). Spring forecast of economic trends 2021. *Ljubljana: IMAD*. Retrieved from: https://www.umar.gov.si/fileadmin/user_upload/napovedi/pomlad/pomladanska_2021/angleska/Spring_Forecast_of_Economic_Trends_2021_01.pdf

IMF, Fiscal Monitor Database. (2020). Retrieved from: http://www.imf.org/en/Publications/FM

IMF. (2022). Policy responses to Covid-19: Policy tracker. *imf.org*. Retrieved from: http://www.imf.org/en/Topics/imf-and-covid19/Policy-Responses-to-COVID-19#S

IUS-INFO. (2023). *Spremljamo covidne ukrepe* [Monitoring the Covid Measures]. Retrieved from: https://www.iusinfo.si/medijsko-sredisce/v-sredis cu/259417

Jaklič, A. & Koleša, I. (2020). *Tuji investitorji o slovenskem poslovnem okolju 2020 [Foreign investors about the Slovenian business environment 2020]*. Ljubljana: Center za mednarodne odnose, Fakulteta za družbene vede, Univerza v Ljubljani [Centre of International Relations, Faculty of Social Sciences, University of Ljubljana].

Miró, J. (2022). Responding to the global disorder: The EU's quest for open strategic autonomy. *Global Society*. https://doi.org/10.1080/13600826.2022.2110042

OECD. (2021). *OECD International Direct Investment Statistics*. Retrieved from: https://doi.org/10.1787/idi-data-en

OFT. (2009). *Government in markets: Why competition matters – A guide for policy makers*. Office of Fair Trading, UK. Retrieved from: https://assets.publishing.service.gov.uk/government/uploads/system/uploads/attachment_data/file/284451/OFT1113.pdf

PISRS. (2021). *Prikaz veljavnih predpisov, sprejetih za preprečevanje širjenja bolezni Covid-19* [An overview of valid regulations, taken to prevent the spread of the Covid-19 disease]. Retrieved from: http://www.pisrs.si/Pis.web/aktualno

Poulsen, L.S. & Hufbauer, G.C. (2011). Foreign direct investment in times of crisis. In *Working Paper Series WP11–3*. Washington: Peterson Institute for International Economics.

Reeskens, T. & Muis, Q. (2021). A new democratic norm(al)? Political legitimacy amidst the Covid-19 pandemic. In E. Aarts, H. Fleuren, M. Sitskoorn, & T. Wilthagen (Eds.), *The New Common* (pp. 189–195). Cham: Springer. https://doi.org/10.1007/978-3-030-65355-2_27

STA. (2020). *Koronavirus: Ukrepi za pomoč gospodarstvu in prebivalcem* [The coronavirus: Measures in support of the economy and inhabitants]. Retrieved from: https://www.sta.si/v-srediscu/koronavirus-pomoc

Stoddard, O. & Noy, I. (2015). Fire-sale FDI? The impact of financial crises on foreign direct investment. *Review of Development Economics*, *19*(2), 387–399.

UNCTAD. (2020). World investment report 2020. In *International Production beyond the Pandemic*. Geneva: United Nations.

ZDR-1. (2013). Zakon o delovnih razmerjih [Labour Relations Act], Official Gazette RS, No 21/13, 78/13 – corrected 47/15. Retrieved from: http://www.pisrs.si/Pis.web/pregledPredpisa?id=ZAKO5944

ZIUZEOP. (2020). *Zakon o interventnih ukrepih za zajezitev epidemije COVID-19 in omilitev njenih posledic za državljane in gospodarstvo* [Act Determining the Intervention Measures to Contain the COVID-19 Epidemic and Mitigate its Consequences for Citizens and the Economy], Official Gazette RS, No. 49/20, 61/20, 152/20. Retrieved from: http://www.pisrs.si/Pis.web/pregledPredpisa?id=ZAKO8190&d-49683-p=2

ZIUZEOP-A. (2020). *Zakon o spremembah in dopolnitvah Zakona o interventnih ukrepih za zajezitev epidemije COVID-19 in omilitev njenih posledic za državljane in gospodarstvo* [Act on Amendments and Supplements to the Act on Intervention Measures to Contain the Covid-19 Epidemic and Mitigate Its Consequences for Citizens and the Economy], Official Gazette RS, No. 61/2020. Retrieved from: https://www.uradni-list.si/glasilo-uradni-list-rs/vsebina/2020-01-0901?sop=2020-01-0901

12 World post-COVID-19

Looking ahead

Katarzyna Mroczek-Dąbrowska, Aleksandra Kania, and Anna Matysek-Jędrych

Introduction

The COVID-19 pandemic has changed the face of the modern world in terms of health protection and the political, economic, and social spheres. The spatial extent, the number of infected and deceased people, the duration, and the long-term effects of the pandemic – comparable to the recession caused by the "Great Depression" of 1929–1933 – make it possible to speak of it as a macrosystemic event.

The pandemic has brought unprecedented challenges with wide-ranging effects on the world's economy. Lockdowns, travel restrictions, and supply chain disruptions had profound consequences that will be felt long after the pandemic ends. The changes that have occurred concern both the macro-sphere (economic policy, the operation of large multinational corporations, strategic and operational changes that have affected both home and host markets) and the micro-sphere (consumer behavior, purchasing patterns, and the operation of small and medium-sized enterprises).

In the economic history of the world, the COVID-19 crisis appears to be a unique event – a simultaneous shock to aggregate demand and supply. The COVID-19 shock had a substantial impact on the financial system and its stability even though – unlike the 2007–2012 crisis – the source of the shock lay outside of the system. The pandemic's negative short- and medium-term economic impact and the necessary restrictions reducing its scope has been partly limited by public measures in the area of fiscal and monetary policy. However, only time will tell how effective these measures were in the long term. At this point, only one thing remains certain: the COVID-19 pandemic, with its short-term disruptions, triggered long-term changes in how the world lives and does business.

The book's focus

The volume was written at a particularly challenging time when the global economy is at a crossroads, and companies need increasing skills to build resilience for volatile ecosystems. It remains an open question to what extent current developments and companies' anxiety, which forms the analysis background in several chapters of this volume, shape the companies' strategies for managing crises. Our intention, though,

DOI: 10.4324/9781003345428-12

was to deliver a volume that would enable the readers to better understand crisis management and resilience building in the CEE context.

The book's central theme is the contemporary approach to crisis management, emphasizing the CEE countries. All chapters, whether they refer to macro-, meso-, or micro-perspectives, always show how businesses or business trends change due to an unexpected crisis. We sought to answer the following questions in the volume:

- how the nature and frequency of crises shift the business environment,
- how companies build their resilience capacity in a digitalized era,
- what role institutions play in making the resilience capacity of companies, and to what extent the institutional changes 'forced' by the COVID-19 pandemic crisis structure the firm-friendly business environment,
- how crises – global and regional – change the global trends we have observed in business in the last 20 years (e.g., offshoring vs. reshoring, globalization vs. deglobalization vs. slowbalization, etc.).

The added value of this volume

The volume stands out as a complex and multidimensional research workshop that draws its roots from distinct yet simultaneously interlinked research areas.

To diagnose the strategic behavior of enterprises, it is necessary to embed considerations first in political or macroeconomic issues. Understanding the mechanisms of the spread of the crisis from the medical sphere to the financial area and, finally, the real economy provides the basis for inferences about the effectiveness of the adopted strategic decisions among companies. Research into the policy decisions made in the face of the crisis, the large-scale institutional changes implemented, or the structuring of aid measures by governments, central banks, or supranational organizations helps to outline the research context for corporate strategic and operational management.

The research on adopting strategies in answer to a volatile and unpredictable environment allows scholars to specify generic conclusions to companies' resilience in times of crisis. It will significantly enhance our knowledge by showing how companies build their resilience capacity for 21st-century crises and how institutions can help (or hinder) a company's adaptive capacity during the crisis. The book also answers the crucial question of how global trends alter as a direct effect of the recent crises.

What is more, the volume presents both economic and managerial perspectives to managing crisis where common denominators are focused on company resilience and CEE context. Additionally, economic and managerial perspectives are supplemented by the geopolitical view and behavioral and psychological dimensions.

The authors contributing to this volume represent leading Polish universities, including Poznań University of Economics and Business, Cracow University of Economics, and Vistula University, and a triple-crown accredited Slovenian university – the University of Ljubljana. All the authors contributing to this volume have broad international experience and have published in highly recognized international journals. They all are part of global research networks (e.g., EIBA, AIB, IT&FA, SUERF) and undertake international projects. The chapters thus offer an informed, well-researched, and comprehensive insight into the specificity of the CEE economies and business environment, written by leading experts in the field. Please note that gender balance has been maintained, and young, mid-career researchers were invited to contribute to bringing new and innovative perspectives to the volume.

The book's highlights

The book offers an interdisciplinary take on current developments and processes that shape and influence contemporary crisis management practices and a company's agility in the face of crises. The volume addresses the most topical issues delineating public discourse on firms' resilience. In this way, this volume 'connects the dots' and uncovers the missing links necessary for any reader wishing to understand the specificity of contemporary companies' responses to unexpected occurrences like pandemics or geopolitical crises.

Looking ahead

The book provides answers to many vital questions that attract the attention of both business and political leaders these days. It also prompts new ones as it is becoming more and more apparent that unexpected economic shocks, the so-called black swans, such as the Global Financial Crisis of 2007, BREXIT of 2016, and now the COVID-19 pandemic, are taking on a cyclical and repetitive nature and may soon become the norm of a new, less predictable reality.

It is worth noting the megatrends that have emerged in recent years and are being accelerated by the impact of the pandemic on the global economy, the society of individual countries, the sphere of technology, etc. One of the trends more strongly highlighted by the pandemic is the wave of disinformation or misinformation, a consequence of the spread of populism in the last decade and the waning faith in experts. These waves are a fundamental obstacle to taking collective, coordinated corrective action in the context of the COVID-19 pandemic crisis. However, this may also have broader implications concerning, for example, the implementation of the Global Sustainable Goals (SDGs). Another trend relates to the proliferation of the digital economy already observed before the pandemic. The pandemic period fostered the spread of digital behaviors such as remote working and learning, telemedicine, and remote service delivery. COVID-19 has been also a litmus paper for global cooperation and globalization as such. There is no doubt we will experience deep structural changes in the way multilateralism operates to reflect the very different world.

The recent disruptions to the global economy (COVID-19 pandemic, Russian invasion in Ukraine, unprecedented inflation growth) indicate that companies in the future might have to further develop knowledge and critical skill sets to respond to highly volatile, uncertain, complex, and ambiguous (VUCA) situations. As the

World Economic Forum predicts, by 2024, the global income gap between developed and developing countries will widen significantly, resulting in yet increased global divergence. Society is reported to fear geo-economic confrontations, debt crises, and environmental perils. The uncertainty also affects international relations as both disruptions to global value chains caused by the COVID-19 pandemic and the nations' resource dependence revealed by the Russian invasion of Ukraine shook the way globalization is now perceived. The definition of globalization, as we know it, is being questioned.

In early 2020, Kristalina Georgieva, Managing Director of the International Monetary Fund (IMF), identified rising uncertainty as the leading theme for the start of the new decade. The World Uncertainty Index – a quarterly measure of global economic and political uncertainty spanning 143 countries – shows that while uncertainty has now decreased by roughly 60% from the peak observed in the first quarter of 2020, it remains approximately 50% above its historical average for 1996–2010 (World Uncertainty Index, 2022).

Right after we could feel the COVID-19 pandemic diminishing, in February 2022, the global economic landscape deteriorated further and became even more unpredictable due to the Russian invasion of Ukraine. The war additionally increased the previously high prices of raw materials and fuels and weakened the Polish zloty, which resulted in further growth of costs of economic activity in Poland. At the same time, the outflow of workers from Poland to Ukraine – mainly men who returned to their country to fight in its defense – exacerbated problems in the labor market, primarily in construction, transport, and industry. In the short term, these challenges will be partly limited by the influx of refugees, which on the one hand is much larger than the outflow of Ukrainians. Still, on the other hand, over 90% of people seeking refuge in Poland are women and children.

Alongside the Russian invasion, the EU and the US started fighting higher inflation rates. Higher inflation means not only building up pressure on wages and thus higher production costs but also higher interest rates, which will gradually increase the costs of new and already existing debts for companies and limit consumer demand. Although in the latter case, the demand generated by refugees and additional government fiscal transfers might act in the opposite direction.

In the face of these shocks, we could see that some companies worldwide began to ask themselves whether they should increase the local concentration of production by reshoring or relocating their operations to a geographically close country (nearshoring). Since February 2020, as the COVID-19 crisis deepened, there has been a visible increase in trade policy activism. Some countries responded to the COVID-19 pandemic by introducing export bans and restrictions to prevent internal shortages at the national level (Evenett et al., 2020).

The COVID-19 pandemic has strengthened countries' mandate to move production closer to home. The protection of broadly understood strategic sectors motivates governments to create mechanisms to support the relocation of production. Further efforts to relocate production can be expected shortly. Factors contributing to this include, inter alia, the unflagging international geopolitical tension and the promotion of "green transformation" at the EU level, which may contribute to shortening supply chains. However, changes in automation, production quality issues in some developing countries, and the importance of market proximity to timely deliveries will remain critical.

We will also most likely experience the continuation of the 'friendshoring' trend that has emerged in recent years. Negative public opinion on continuing to operate in an 'unfriendly' country can have an indirect positive business impact by leading to creation of new relationships with partners who follow similar beliefs and values. Russian invasion in Ukraine confirmed that increasing political or public pressure can persuade companies to relocate their activities, even if it means higher costs and reduced competitive advantage. Ideally, such a move should be counterbalanced by preferential tax treatment or other incentives introduced by the government. It should be noted, however, that 'friendshoring' may work both ways. We can already see, for example, that Russia is looking for other, less hostile destinations in Asia and is shifting exports to China and India.

Companies will most probably also look for more diversification. Instead of sourcing from one country, they will source more from others. Why, in some cases, will we likely see diversification instead of reshoring? The main incentive for moving a business is the existence of competitive advantage in relocating. Therefore, the absence of such an advantage and increased production costs may make enterprises reluctant to relocate their operations. Diversification of suppliers may seem more reasonable in such cases.

It should also not be forgotten that essential commodities are immensely difficult to replace. The appetite for local components is growing. While it would be beneficial to reduce dependence on some imported products, such as e.g. the rare earth metals for the EU, having only minimal resources, the extraction of which is associated with enormous costs, is not enough to become self-reliant and avoid importing goods altogether.

Another factor that makes relocation a challenge is the apparent lack of skilled workers worldwide. In the past, the wage gap between the US, EU, and China has been smaller, making labor costs a less significant factor when deciding on relocating to these regions. However, with rising inflation wages will again play a larger role while considering reshoring.

Finally, with the price rises we already see, and with wages lagging behind inflation, we will get to the point where clients simply cannot afford to buy. Businesses are already reporting that it is increasingly difficult to base prices on production costs. In the future it all comes down to customer preferences – in case they would rather buy cheaper products from overseas, the relocation trend will quickly shift back to nearshoring or offshoring.

However, looking at the overall picture, the benefits to international business still persist and supply chains remain intact for the time being. It's about changing routes, diversifying suppliers and regions, and increasing inventory. It is not the time to cancel globalization. Right now, the idea is to plan further than ever before, creating new opportunities.

Acknowledgments

This contribution draws on the final results of the 'Determinants of company's adaptability to crisis situation – the case of Covid19' project. The project was co-financed by the Polish National Agency for Academic Exchange within the Urgency Grants program.

References

Evenett, S., Fiorini, M., Fritz, J., Hoekman, B., Lukaszuk, P., Rocha, N., Ruta, M., Santi, F. & Shingal, A. (2020). *Trade Policy Responses to the COVID-19 Pandemic Crisis: Evidence from a New Dataset, VoxEU.org*, 11 December. Retrieved from: https://cepr.org/voxeu/columns/trade-policy-responses-covid-19-pandemic-evidence-new-dataset.

World Uncertainty Index. (2022). Retrieved from: https://worlduncertaintyindex.com.

Index

Note: Page numbers in *italics* indicate a figure and page numbers in **bold** indicate a table on the corresponding page.

For Product Safety Concerns and Information please contact our EU
representative GPSR@taylorandfrancis.com
Taylor & Francis Verlag GmbH, Kaufingerstraße 24, 80331 München, Germany

www.ingramcontent.com/pod-product-compliance
Ingram Content Group UK Ltd.
Pitfield, Milton Keynes, MK11 3LW, UK
UKHW022124190926
475702UK00013B/1630
9781032385242